Pennsylvania Clocks and Watches

PENNSYLVANIA CLOCKS AND WATCHES

Antique Timepieces and Their Makers

JAMES W. GIBBS

THE PENNSYLVANIA STATE UNIVERSITY PRESS
UNIVERSITY PARK AND LONDON

Library of Congress Cataloging in Publication Data

Gibbs, James W.
    Pennsylvania clocks and watches.

    Includes index and bibliography.
    1. Clock and watch making—Pennsylvania—History.
2. Pennsylvania—Industries. I. Title.
TS543.U6G53   1984   681.1'1'09748   83-62539
ISBN 0-271-00367-7

Contents

Preface

When the late George H. Eckhardt was writing *Pennsylvania Clockmakers*, he was under a time schedule which permitted him to include only a few southeastern counties and some other material on hand. Together, we had planned many joint projects, the major one being a second book embracing all of the clockmakers of Pennsylvania. His untimely demise prevented the realization of this project, but as a labor of love I have tried to do it for him. Therefore, this book is dedicated to his memory and to all those helpful persons who cheerfully contributed material.

Two past presidents of Pennsylvania chapters of the National Association of Watch and Clock Collectors read the manuscript of this book for the Penn State Press and made valuable editorial suggestions; they are Eugene E. Smeltzer (Allegheny Chapter) and Julius B.B. Stryker III (Bucks County Chapter).

Finding photographs of all the clocks that I thought merited special attention in this book was a long and, at times, difficult process. I wish to thank here those persons who aided my search. Unfortunately, in some cases the only available photographs were in less than desirable condition, yet these had to be used to avoid any sorry omissions.

Fig. 1. Typical early thirty-hour clock. Peter Stretch, Philadelphia, circa 1725–40.

Introduction

Just over three hundred years ago the short pendulum clock was conceived in Holland. This concept was quickly brought to England by Johann Fromanteel and was
adopted by his father, Ahasuerus. With the advent shortly thereafter of the long pendulum, the tall case clock steadily became the popular acme of the clockmaker's craft.
The birth of the eighteenth century saw the inception of clockmaking in this country. Across the years, American clocks were so well constructed that large numbers of
them still exist, faithfully discharging their continuous duty. Traditionally, American
clockmakers favored the recoil escapement, which required no significant mechanical
or design change in tall case clocks, though these were gradually phased out in this
country before the Civil War.

Prior to the advent of mass-produced shelf clocks in New England, the production
of tall clocks depended on the skill of tradesmen such as brass and bell founders,
wheel and pinion cutters, catgut and chain makers, and casemakers. These craftsmen,
using hand tools, combined their talents in such a manner that the last one in the sequence, the clockmaker, could produce only a few clocks a year. The definition of a
clockmaker requires latitude but generally applies to the one who finished all the
parts as required, assembled them, inserted the movement parts into a suitable case,
put his name on the dial, and sold the complete clock.

Because the demand for tall clocks increased, and perhaps for other reasons, many
of the clockmakers began importing clock components, primarily from England.

These would include finished dials, false plates, brass wheels in blank or cast form, steel rods for pinions or rough-cut pinions or pinion wire, rough cast brass forms for plates, and other miscellaneous metal parts. This is not to disparage our clockmakers, for they still labored with the parts before assembling a finished movement; nor does it assert that the importation practice was universal, for there were renowned clock-makers who made every part of the clock except the glass. Estate inventories and other records indicate that quite a few Pennsylvania clockmakers owned wheel-cutting engines.

Most clockmakers had a favorite cabinetmaker, who often made his required cases to the specification of the buyer. No standardization of cases as to style or size evolved, although Chippendale, Hepplewhite, and Sheraton designs are readily identifiable. Design, dimensions, and decoration of the cases exhibit considerable variation and individuality.

Native woods, such as walnut, cherry, and maple, and imported mahogany were often the primary case woods; these woods were employed whenever secondary woods were required. Occasionally, bizarre additions were applied to otherwise beautiful wood cases (as seen, for example, in figure 4).

By the end of the Revolutionary War, the brass and silvered dials had generally given way to the less expensive, painted iron dials. A notable exception, the German wag clocks (to be mentioned again later) were almost always equipped with a painted wooden dial. Calendars and moon phase attachments continued to be popular on Pennsylvania clocks.

The reader may be wondering if this book will consist of more than a simple compendium of previously listed clock- and watchmakers. I hope you will find more than that. Initially, both the county clerk and the research librarian of the library in the county seat of each of the sixty-seven Pennsylvanian counties were contacted, as were local historical societies, to obtain factual data on any horological activities within the county. Thus, information from local history books and old newspapers became available. Valuable leads to other sources sometimes led to descendants of early clockmakers; these sources put us in contact with family historian-genealogists of the two most prolific families of clockmakers in the Commonwealth.

Some special circumstances set clock- and watchmaking in Pennsylvania apart from similar activities in other areas. Primary interest centers on the period of 1700 to 1830–40. While early clockmaking tended to concentrate along the New England coast and in the mid-Atlantic colonies and South Carolina, craft clockmaking flourished to a greater degree in Pennsylvania. Perhaps the virtue of thriftiness gen-

2   3

Fig. 2. Eight-day astronomical clock by David Rittenhouse, circa 1780.

Fig. 3. Unsigned eight-day clock, undoubtedly designed to the buyer's specification because the ball and flame finial is unusual.

Fig. 4. Jacob Young clock, circa 1844. The grain painting, probably added later, is a bit garish for contemporary taste.

erally attributed to the New England area can account for this. South Carolina, essentially Charleston, was well populated with cultured French, many of whom rapidly became wealthy from indigo and rice. Sudden wealth usually demands sudden luxuries; thus, it was quicker and more fashionable to import European clocks. By offering religious freedom, Pennsylvania was blessed with a more heterogenous ethnic and religious population. Men engaged in trade and commerce in Philadelphia soon were able to afford finely made clocks in handsome cases. Those farther inland, who tended to accumulate wealth by the sweat of their brows, were anxious to "bespeak" a tall clock as an important piece of furniture in their homes. Importation was of little concern, as there was a good possibility they knew a clockmaker within a reasonable distance.

A partial list of the pioneer clockmakers of Pennsylvania would include Abel Cottey (1655–1711), Peter Stretch (1670–1746), and Dr. Christopher Witt (1675–1765), all from England; Benjamin Chandlee (1685–1745) from Ireland; Christopher Sauer (1693–1731) and Hendrick Heilig (1700–75) from Germany; Augustine Neisser (1717–80) from Moravia; and John Wood, Sr. (d. 1761). All were makers of tall clocks; their craft flourished until the decade of 1830–40, when it declined drastically. That decade and the few years before saw a desultory attempt made by a comparatively small handful of makers to produce shelf clocks. They often attempted imitations of the pillar and scroll case, but hand-craft methods were no competition for mass-produced Connecticut clocks. The isolated making of shelf clocks is still unresolved in any satisfactory manner. Did the ethnological population drawn from England, Scotland, Ireland, Wales, and France affect clockmaking? Yes, in a pull-push manner. Coming from the more advanced, well-to-do European countries, these folks either brought clocks (usually uncased) or desired them as soon as financially possible as a piece of cherished household furniture. These people brought to Penn's Land diverse artisans, some of whom were or became clockmakers and clock casemakers.

Geographically, there were three principal clockmaking areas: the three original counties of Chester, Philadelphia, and Bucks; a sweeping semicircle stretching from Easton, through Bethlehem, Allentown, Reading, and Lancaster to York; and Pittsburgh. So much of the state is mountainous, forested, and lightly populated that it is amazing that forty out of the sixty-seven counties were blessed with some horological activity. Yet geography and topography clearly did nothing to inhibit the development of factories like those of Connecticut.

Some of the more affluent emigrants from England, especially the Quakers, prob-

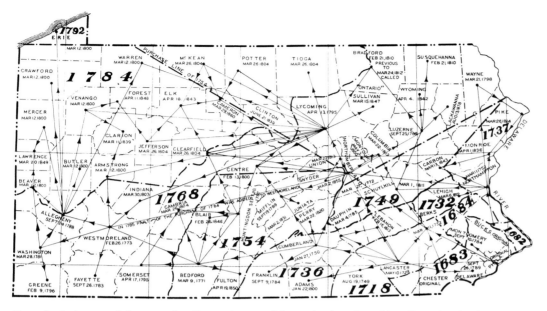

Genealogical map of the counties. Large dates and heavy broken lines identify major land purchases from Indians. (Compiled and prepared by the Pennsylvania Bureau of Land Records)

ably brought clocks along or ordered them later, particularly from Thomas Wagstaff of London. The number of authenticated makers in the English-settled counties, however, shows that these clocks created no imbalance of trade. The same can be said of the imported German wag-on-the-wall clocks, many of which were eventually housed in American-made cases. They were not copied for use in tall clocks, but a few clockmakers in the Allentown area did adapt the movement for use in shelf clocks, usually the pillar and scroll types.

This introduction draws to a close with two questions. First, what—if anything —did Pennsylvania contribute to clockmaking? Second, did clockmaking have any significant economic impact on the Commonwealth? It must always be borne in mind that Pennsylvania clocks were produced by individual artisans of such ability that technological advances were neither necessary nor created. Elsewhere, notably in Connecticut, sales appeal and demand sired mass production, which saw wood

Fig. 5. Unsigned clock, circa 1785, with so-called Pennsylvania Dutch decoration.

movements supplanted by riveted strap brass movements, which in turn were superseded by stamped brass movements. Weights gave way to springs, first brass, then steel. Sizes, styles, and shapes became legion. There could be but one outcome when mass production challenged hand crafts with such overwhelming success: Pennsylvania became noted for individual quality. Connecticut is known as the birthplace of mass production in this country.

William Penn Country

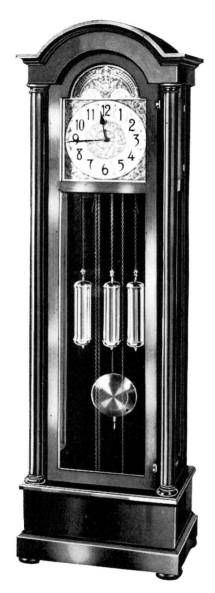

Fig. 6. This is clock No. 80 described in text. Courtesy of E.F. Tukey.

Philadelphia County

Philadelphia County, one of the three original counties established in 1682, was named for a Biblical city in Asia Minor. Here Penn came to establish his "greene countrye town"; here he adopted his Frame of Government; here the Declaration of Independence was signed. Philadelphia was center of events for the colonies in the War of Revolution. Washington here took the oath of office as president for his second term. Early settlers were predominantly English Friends, or Quakers, to be followed by Germans, Scotch-Irish, Welsh, and lesser numbers of every other nationality attracted by the tolerance and freedom provided by Penn. Here is Gloria Dei, or Old Swedes' Church, dedicated in 1700, the state's oldest house of worship. The first Presbyterian Church in America was organized in 1698; the first Mennonite Meeting House was erected in 1708; and a Roman Catholic Chapel was constructed in 1732. Philadelphia is a city of firsts: the first American play was written by a Philadelphian; the city housed the first Masonic Lodge in 1730, the first magazine in 1741, the first newspaper in 1719, the first paper mill in 1690, the first United States Mint, the first bank, the first insurance and trust companies in America, the first building and loan association, the first medical school in 1765, the first hospital in 1751, the first women's medical college, and the first city directory. Historic buildings of all sorts abound.

All of these factors, plus the fact that for many years Philadelphia was the largest English city in the Empire other than London, suggest a large population of artisans in all sorts of crafts, including clockmaking. Early compilers, however, exaggerated the number of clockmakers and imprudently designated many watchmakers by listing over three hundred names. Because the county and city of Philadelphia are geographically the same, makers in such early separate communities as Frankford, Germantown, and Lower Dublin are included in this chapter. It is the most difficult chapter to compose because of the tremendous number of names ascribed as makers. Here the author performs the greatest amount of arbitrary decision making, founded on educated guesses based on currently available information.

Although Thomas F. Albright was listed in directories from 1835 through 1847 as a clock- and watchmaker, no clocks bearing his name are reported, and by 1835 the twilight of individual makers was approaching. It is more likely that he was a clock and watch repairer as a sideline to a jewelry store. This hypothesis is strengthened by the existence of his watch papers, which carry the message: "Clock and watch maker. Gold and silver patent lever, lepine and plain watches, jewellery and silver were of the newest patterns."

The entry for the American Chime Clock Company in Brooks Palmer's *Treasury of American Clocks* states that the operation was in "Nicetown, Pa. 1916–22." The entry reads: "Sold clock cases for grandfather and banjo in knockdown packages. Put together and movements supplied by purchasers. Louis Breitinger of Germantown, Pennsylvania was president. Blue print sets in E.F. Tukey collection." No new information was developed until March, 1975, when Mr. Tukey thoughtfully and generously gave the author copies of company brochures and letters, which, while not lifting the curtain on the whole story, greatly expands upon the preceding quotation.

Primarily, the dates are too narrow because the company had a much longer existence. Unfortunately, none of the brochures are dated, but one contains customer endorsements dated as late as September 25, 1924, suggesting that the brochure was issued in 1925. Included are one statement that the company had been making clocks for forty-eight years and another that it had been a leader in its field for almost fifty years. Accepting these statements as correct establishes the founding of the company as in approximately 1875. There is also a letter, dated February 1, 1932, from L.A. Breitinger to a customer, which establishes a span of nearly sixty years. The precise relationship of the American Chime Clock Company and the American Cuckoo Clock Company is not known, other than that both were founded and operated by members of the Breitinger family. The Cuckoo Company lasted until World War II. If we assume the Chime Company did likewise, then it was in existence nearly seventy years.

Secondly, it is clearly inferred that the American Chime Clock Company produced only knockdown clock case kits. It did that, of course, but it also did more. They sold movements and dials as components for use either with their cases or with cases the customers might already have. Its catalogs also offered good quality eight-day striking and chime hall clock movements, inexpensive, imported grandfather's clock works with enameled wooden dials (wags-on-the-wall) and complete hall clocks. The previously mentioned brochure called particular attention to their solid mahogany hall clock (No. 80), with fine metal dial and three-weight Westminster chiming movement, selling for $149.75 net. It was pointed out that the clock was sold with the fullest guarantee of absolute satisfaction in every detail, and that the low price was made possible only because of their highly specialized quantity production and their forty-eight years of making clocks. "BUILT ON HONOR AND SOLD BY THE GOLDEN RULE."

While the early records of the company are no longer available, there were probably tens of thousands of American Chime clocks assembled, manufactured, and sold throughout the United States. They were merchandised through the usual jobbing trade and available directly to large users such as department stores and mail order houses; the clocks were also given as premiums with subscriptions to newspapers and magazines. The history of the company is quite interesting in the annals of American clockmaking.

The American Cuckoo Clock Company had its beginning in the mid-1890s. At that time Breitinger and Kunz (later known as Breitinger and Sons) had a retail store at 37 and 39 N. Ninth Street, Philadelphia. They were very large importers of cuckoo clocks from the Black Forest of Germany. So many of the imported clocks, however, arrived in a damaged condition that the firm decided to attempt to manufacture cuckoo clocks in this country. They set up a manufacturing establishment on the upper floors of the Ninth Street building, and here they fabricated the wooden cases and employed European wood carvers to embellish the ornamental frame work. The movements, bellows, and certain other small components were imported.

The business so prospered that the activity soon outgrew the space available. The American Cuckoo Clock Company was organized and set up factory operations in a building at the corner of Randolph Street and Fairmount Avenue in the 1900s. The building was occupied until 1912, when the company moved to a still larger building at 1669 Ruffner Street, its final location in Philadelphia.

At the outset of World War I, the importation of movements was cut off and within a short time the supply on hand was exhausted. Therefore, for a few years all activity ceased. As things returned to normal after the war, the importation of move-

7

8

9

ments was resumed, although changing public tastes resulted in a much smaller volume.

In the meantime, the company had begun importing fine German chiming clock movements and the manufacture of mahogany cases for them. These cases were made for their own use and that of the other importers. Throughout the 1920s the manufacturing, marketing, and servicing of fine chiming clocks was the chief business of the company, although cuckoo clocks were handled to some extent. Changing economic conditions in the 1930s affected both these lines, and the outbreak of World War II cut off the supply of both cuckoo clock and chiming clock movements. This, together with the severe materials allocation during the Second World War, led to the final discontinuance of all manufacturing and assembling operations.

The Angelus Clock Company was incorporated on March 20, 1874, in Philadelphia at 136 S. Sixth Street. While it remained viable only a year or so, it is curious that a century later no procedings in merger, sale, or dissolution have been filed, so the incorporation remains open on the records of the Pennsylvania Department of State, Corporation Bureau. Typical Angelus clocks were cased in marbelized wood, carved or turned to simulate the front of a cathedral. The cases were twenty-eight to twenty-nine inches tall and about fourteen inches wide. Figures 7, 8, and 9 show two typical examples. The brass, spring-driven, eight-day movement was arranged to strike twelve strokes on the canonical hours of six A.M., noon, and six P.M. Obviously a novelty clock, the Angelus was designed specifically for the Roman Catholic trade. Its appeal was apparently not directed to churches, convents, and missions, but rather to the parishioners as a house clock that sounded the bells to prayer in synchrony with those rung at the churches. Considering the number of Roman Catholics, it is difficult to hazard a guess as to why the venture was so unsuccessful, unless the retail price was too high.

> LAWRENCE ASH, Clock & Watchmaker, (Late from Mr. Edward Duffield's) Having set up his Business in Front-street, six Doors above Market-street, would be greatly obliged to all Gentlemen and Ladies for their Custom, and Recommendation; as it will be his chief Care to finish their Work with the utmost Dispatch. Engraving Likewise performed in all its Branches, in the neatest Manner, by John Sleeper. (*Pennsylvania Gazette*, March 25, 1762)

It is not clear whether Ash was an apprentice or a journeyman to Duffield, but in either event he would have acquired valuable clock experience. For some reason, perhaps political, he moved to Baltimore before the Revolutionary War.

Matthias Baldwin (1795–1866), left fatherless at the age of four, showed an early love for tools and mechanical devices. At sixteen he was apprenticed to Woolworth Brothers, in Frankford, Philadelphia County, to learn the jewelry trade; he served for five years. In 1817 he became a journeyman jeweler with the manufacturing firm of Fletcher & Gardiner at 130 Chestnut Street, Philadelphia. Baldwin started his own business in 1819. Success came slowly, but nine years at the bench gave him a love for accuracy and awakened his creative genius. He finally joined with a machinist and wood-engraver named David Mason in 1825, and they opened their establishment on Walnut Street between Fourth and Fifth. They invented many improvements in the methods of bookbinding, and they also manufactured copper cylinders for printing calico. This enterprise was so successful that it was necessary for Baldwin to

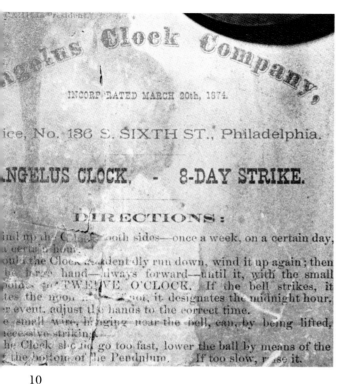

10

Fig. 7. Rough finished Angelus clock, possibly with original tablet. Courtesy of Edward Railsback and John Sweisford.

Fig. 8. Smooth finished Angelus clock, possibly with original tablet. Courtesy of Edward Railsback and John Sweisford.

Fig. 9. Stippled finished Angelus clock with replaced but compatible tablet. Private collection.

Fig. 10. Label found in the clock in fig. 9. Private collection.

move to a larger shop to design and build a vertical steam engine capable of delivering five horsepower. At about this time, reports on British steam locomotive accomplishments stung Yankee pride and stirred Yankee ingenuity. The Peale Museum asked Baldwin, the former watchmaker who reputedly had built a tiny model of a steam locomotive, to attempt the construction of a model locomotive large enough to haul two small cars on a circular track at the museum and carry four passengers. Baldwin succeeded, and on April 25, 1831, his first steam locomotive fulfilled all requirements of the order. His renown caught the attention of the officials of the newly organized Philadelphia, Germantown & Norristown Railroad Company, who commissioned Baldwin to construct a full-size locomotive, which was the "Old Ironsides" of 1832. Its trial was the first movement by an American steam locomotive on a railroad in Pennsylvania; this accomplishment sired what became the Baldwin Locomotive Works and the Philadelphia & Reading Railroad.

All that is known of Samuel Barrow is contained in this advertisement of his Philadelphia shop.

> SAMUEL BARROW, Clock and Watch-Maker, From London, who came over in the Betsey, Captain Brown, from Liverpool, has set up a complete shop, well furnished with materials for his business, in Chestnut street, on the south side, betwixt Second and Front streets, Where he makes, sells and repairs all sorts of repeating, horizontal, seconds or stop and plain watches and clocks of all kinds, according to the newest and most approved methods for exact keeping of time. As he has been some years under the instruction, and wrought for most of the principal watch and clock makers in London, particularly the famous Mr. John Harrison, who made the noted timepiece, he makes no doubt of giving satisfaction to all his employers, by making, finishing and repairing in this city, all kinds of work in his way, in the very best and neatest manner, and on the very lowest terms such work can be performed. (*Pennsylvania Chronicle*, October 7, 1771)

Owen Biddle (1737–99) was a clockmaker, a scientist, and a statesman. He advertised from 1764 to 1770; the following is a typical sample:

> OWEN BIDDLE, Clock and Watch-Maker, Has for sale, next Door to Hugh and George Roberts's Ware-House, of Ironmongery; A Variety of Articles in the Watch-making Business; consisting of Mainsprings, Glasses, Verges, cantred Wheels and Pin-

ions, Buttons, leaded and unleaded; Silver and Pinchbeck Bows, and Pendants, & c. & C. Clocks and Watches, made and repaired in the best Manner, and on the most reasonable Terms. (*Pennsylvania Chronicle*, November 30, 1767)

Philadelphian Biddle temporarily laid aside his Quaker beliefs of neutrality and was in 1775 appointed a member of the Pennsylvania Committee of Safety. His younger brother Clement did likewise and was put in charge of erecting a powder mill on French Creek in Chester County. In 1776 Biddle and the other members of the Committee of Safety were charged with initiating the Pennsylvania State Gun Factory in Philadelphia, but in December the operation was moved to the French Creek Powder Mill. Benjamin Rittenhouse was employed there as a gun lock maker.

Lawrence Birnie advertised in the mid-1770s as an experienced tradesman.

LAWRENCE BIRNIE. Watch and Clock maker from the city of Dublin, begs leave to acquaint his friends, and the Public in general that he served a regular apprenticeship to his father William Birnie, late of Temple Patrick, and afterwards experienced a considerable share of knowledge with some of the most eminent Watch Makers in England and Ireland; and as he has opened a shop at his lodgings in the house of Mrs. Faries in Arch Street, near Second Street, where he intends carrying on said business in all its various branches, particularly making and repairing all sorts of repeating, horizontal, and plain gold and silver watches. (supplement of the *Pennsylvania Packet*, October 24, 1774)

Birnie advertised the following year in search of an assistant; he also continued to solicit business for his shop, now located on Second Street. In 1776 the Pennsylvania Committee of Safety commissioned Birnie to build an air furnace and a mill for cutting files to be used in a gun lock factory. He was thus among a group of horologists whose talents were used to support the war effort.

James Boss was listed in the 1846–47 McElroy's Philadelphia City Directory and is famous for his invention of the gold-filled watch case, which was patented in 1859. His story is more fully related in the chapter on watch case makers.

Henry Bower was apparently an active clockmaker at the end of the eighteenth and the beginning of the nineteenth centuries. Plate 102 in Brooks Palmer's *Book of American Clocks* shows a dwarf tall clock constructed by him. If the dating is correct, Bower must have been one of the earliest American makers of what is now popularly called a grandmother's clock.

What year Aime Brandt and Louis Matthey arrived in Philadelphia from Switzerland is uncertain. The following advertisement suggests it was a reasonable length of time before 1795.

> BRANDT & MATTHEY, Watch Makers, and Clock Makers, From Switzerland, North Second, at the corner of New Street, No. 158, Respectfully inform the public in general, and their Friends in particular, that they have received by the latest arrivals from Europe, a large assortment of elegant and most modern Gold and Silver Watches, Watch-makers Tools, & c. which they offer for sale at a most reasonable price. Likewise take in to repair, all sorts of Clocks and Watches, and hope to maintain the good opinion of the public and their friends, which they have hitherto liberally experienced. (*Pennsylvania Packet*, October 3, 1795)

Fig. 11. Calendar watch signed "Aime Brandt, Philadelphia." Private collection.

The partners were listed as clock- and watchmakers in the 1797 to 1799 directories, although apart from their self-styled qualifications, there is no positive proof they really were makers. Aime and Charles Brandt, singly and in partnership, were listed in directories from 1800 through 1831. Indeed, watches signed "Aime Brandt, Philadelphia" are known. Figure 11 displays one of them.

Amable Brazier has been described as a French watchmaker and jeweler who was listed in directories from 1794 through 1833. According to his own advertisement, he spelled his name with an "s," rather than with a "z."

> Brasier, A., Clock and Watch Maker, Informs his friends and the public in general, that he has removed from No. 7 to No. 23, north Third street, where he continues to carry on the clock and watchmaker's business, and has for sale an assortment of Warranted Watches, consisting of elegant gold, plain, enamelled, and fancy watches, for ladies, double cased, capp'd and jewelled, and a great variety of silver watches, warranted, at the most reduced prices. (*Federal Gazette*, Philadelphia, April 21, 1796)

None of his watches have been reported; in all likelihood they were imported.

Breitinger & Kunz was a firm mentioned in the description of the American Cuckoo Clock Company. The precise dates of the firm have not been established, but it evidently handled both clocks and watches. A Victorian wall clock in walnut which bore that name was sold at auction a few years ago. More recently, one showed up for repair and the owner said her father had bought it in 1929 from Breitinger's store on Ninth Street (Mr. Kunz had died at some earlier date). Figure 12 shows a watch bearing the firm name. The manufacturer has not been identified. From facts thus far developed, it appears doubtful that the firm was a manufacturer, although the clocks might have been assembled there.

William Brewer's name appeared in directories from 1791 to 1825.

> WILLIAM BREWER, Clock and Watch-maker, takes this method to inform the public, that he hath opened a shop in Chestnut-street, between Front and Second-streets, and nearly opposite Joseph Saunders's; where he purposes making and mending all kinds of clocks and watches; being many years conversant in that business, hopes by his attention to please, and the most reasonable charge to merit the notice of his friends, and the public in general, whose favours will be greatly esteemed, and thankfully received, by their friend.
>
> N.B. He has for sale, a neat assortment of broad cloths on the most reasonable terms, for ready money. (*Pennsylvania Journal*, September 28, 1774)

There has been no previous directory listing of a Germantown clockmaker named John Brocker. Nevertheless, at least two of his tall clocks are in existence and he is therefore included here, if for no other reason than to challenge a future researcher to learn more about him.

Only two of the five earlier clockmaker authorities mentioned John Brooke; and they placed him in New York City circa 1830. There is nothing to substantiate this and it may be an error. He apparently did work in Germantown, as a tall clock bearing his name and "Germantown" on the dial is in a private collection and is consistent with the period of about 1820 to 1830.

S.P. Burdick invented a patent lever, an eight-day cathedral gong, and a musical clock using a music box. Examples of his production are quite rare. He worked during the 1870s and 1880s.

Charles Campbell was listed in directories from 1794 to 1803. That he was an extensive newspaper advertiser offers an advantage to his researchers.

> CAMPBELL, CHARLES. Watch Maker. The Amateurs of Mechanism. An Astronomical and Musical Clock, Shewing the Sun's diurnal motion, its rising and setting through the year by a

Fig. 12. Watch bearing the name "Breitinger & Kunz, Philadelphia." Private collection.

moving Horizon, and pointing to a graduated arch from which mean-time may be calculated with facility. Likewise, showing the Phases of the Moon, its celestial appearance, age and southing. In the center, the indexes point to hours, and minutes, with an extra index pointing to the days of the month through the year without shifting, and marking at the same time the Sun's situation on the Zodiac. In the body is displayed a complete Orrery, moved by the clock, shewing the motion of the Planets making their revolutions round the Sun according to the Newtonian System. Its external appearance is finished in a stile of elegance almost equal to its intrinsic value, its Musical part is moved by the clock and by shifting an index will play alternately twelve tunes. The Pendulum is scientific, compound and very heavy. This invaluable clock is in complete order, will be warranted, and is for sale by Charles Campbell, Watch-Maker, No. 3, South Fourth Street.

N.B. At the above place are always for sale large collection of curious, elegant and plain gold and silver watches and a variety of clocks, & c. (*True American and Commercial Advertiser*, Philadelphia, July 2, 1798)

CAMPBELL, CHARLES, Watch Maker, Has removed to the Shop formerly occupied by Mr. John Wood, No. 55, corner of Front and Chestnut Streets: Where he will thankfully receive and execute orders with neatness and dispatch. He has constantly on hand, A Neat and Large Assortment of Clocks and Watches. Wanted, A Journeyman: Also, one or two Apprentices of respectable parents. For Sale, A large quantity of Watch Glasses, Wholesale and Retail. (*Gazette of the U.S.*, November 24, 1798)

Fig. 13. Unique hood and dial of a tall clock by John Brocker, Germantown, Pa., made before 1811.

Campbell advertised the same year that he had moved his business to another location and that he wanted a journeyman; the following year he notified the public that his shop was now in Germantown and that he had engaged "an experienced Watch-Case Maker, from London" to outfit his large assortment of timepieces. While it is obvious that he sold a considerable quantity of imported clocks and watches, it is equally apparent that he was skilled in their manufacture, or at least in their assembly, as he twice advertised for apprentices. The advertised sale of the astronomical clock in 1798 is intriguing because there is no suggestion of its maker. The ability to construct an orrery in America at that time was limited to only a handful of craftsmen—one of them being David Rittenhouse, who had died two years previously. Could this have been a Rittenhouse clock not purchased during the maker's lifetime by whomever had commissioned its construction? Of course, it could have been an import; whatever, it is unlikely that Campbell constructed the clock. Watch papers of Campbell's are reported in collections.

Isaac Campbell was listed in the 1813 directory as a watchmaker, in directories of 1818 to 1822 as a watch case maker, and in directories of 1821 to 1824 again as a watchmaker.

William Cannon served as an apprentice to an unknown clockmaker, probably in the 1720s and 1730s; he may even have been a journeyman. He later returned to his native town of Burlington, New Jersey, where he plied his trade until his death in 1753. Interestingly, an even better-known clockmaker, Joseph Hollinshead, was administrator of the estate.

John Carrell advertised in the late eighteenth century as a jeweler and tradesman.

> CARRELL, JOHN, Clock and Watch Maker, In Front street, six doors below Market street, Has for Sale, Eight-day Clocks, Japanned clock faces, Gold and silver watches, Patent seconds watches. An assortment of clock and watch maker's tools and materials imported immediately from the manufactories, and sold on reasonable terms. Also, all kinds of gold and silver work and jewellery done in the neatest manner. An Apprentice wanted. (*Pennsylvania Packet*, October 3, 1786)

> CARRELL, JOHN. Watches and Clocks, Made and carefully repaired. Also, all kinds of Work in Gold, silver and Jewellery, Done in the neatest manner, and at the lowest prices, By John Carrell, In Front street, six doors below Market street. He has for sale, Gold, silver and pinchbeck watches, Patent second and day of the month ditto, Eight day and 30 hour clocks, Cast clock, brass forged, iron and slit pinions, Watch main springs, pendants, glasses, keys, chains & c. Black lead crucibles of all sizes, Buckle chapes by the doz, or pair, Plated bitts, stirrups, and spurs, Silver mounted swords and belts, Ladies and gentlemens pocket books, Penknives, plated buckles, & c. & c. A small invoice of Clock and Watchmakers tools and Files to be sold very low. Any person wanting a Watch of any quality or description, may be furnished at as low a price as he could purchase it in England. (*Pennsylvania Packet*, September 29, 1787)

John and Daniel Carrell advertised as watch- and clockmakers, goldsmiths, and jewelers.

Fig. 14. Compare the hood and dial of this John Brocker clock and the one in figure 13. Courtesy of Mr. and Mrs. James Barthold.

> JOHN & DANIEL CARRELL, Watch and Clock-Makers, Goldsmiths, and Jewellers, In Front street, seven doors below the Coffee-house; Have for sale Silver watches capp'd and plain, of various prices; eight day and twenty-four hour clocks; clock dials, neatly japann'd with or without moon-plates; cast clockwork in setts; clock-bells; clock pinions, ready split; watch dial-plates, main-springs, glasses, pendants, verges, pinion-wire; gold, gilt and steel watch-hands; chains, seals, and trinkets; buckle chapes and money-scales. An elegant gold repeating watch to be sold cheap. Also, an assortment of clock and watch-makers' files, gravers, & c. All kinds of plate-work and jewellery, done in the neatest manner—Clocks and watches made and carefully repaired. (*Pennsylvania Evening Herald*, October 29, 1785)

While enterprising entrepreneurs, the Carrells can scarcely be recorded as makers.

> CHARTER.—Wants Employment, A Person turned of fifty years of age, can handle a file in brass or silver, in a midling way, or the pen if required, and knows something of accounts, or is willing to attend in a store, so far as his ability and strength will permit; can have a character for his good behavior and honesty. Any one this may suit, by enquiring at Mr. Charter's watch-case maker, in Locksley's alley, in Arch above Third street, and facing the Friends Burial Ground. (*Pennsylvania Packet*, March 14, 1785)

Benjamin Chandlee is fully described in the Chester County chapter.

Simon Chaudron, Simon Chaudron & Company, Edward Chaudron, and Chaudron & Rosch are all listed as watchmakers, jewelers, and wholesale and retail dealers in clocks and watches between 1798 and 1816. It is fairly obvious that none were makers. In 1819 Simon moved to the exiled French colony at Demopolis, Alabama, where in his first advertisement he claimed long experience in repairing clocks, watches, and chronometers, thus indicating he had some horological skill.

John Child (1789–1876) was regularly classified in directories from 1813 through 1847 as a clock- and watchmaker. That he made watches is doubtful; he more likely was a repairer. This theory is strengthened by the existence of his watch papers. There can be no doubt that he made clocks, at least one of which still poses some mysteries. This clock is owned by the Library Company of Philadelphia.

A letter was received from John Child of Philadelphia offering to sell to the Li-

16

Fig. 15. Full view of the huge clock by John Child, Philadelphia. Permission from the Library Company of Philadelphia.

Fig. 16. Dial of the clock in fig. 15. Permission from the Library Company of Philadelphia.

15

brary Company a clock with an alarm to ring at sundown. Mr. Norris, a member of the committee on repairs and improvements, reported the purchase of the astronomical clock on May 7, 1835, for $125.00. The "astronomical" description raises questions, for the clock does not contain any of the features usually appertaining to such an instrument. It is an ungainly monster: the case is 92 inches tall, 44 inches wide, and 12 inches deep. Apparently it is of plain white pine which has been stained walnut and can be dated somewhere between 1870 and 1890. The high dial, 24 inches in diameter, holds more mysteries. The right and left winding arbors handle the time and strike weights. The center winding hole leads to an extra portion, which was originally attached to the movement and which had a winding drum for some unknown purpose. There is no explanation for the small hole at the top of the dial. What appears to be a third hand pointing to four is actually the tail of the minute hand. Finally, there is no explanation for the oddly calibrated scale between 4:30 and 7:30 unless, in some way, it tied in with the sundown alarm feature. There is a plausible excuse for a sunrise alarm, but for a sundown alarm?

Mention of tower or turret clocks has been sadly missing, so it is fitting to note one that looks benevolently out over this whole county. In the tower of City Hall is the great clock, 361 feet above the pavement. The diameter of each of the clock's four faces is 26 feet; they are all lighted at night. The length of the minute hand is 10 feet, 8 inches, and its weight is 225 pounds; the length of the hour hand is 9 feet, and its weight is 175 pounds. The hour marks are each 38 inches long and 14 inches wide. The total weight of the complete clock installation is over fifty tons. The clock was designed by Professor Warren O. Johnson for the Pneumatic System of Tower Clocks. The city contracted with the Johnson Temperature Regulation Company of Madison, Wisconsin, to install the clock. The contract was dated June 22, 1898; the clock was started on December 31 of the same year and has kept accurate time ever since.

Benjamin Clark was consistently listed in directories as a clock- and watchmaker over the lengthy span of 1793 to 1848. Likewise, he frequently advertised himself as such.

CLARK, BENJAMIN, Clock and Watch Maker, The corner of Front and Market Street, Has just received by the Dolly, Capt. Smith, from Liverpool, a general assortment of warranted Silver and Pinchbeck Watches, With tools, files and materials, japanned clock faces, clock bells, cast and forged work, with slit pinions. Chains, strings, seals, and keys. (*Federal Gazette*, November 19, 1791)

Fig. 17. Mahogany tall case clock with dentil molded scroll top, reeded columns on the hood, and reeded quarter columns on the case. Made by Benjamin Clark, Philadelphia, circa 1780–90. Height 8′1″.

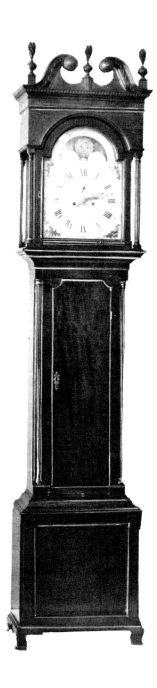

CLARK, BENJAMIN, Clock and Watch Maker, The corner of Market and Front streets, Has just returned from the country, and opening a large assortment of Cap'd and Jewelled, cap'd and plain Watches, Tools and Materials, Consisting of Japanned clock faces, eight day and thirty hour, cast brass forged work, and slit pinions, bell, bench, hand and tail vices, shears, clock and watch plyers, sliding tongues, cutting nippers, large and small screw plates and screw drivers, watch faces, files assorted, main springs, glasses, clock and watch hands, fashionable gilt and steel chains, seals and keys, silk strings, & c. & c. (*Federal Gazette*, November 6, 1793)

CLARK, BENJAMIN, Clock and Watch-Maker, Has removed to No. 36, Market Street, Where he has for sale at the above place, Spring and other Clocks, Gold and Silver Watches, Tools, Files, and materials; steel and gilt chains, Seals and Keys, Strings, & C. Clocks and Watches repaired as usual. (*Pennsylvania Packet*, June 4, 1800)

Benjamin Clark provides a good example of how misleading superficial references in early directories and advertisements can be. The reader will undoubtedly conclude that he is not a proven maker, unless he believes that the picture of this one clock (fig. 17) proves otherwise.

Ephraim Clark, father of Benjamin and also a prolific advertiser, was listed as a clock- and watchmaker in directories from 1785 to 1811.

EPHRAIM CLARK, Clock and Watch-Maker, The South-east Corner of Market and Front streets, Has for Sale, A Large assortment of Watches, capt and jewel'd; plain capt and other warranted Watches; an Assortment of Clocks, moon and plain arch'd; likewise A Quantity of Clock and Watch-makers Tools and Materials; consisting of Clock and Watch Plyers; Hand and Tail-Vices; Sliding Tongs; blow Pipes; double Tweesers; Hammers; Pincers; Gages; Clock and Watch-Turnbenches; Bench-Vices; Spring Saws; cutting Nippers; Screw-Keys; Screw-Drivers; Watch and Clock; Watch-Brushes; Broaches for Clock and Watch-Makers; adjusting Tools; Engravers; regulating Springs; magnifying Glasses; Clock and Watch Fobs; gilt and steel Chains; main Springs; Watch-Glasses, double and single ground; Fusee Chains; Hands; silver Pendants; Dial-Plates; large and small steel Wire; steel and brass Keys; an Assortment of other

Things in his line of business. Watches and Clocks repaired as usual. (*Independent Gazetteer*, Philadelphia, August 20, 1785)

In an advertisement of November 19, 1791, Clark announced that he was the successor to Mr. John Wood, who had been a distinguished clockmaker. In an advertisement of November 7, 1793, Clark wrote "that a Journeyman and Apprentice [was] wanting." This is evidence of his own skill and a trade expanded by retention of many of Wood's former customers.

One of the horological pioneers of Philadelphia, Clark began manufacturing high case clocks at Nos. 1 & 3 South Front Street in 1785, soon after his arrival from England. He quickly took his son Benjamin into partnership, and they formed a successful clockmaking firm. They changed their location several times until 1806, when Charles, Benjamin's son, was admitted. Son Jesse was later taken on. These latter two left the firm in 1811, and Ellis, another son, was admitted. Ephraim Clark was then retiring, so the new firm was styled by Benjamin and Ellis Clark. They were then located at the southeast corner of Front and Market Streets. In addition to their clockmaking business, they imported on an extensive scale castings and forgings for high case clocks, and sold large quantities of them to the Pennsylvania clockmakers. At one time they were much the largest importers of these materials in America. As the demand for high case clocks slowed, the firm's business declined, until about 1845 when it closed.

Abel Cottey, born in England in 1655, arrived in Philadelphia in 1682 and his name was immediately added to the list of clockmakers. He appears to have been the first confirmed clockmaker in Pennsylvania and possibly in all of Colonial America, as there survives a clock by him dated 1709. He was, of course, closely followed by Peter Stretch of Philadelphia; Benjamin Bagnall (a fellow Quaker) in Boston; William Claggett in Boston and Newport, Rhode Island; and Isaac Pearson of Burlington, New Jersey. Pendulum clocks had been introduced into England from Holland before Cottey emigrated to the colonies. From whom he learned the trade is not known, but he did bring the art with him, making tall clocks with eight-day brass movements. His 1709 specimen has an eleven-inch, square dial with skillfully engraved corners. It has protecting rings around the key holes and has a second hand and a calendar ring. His apprentice, Benjamin Chandlee, married Cottey's daughter Sarah, and so inherited from Mrs. Cottey a house and a lot in Nottingham, Chester County. When Abel Cottey died in 1711, the inventory of his estate listed many items associated with watchmaking. Although it is fair to assert that he was not a

Fig. 18. Bracket clock, circa 1810, with unusual feature of moon phase, signed by John Crowley. Courtesy of Edward Railsback and John Sweisford.

Fig. 19. Rear view of the clock in fig. 18. Prolific engraving on back plate suggests English origin, but type of decoration and stylized eagle of the period are equally suggestive of the United States. Courtesy of Edward Railsback and John Sweisford.

watchmaker, he may have done repairing along with his clockmaking, as there is no evidence of anyone else capable of it in Philadelphia at that time. He constructed at least twenty-one clocks.

Although Robert Coupar was not a maker, his advertisement may establish him as America's first horological consignment merchant.

> ROBERT COUPAR. Opposite the Friends Meeting House, in Second street, Hath for sale a few very neat skeleton watches, silver and pinchbeck, chased and plain, with a variety of common construction of various prices, all of which will be sold very low, as they are upon commission from one who exports those articles upon the best terms from London. (*Pennsylvania Packet*, August 15, 1774)

The Crow family of clockmakers is properly associated with Wilmington, Delaware, yet one of them, Thomas, had some ties with Philadelphia. He appears to have worked in about 1797 and again in 1805–7, and he advertised in Philadelphia newspapers.

> THOMAS CROW, Clock and Watch-Maker, in Wilmington, New Castle county, hath for sale, Watch Springs, by the dozen or small quantity. He puts Springs in Watches at Twelve Shillings each, the former price, and warrants them good for one year. Clock-Makers may be supplied with large Springs for Table or Musical Clocks of any sizes. (*Pennsylvania Gazette*, August 14, 1782)

That he worked from 1770 to 1824 would indicate by rule of thumb that all his tall clocks would have enameled dials, yet some of his clocks have brass dials, which were uncommon after the Revolutionary War.

John Crowley was listed as a clock- and watchmaker in directories from 1803 to 1825. He was one of the early makers to offer bracket clocks. The clock (figure 18) has a painted dial and a mahogany case of typical English style. It even has a fusee movement and a time and hour strike, and it dates about 1810.

The description of the bracket clock and the absence of good American-made clock springs in Crowley's time together lend credence to the hypothesis that he was an importer. The owner of this clock, however, believes that Crowley may have been one of the few clockmakers of his time to make his own movements, including cutting the fusees and cases.

Frederick Dominick purported to be a clock- and watchmaker in his advertisements appearing between 1766 and 1777.

> FREDERICK DOMINICK, Clock and Watchmaker, in the southwest corner house of 2d and Vine Streets, makes and repairs all kinds of clocks and watches, in the neatest and best manner. All those who will favour him with their custom may be assured that he will serve them faithfully at the cheapest price. He hopes especially that his countrymen, the Germans, will give him their custom; their kindness will ever be recognized with thanks. (*Staatsbote*, July 12, 1768)

He apparently made some tall clocks, as his #9 is reported.

English-born James Doull made both tall and Massachusetts shelf clocks in Charleston, Massachusetts, circa 1790–1820. One of his tall clocks is illustrated in the *Book of American Clocks*. He moved to Philadelphia, where he was listed rather regularly in directories from 1823 to 1840 and from 1845 to 1849. Here he seems also, judging from figure 20, to have made banjo timepieces.

Burrows Dowdney advertised as a clock- and watchmaker from 1768 to 1811.

> BURROWS DOWDNEY, Watch and Clock Maker, in Front-Street, a few doors above the Drawbridge, in the Shop lately occupied by Mr. Emanuel Rouse, Makes and repairs all Kinds of Clocks and Watches, after the neatest and best manner. (*Pennsylvania Chronicle*, May 16, 1768)

In the State Department in Washington, D.C., there is a Philadelphia Chippendale tall case clock, circa 1770. The case is attributed to Thomas Affleck, Philadelphia's greatest cabinet maker of the pre-Revolutionary period. The broken pediment hood is ornamented with applied carving over the arched dial. The clock itself, made by Burrows Dowdney of Philadelphia, has a moon phase face with unique eyes that wag with the swing of the pendulum.

Edward Duffield (1720–1801), born in Philadelphia, was one of the earliest clockmakers in that city. The identity of his teacher is not known, but he began business when he attained his majority in 1741, in a shop at the northwest corner of Second and Arch Streets. Neighbors dropped in so frequently to ask the time that his

20

Fig. 20. Earliest known Philadelphia banjo clock (completely original) by James Doull, circa 1825. Woods are mahogany, yellow poplar, and cedar. Private collection.

Fig. 21. James Doull clock in the style of Massachusetts shelf on shelf. Both case and dial appear to be reproductions. Courtesy of Edward Railsback and John Sweisford.

life-long friend, Benjamin Franklin, suggested he make a two-faced clock, placed obliquely at the corner of the store, so as to be seen from both directions. This was the first public clock in Philadelphia, so it became the time standard. Duffield was a respectable citizen, a well-read fellow, and an excellent clockmaker. He was equally adept at tall case and tower clocks. Moreover, one known piece of his work was what today would be called a grandmother's clock. One of his clocks can still be viewed at the American Philosophical Society, of which he was a member.

It has been averred that Duffield was the first watchmaker in Pennsylvania; at least, a watch bearing his name was exhibited in Philadelphia in 1950. He also produced various instruments for Franklin to use in his experiments. In 1747 he moved out to Lower Dublin, Philadelphia County, to live at "Benfield," a tract of land purchased by his grandfather, Benjamin Duffield, in 1683. During the British occupation of Philadelphia, the Franklins spent many days at Benfield. The versatile Duffield made the first medals ever executed in the province to honor the victory over the Indians at Kittanning in 1756. He succeeded Thomas Stretch as caretaker of the State House clock in 1762, and was, in turn, succeeded by the renowned David Rittenhouse in 1775. He was a delegate to the first General Convention of the Protestant Episcopal Church, held in Philadelphia in September, 1785. In 1793 the Lower Dublin Academy obtained a charter, and Duffield became one of the trustees. He gave to the Academy his famous two-faced clock; a dormer window was made for it and a thirty-pound cannon ball served as the weight.

The partnership of Dungan & Klump was formed in 1909 for the express purpose of producing the Dickory Dickory Dock Clocks, now popularly referred to as Mouse Clocks. This enterprise enables Pennsylvania to lay claim to a unique horological fame—the design of the only American production clocks employing vertical dials. By 1915, however, the name of the partnership disappeared from the Philadelphia business directory.

Elmer Dungan was born in Flourtown on December 25, 1861, and died in Fort Washington on September 10, 1930. Although he never finished high school, he was blessed with ambition, energy, and genius, which brought him success in such varied fields as the furniture, jewelry, publishing, and bowling businesses. Furthermore, he was an ardent clock collector. Because his daughter Emily greatly favored the Dickory, dickory clock nursery rhyme, Dungan proceeded to design and patent a mouse clock, the mechanical embodiment of the rhyme, which he arranged to have made for her.

A family friend, Charles M. Klump, who was also in the publishing business, envisioned the commercial possibilities of the clock. This led to the partnership. All their models were wall clocks. The first model was 43½ inches tall, was patented on February 16, 1909, and was produced by the New Haven Clock Company for Dungan & Klump, originators and manufacturers, 1208 Chestnut Street, Philadelphia, Pennsylvania. These clocks failed to perform satisfactorily, so Dungan created a second model, which differed from the first only in the release mechanism. Both models had the movement at the bottom, the mouse release mechanism at the top of the case, and the two-day, full-strike movements; the second, however, also had mechanical difficulties. Consequently, Dungan completely redesigned the clock, and a third model, patented on July 12, 1910, had both movement and release device at the top of the case. These were produced by the Sessions Clock Company. Dungan and Sessions personnel created yet a fourth model, patented on September 13, 1910. The case, reduced to 35¼ inches and made of oak, was simpler in design and construction, and therefore cheaper to make. The full-striking, lever escapement was changed to a single strike at one o'clock, eight-day, pendulum movement, and was therefore more reliable. No accurate production figures are known, but possibly up to 2,000 clocks were made. Klump died shortly thereafter, and Dungan lost interest in the project. Later, though, to help his son Warren, he designed a fifth model. This clock, only 15½ inches high and wearing a round dial, sounded no strikes and sported a moving mouse, although this one did not point out the time as previous models had. Only a test lot was produced.

Dungan left a heritage for collectors who are lucky enough to own an original Dickory Dickory Dock Clock or a fine Horolovar Company reproduction; he also offered another gift. Motorists driving north on Bethlehem Pike through Fort Washington may see in the gable of the Dungan home the dial of a tower clock he designed and had built for the benefit of travelers. For the complete story, the reader is advised to see the *Bulletin* of the National Association of Watch and Clock Collectors, Inc., Supplement 4, Summer 1966, entitled "Elmer Ellsworth Dungan and the Dickory Dickory Dock Clock." This extract is available by the kind permission of the author, Charles Terwilliger.

John Dupuy advertised from 1769 to 1774 as a clock- and watchmaker.

JOHN DUPUY. Just imported in the ship Mary and Elizabeth, Captain Falconer, and to be sold by John Dupuy, in Second-street, the fourth door below the Friends meeting house, Philadelphia. A Considerable number of handsome Silver Watches of

22

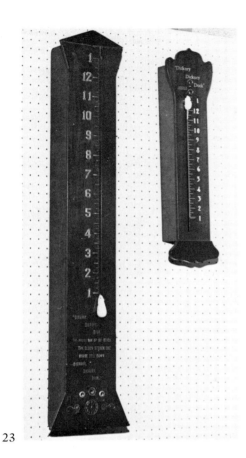

23

Fig. 22. Clock by Edward Duffield, probably made on special order because the case, constructed of Santo Domingan mahogany, has cloth-covered open work to allow a louder sound to emit from the bell. Private collection.

Fig. 23. The first model of the Mouse Clock is on the left; the fourth model is on the right. Courtesy of Edward Railsback and John Sweisford.

various kinds and prices; also may be had, watch main springs, silver pendants, watch crystals, inside and outside chains, enamelled dial plates, brass and steel watch keys, jointed and common sorts, pyramid chrystal seals, swivel cornelian ditto set in silver, with various other kinds of materials in the watch way. Likewise a curious assortment of gold and silver hat bands, buttons and loops, with buckles, all of an elegant kind and newest fashion. . . . He still continues the business of clock and watch making and mending as usual, and will make it his particular care and study to give satisfaction to all those who chuse to employ him.

    N.B. At the same place may be had, all kinds of plate and jewelry, imported in the ship Richard Penn, from London; also money scales and weights properly regulated. (*Pennsylvania Packet*, May 9, 1774)

John Ent advertised in 1763 as a tradesman in Philadelphia.

> JOHN ENT, Having set up his Business in Second-street, Philadelphia, between Arch and Race-streets, next Door but one to Leonard Melchior's Tavern, and opposite to Mr. Anthony Morris, Brewer; Makes and repairs all Sorts of Clocks and Watches, in the best and neatest Manner, as well as performed in London. N.B. He likewise undertakes clocks by the Year, at a moderate Price. (*Pennsylvania Gazette*, July 28, 1763)

David Evans conducted business in Philadelphia from 1770 to 1773, then opened a shop in Baltimore and served there until 1790. He was a nephew of David Rittenhouse, from whom he undoubtedly received a first-rate training and for whom he made tall clock cases. No information concerning his clockmaking activity in Philadelphia has been found. An early advertisement of his (below) is for his Baltimore shop. It is unique that while he was a clockmaker, he served watch customers by employing English watchmakers.

> DAVID EVANS. Clock and Watch-Maker, from Philadelphia. Informs his friends and the Public, that he has opened Shop, at the Sign of the Arch-Dial and Watch, next Door to Messieurs Shields and Mattison, Hatters and adjoining Mr. Francis Sanderson's Coppersmith, in Gay-Street; where he makes musical, horizontal, repeating and plain Clocks, in the neatest manner, and newest fashion, and at the lowest prices. He likewise makes

Watches (having employed workmen, regularly bred to the different branches of Watchmaking in London) which he engages to be as good and equal in quality to any imported. Watches repaired, shall be warranted for several years, cleaning once a year, and accident or abuse excepted. As a proof that his intentions are just, he further engages, to return the money for repaired or new work, in case they should not perform. As he had just begun business, he will do the utmost in his power to merit the approbation of these gentlemen and ladies who will please to favor him with their custom, and their favours shall be gratefully acknowledged by their humble servant, David Evans. (*The Maryland Journal* and *The Baltimore Daily Advertiser*, August 20, 1773)

Matthias Eyre was an interesting practitioner of a craft supportive of watchmaking—springmaking. Indeed, he must have been one of the earliest such artisans in America.

MATTHIAS EYRE. Watch-Main-Springs, Made in Philadelphia, are sold by the Manufacturer, Matthias Eyre, at his House in Third-street, below South street, and by John Wood, Watchmaker, in Front street, at the corner of Chestnut-street; where Watch-makers and others may be supplied with any Quantity of Springs, much cheaper than they can be afforded when imported from England; from which Circumstance, and the good Quality of the Springs, the Maker hopes for the Encouragement of the Watch-makers in this and the neighbouring Provinces, whose Orders will be gratefully received and faithfully executed. (*Pennsylvania Journal*, February 1, 1775)

William Faris was not only the most important clockmaker in the whole history of Annapolis but was perhaps the most multifaceted and interesting one in all Maryland. He is mentioned in *Maryland Silversmiths, 1715–1830*:

The most picturesque figure among eighteenth-century Maryland silversmiths is William Faris of Annapolis. Silversmith, watchmaker, clock maker, designer, portrait painter, cabinet maker, tulip grower, tavern keeper, dentist, diarist and gossip, he arrests and deserves our attention. In addition to his sundry notices and advertisements in the newspapers, we have his diary, . . . his account books, and what to the lover of old silver is even more interesting, a book of drawings with his beautiful designs for silver, probably the only existing example of original working drawings and patterns of an eighteenth century American silversmith which has come down to us, and one which shows that he was a craftsman and artist of no mean ability.

Faris was born in 1728, probably in London, and his early days were spent in Philadelphia. He was the son of Abigail and William Faris; his father, a London clockmaker, died in an English prison because of his Quaker beliefs. The six-month-old William and his widowed mother fled to the colonies, arriving in Philadelphia in the spring of 1729. Abigail Faris brought to this country the five clocks made by her husband in London. The subsequent tale was recorded in 1939 by the late Charles T. Stran, a great-great-grandson of William Faris.

> Widow Abigail . . . sold some of the clocks to obtain money. One was sold in Philadelphia and was lost sight of until quite by accident it was discovered by Mrs. Thomas P. Stran, who was Kate Abrahams. She and Mr. Stran were visiting a friend in Philadelphia many years ago and she noticed that her host wound a tall clock in his possession left-handed (from right to left). As all the Faris clocks were supposed to be wound left-handed she examined this clock and discovered the name of William Faris, London, inside the case.[1]

Widow Faris married John Powell, a Presbyterian, in 1735 and was apparently widowed again, for in 1738 she married Philip Petro, an Episcopalian. William was obviously not raised in his father's religion, so the Quakers in the colonies were denied a distinguished clockmaker and craftsman.

> On 31 October, 1749, it is recorded that "William Faris of Philadelphia, Clockmaker, son of Abigail Petro (or Pedro) of the same City, Shopkeeper" purchased a plot of ground in Philadelphia. The deed was witnessed by Abigail Petro, Widow. William Faris was then just twenty-one years old, and if he was buying property, it is possible that he had for some time been a successful clockmaker in his own right—or had inherited money from England.[2] Having been thrice widowed, Mrs. Faris Powell Petro valued an independent income so maintained a little shop at the corner of Market and Water Streets for selling miscellaneous merchandise until she died sometime after 1755 but before April, 1763, when her son sold his property preparatory to moving to Annapolis. . . .

1. Lockwood Barr, "William Faris, 1728–1804," *Maryland Historical Society Magazine*, December 1941.
2. Ibid.

When and where William Faris learned clockmaking may never be established, but there is circumstantial evidence worthy of being put into this record. Most of the early Philadelphia clockmakers, silversmiths, cabinet-makers, and other master craftsmen of that period, had their shops on Front, Second and Third Streets, within the confines of two blocks South of Market Street. Peter, William, Isaac and Samuel Stretch, Henry Flower, Francis and Joseph Richardson, John Wood and others, all clockmakers of the 1720–50 period, lived within a stone's throw of each other. William Faris' name is associated with Stretch and also with that of Henry Flower, who in 1747 witnessed papers for Faris. Henry Flower had his shop on Second Street between Black Horse Alley and Chestnut Street.

If Faris by 1749, when he was only 21 years old, had accumulated sufficient money to buy property upon which he subsequently erected a home and other buildings, he must have been working successfully for several years as a clockmaker. During the ten years that followed he evidently continued to work in Philadelphia, although search of the newspapers does not disclose announcements by him. This is strange, if he was in business for himself, for in subsequent years he was a prolific advertiser.

On October 8, 1754, there was recorded a mortgage for 50 pounds given by "William Fareis of City of Philadelphia, Clockmaker" to one James Bagley. On 1 May, 1755, "William Faris of the City of Philadelphia, Watch-maker, to Robert Greenway, Merchant" gave a mortgage for 108 pounds on the Spring Garden property. A witness to his mortage was Isaac Stretch, a member of the famous clockmaking family by that name.[3]

It is curious that in one document he refers to himself as a clockmaker and in the other, as a watchmaker. The reason why Faris left Philadelphia, a thriving commercial and political center, for Annapolis, then a little seaport of about twelve hundred inhabitants, also remains unexplained. His earliest advertisement in Annapolis appeared in the *Maryland Gazette* of March 17, 1757.

WILLIAM FARIS
Watch-Maker, from Philadelphia

At his Shop near the Church, next
door to Mr. Wallace's, in Church
Street, Annapolis.

Cleans and Repairs all Sorts of Watches and Clocks as well and
neat as can be done in any part of America; And takes the same

3. Ibid.

Prices for his Work as are taken in Philadelphia.
He also makes Clocks, either to Repeat or not, or to go either Eight Days or Thirty, as the Purchaser shall fancy, as good as can be made in London, and at reasonable prices. And all Gentlemen who shall be pleased to employ him, may depend on having their Work done with all possible Dispatch, by

Their humble Servant,
William Faris

Henry Flower advertised between 1753 and 1775. These two advertisements suggest that he made, repaired, and gilded watches, and may hint at retail jewelry on a small scale.

HENRY FLOWER. In Second-street between Black Horse Alley and Chestnut-street, Philadelphia, makes and repairs in the neatest manner, all sorts of watches, either of the Repeating, Horizontal or plain kinds. (*Pennsylvania Journal and The Weekly Advertiser*, August 30, 1753)

HENRY FLOWER, Watchmaker, at the sign of the Dial, in Second-street, between Black-horse Alley and Chestnut-street. Makes and repairs all sorts of watches and clocks in the best manner. Likewise gilds sword hilts, watch movements and Pinchbeck cases, chased or plain, snuff-boxes, watch-chains or anything of the kind. N.B. Any person may be supplied with watch-chains, either gold, silver, or Pinchbeck, of the best fashion. (*Pennsylvania Gazette*, September 18–25, 1755) [Pinchbeck, i.e. Derived from the inventor's name, an alloy of copper and zinc resembling gold; a yellow metal composed of three ounces of zinc to the pound of copper.]

A tall clock bearing his name is illustrated in the *Book of American Clocks*.

Until recently little information was available concerning mantle clocks labeled "Globe Clock Co." and tall clocks labeled "The Franklin Clock Company." Both can be attributed to an obscure but gifted designer-maker named Stephen Pavky, of Philadelphia. Around 1921 he developed an 8-day mantel clock; this unique piece had two trains (instead of the usual three), with a strike and chime operating off the same train. Probably only a few hundred were made and then sold in the local department stores. The label "Globe Clock Co." was used, although some may have had no identification.

Pavky soon designed and began production of tall clocks; these also featured the single strike and chime train, although they were powered by three weights, two of which together activated the unique train. The strike and chime hammers received their power from the second wheel, which resulted in some underpowering. The wheel taking off power to the chime mechanism was designed with several teeth absent. One wonders how many do-it-yourself collectors and even experienced collectors, not cognizant of the purpose, tried to replace the teeth. Westminster, Oxford, and Whittington chimes were available. These clocks could be troublesome, so eventually Strawbridge and Clothier was the sole remaining retail outlet, for only they could provide service.

In 1931 the name on the clock was changed to the "Franklin Clock Company," and in 1935 Pavky created an electric version of the tall clock. This also incorporates some unique features: a deadbeat escapement, a forty-inch pendulum, and a small electric motor. Ordinary house current supplies all needed power. During the striking sequence, the motor drives an endless ladder chain to the center, which raises three light shell weights, with a friction spring to prevent overwinding. The weights move through a total distance of about four inches; their combined weight powers the time train. Thus, the clock will run without striking or chiming for several hours after an electric power stoppage. Amazingly, the strike is self-correcting upon power restoration.

The electrics also had their idiosyncrasies. Even so, clock manufacture continued until the early 1960s.

Benjamin Franklin (1706–90), "Mr. Philadelphia," designed a three-wheel timepiece. The working model may have been made by his close friend, Duffield, or perhaps by another friend, Gawen Brown of Boston. The design was improved in England by James Ferguson about 1758.

Alexander and Robert Fraser appear to have been Philadelphian clockmakers prior to 1799; they later performed their trade in Paris, Kentucky, and then in Lexington, Kentucky.

William Fraser (1801–77) was at work in Philadelphia by the 1820s, and perhaps earlier. He served first as an apprentice, then as a journeyman to Solomon Park, who operated a clock manufactury from 1802 to 1822. Fraser later returned to Lancaster County, where he continued his craft.

Jacob Gaensle was born in Wurtemburg, Germany, in 1721, and emigrated to America in 1743. This clockmaker settled (quite naturally) in Germantown, where he lived until 1765. One thirty-hour, one hand, tall case clock is reported.

Fig. 24. A fairly short (seven foot) but well-proportioned handsome clock signed "Phillip Garrett, Philadelphia." Case is mahogany with satinwood inlay. Besides calendar ring, it has a rocking ship atop the dial. Private collection.

Phillip Garrett was listed in the 1801 through 1835 directories as a clock- and watchmaker and a machinist at various locations. At least two tall clocks bearing his name survive, one of which is seen in figure 24.

Thomas Gibbons advertised as a maker and repairer of watches and clocks.

THOMAS GIBBONS Watch Maker from London. In Front-street below the Draw-bridge, makes and mends all sorts of clocks and watches, in the neatest manner where gentlemen may have their work done with Expedition. (*Pennsylvania Journal* or *Weekly Advertiser*, November 21, 1751)

Jacob Godschalk is properly connected with Montgomery County, as he was a resident of Towamencin Township, a contemporary of Rittenhouse, and a fellow Mennonite. He was, however, equally connected with Philadelphia. Biographical data on Godschalk is scarce, but his many fine clocks speak for him. In 1945 a Jacob Godschalk Towamencin tall clock stood in the home of Mary Washington, Fredericksburg, Virginia, on loan from the Mabel Brady Garvan Collection. Another of his clocks was the property of John Bringhurst of Trappe, Pennsylvania. When General Washington encamped at Pennypacker's Mills in the autumn of 1777, he must have seen a Godschalk clock owned by Samuel Pennypacker. His Towamencin clocks have English-style spandrels, and some of the dials are decorated with punch marks and a wind rose design.

For any of several possible reasons, Godschalk moved to Philadelphia in the late 1760s. Tax lists show him as a resident of the east part of Mulberry Ward; his shop was on Arch Street between Second and Third. He was listed in 1774 as a clockmaker, but in 1780 he was called a watchmaker. Once in Philadelphia, he changed the spelling of his name to Godshalk. He may have assisted his famous contemporaries, Duffield and Rittenhouse, in the care of the State House clock. On December 8, 1770, Godshalk married Elizabeth Owen, a widow with a son Griffith. Griffith apprenticed to his stepfather in April 1773 for a term of seven years. During the Revolutionary War, Godshalk was a second lieutenant but probably saw no active service. Figure 25 shows a Godshalk clock made in Philadelphia. Gone are the English cherub and orb spandrels, but the wind rose and punch mark dial decorations are still present.

It has always been accepted that Godshalk did not move into the city until the late 1760s; there does exist, however, a clock with a rocking ship dial, with wind rose and punch marks, and with dolphin-like spandrels, which is signed "Jacob Godshalk,

25

26

Philadelphia, 1745." There is no ready explanation for this signature. It is doubtful that he was a watchmaker, but the following advertisement states, indirectly, that he was.

> JACOB GODSHALK. Lost on Friday last, between this City and Mr. Daniel Ernst's Tavern on the Five Mile Round, a Silver Watch, with a China Face, No. 2, Maker's name, Jacob Godshalk, Philadelphia. Whoever finds the same and delivers it to the said Godshalk, living in Arch Street, shall have Fifty Shillings Reward. (*Pennsylvania Chronicle*, March 18, 1771)

Godshalk paid taxes for the last time in 1781. Also, in September of that year, the Supreme Executive Council of Pennsylvania had an order drawn in favor of Godshalk for 10 specie, payment for repairing the State House Clock. He must have died shortly thereafter, because the next year's taxes were paid by his estate. His fame as a craftsman, however, was long recognized. For example, one of his clocks was purchased in 1956 for use in a Salem Tavern, a part of the Old Salem, North Carolina Restoration.

Although the Goldsmith Company of Philadelphia is not listed in directories, a photograph of its amusing alarm clock, "The Bachelor's Alarm," patented April 16, 1901, must be included here (fig. 27).

John Gorgas, the first generation of the well-known Pennsylvania Gorgas family of clockmakers, was at work in Germantown for about four decades in the mid-1700s. He married Sophia Rittenhouse, the aunt of David and Benjamin.

Jonathan Gostelowe (1744–1806) made superb clock cases and furniture. Inasmuch as he married a niece of Edward Duffield, it is highly probable that he made some of Duffield's cases, particularly those of carved mahogany.

J.L. Groppengiesser was listed in directories from 1841 to 1850 as a clock- and chronometermaker. A tall clock—one weight, thirty-hour, with a square top hood and a twelve-inch square dial with second hand—is attributed to him, but this must be an anomaly. Still, he was a fine enough mechanic to repair the famous David Rittenhouse clock at Pennsylvania Hospital.

John Gearhart Hagey, the third generation of a renowned family of clockmakers, was born on October 7, 1799, in Lower Salford Township, Montgomery County. Certainly he learned his trade from his father, Jacob, and thereby was an independent clockmaker at an early age. In 1826 he removed from Lower Salford, going first to Mt. Airy and then to Germantown, where he had a clock shop and store. In about

27

Fig. 25. Plain-cased clock that Jacob Godshalk made in Philadelphia to appeal to Quaker customers. The outside hinges on the dial door do not appear to be original. Courtesy of Dr. Douglas H. Shaffer.

Fig. 26. Close-up of hood and dial of the clock in fig. 25, made during or immediately after the War of Independence. Courtesy of Dr. Douglas H. Shaffer.

Fig. 27. The Bachelor's Alarm. Legs of girl serve as minute and hour hands. Private collection.

28

29

30

Fig. 28. The John Hagey clock in Kirk & Nice. Courtesy of J. Malcolm Henderson.

Fig. 29. Dial of Hagey clock in fig. 28. Courtesy of J. Malcolm Henderson.

Fig. 30. Shelf timepiece signed "W.E. Harpur, Phila." It has a fusee movement with the escapement outside the back plate. Courtesy of Edward Railsback and John Sweisford.

1823 he married Elizabeth Nice, who possibly was related to the Nice in Kirk & Nice of Germantown, reportedly the nation's oldest funeral home. Kirk & Nice own a splendid tall clock, signed "John Hagey, Germantown," with moon phase, calendar, and day of week features. The days are quaintly abbreviated "SUN^Y," "MON^Y," etc.

The comparatively few clocks produced by Hagey are all of fine workmanship, including the tall case clocks, which were mostly in Chippendale or Sheraton styles, and the shelf clocks. Hagey was one of only several makers in Pennsylvania to construct this latter type. He is also reputed the inventor of a special type of chimes used in the tall clocks. Like his brothers, George and Jonas, he also sold and repaired watches. He moved into Philadelphia in about 1850, where he owned a large confectionary establishment at the corner of Ninth and Market streets. He died on June 30, 1885; he and his wife are buried in the cemetery of the Church of the Brethren (Dunkard) in Germantown, of which both had been members.

George Hagey, also of the third generation, labored from approximately 1820 to 1850. He worked primarily in Trappe, and later in Sterling, Ohio; there is no record of him in Germantown, yet in Winterthur Museum there is a beautiful tall clock with inlay work and a rocking ship dial bearing the signature of George Hagey, Germantown.

The Hahn Improved Portable Watchman's Time Detector was made in Philadelphia during the 1890s–1900s and was awarded a first prize at the Chicago World's Fair of 1893.

William E. Harper (Harpur) was listed in the 1845 to 1850 directories as a chronometer- and watchmaker. Several watches bearing his name are in private local collections; he also produced shelf timepieces, such as that shown in figure 30. Available evidence suggests that Harper was an importer and a dealer.

John Heilig, born the grandson of Henrick Heilig in 1765, represented the first generation of a multitudinous family of Pennsylvanian clockmakers. Not only a clockmaker, John was also the first silversmith in Germantown, where he was living in 1796. In 1800 he moved to what is now 6374 Germantown Avenue. He was listed in the Philadelphia 1801 and 1802 directories, and he lived until 1841.

John Heilig, Jr. had a shop in Germantown in 1829 and 1830, and survived his father by only one year. Henry, John Jr.'s son, learned his trade in his grandfather's shop but unfortunately died in 1830. Jacob Heilig, the great-grandson of Hendrick, born in 1802, was listed as a clock- and watchmaker in Germantown in 1833. Jacob's brother John, born in 1804, worked in Bridgeton, New Jersey, from 1824 to

1839, and then in Philadelphia from 1841 to 1850. He was generally referred to as a watchmaker. Finally, Albert E. Heilig, born in 1834, succeeded his father Jacob in business in Germantown.

Thomas Howard advertised rather regularly between 1775 and 1789, and was still listed in the 1791 directory as a maker of both clocks and watches.

> THOMAS HOWARD. Made sold and repaired, in the best manner, by Thomas Howard, At his shop in Second-street, between Market and Chestnut-streets, and next door but one to Trotter's Alley, Where he carries on the Clock and Watch-making business in its various branches, and will be much obliged to his friends and the public to favour him with their custom.
>
> N.B. Masters of shallops or others, who bring up watches from the lower counties, or elsewhere, to be repaired, by favouring him with their custom may have their own done gratis. Likewise an apprentice wanted to the said business. (*Pennsylvania Packet*, May 8, 1775)

> HOWARD, THOMAS. A Few Good New and Second Hand Watches, To be sold by Thomas Howard, In Second street seven doors above Chestnut Street, Where he continues to carry on Clock and Watch Making business in its various branches, and will use his best endeavours to make his work give satisfaction to those who employ him. Any person who has had the misfortune to break the horizontal wheel, or cylinder of their watch, by applying to him may depend on having it repaired as well as if sent to London. Shallopmen, Stagemen, and others, who bring watches from the lower counties, or elsewhere, to be repaired, by giving him their custom may have their own done gratis. (*Pennsylvania Packet*, March 31, 1787)

> HOWARD, THOMAS. A Variety of good New and Second Hand Clocks, with or with-out Cases; an elegant musical Chamber-Clock—Also a few new and second-hand Watches, to be Sold by Thomas Howard, In Second street between Market and Chestnut streets, where all kinds of Clock and Watch work are done as usual. (*Pennsylvania Packet*, December 8, 1789)

Although no specimens of Howard's work are known, his earliest advertisement for an apprentice strengthens the supposition that he had maker capabilities. His later bills, indicating more emphasis on repairing and on retail trade, would seem merely to reflect a postwar situation.

William Huston was at work from 1754 to 1771. A number of his clocks are extant; one survives in a local private collection and another in the Philadelphia Museum of Art. Two of his casemakers have been identified as Nathaniel Dowdney and Edwin James, both cabinetmakers.

The Imperial Portable Watchman's Time Protector, patented November 5, 1900, was made in Philadelphia.

Joseph H. Jackson came to America from Wolverhampton, England, in 1801. Settling in Germantown, he served a few months as a journeyman under John Heilig. At that time about twenty-one years old, he decided to establish his own business in Flourtown, now in Montgomery County. There he made clocks until 1810, when he married and moved to Chestnut Hill, a suburb of Philadelphia, where he remained until 1817. Feeling the competition of the area, he bought a farm in Mill Creek Hundred, Delaware, where he reportedly engaged in farming and clock repairing. Two tall clocks exist that bear his name and that location.

Samuel Jefferys was another clockmaker, repairer, and watch importer in Philadelphia just before the Revolutionary War.

SAMUEL JEFFERYS. Watches. Just imported from London, in the Britannia, Capt. Falconer, A Parcel of new Watches, warranted to keep good time, and to be sold at very moderate prices. Clocks made and mended; also repeating, horizontal and plain Watches repaired in the compleatest manner by Samuel Jefferys, in Second-street, between Christ's Church and the Court-house. (*Pennsylvania Journal*, April 11, 1771)

Alexander Landry, a French émigré, offered to make clocks in European style.

LANDRY, ALEXANDER. Clock and Watch Maker from Paris, west side of Second street, above Race street, Begs leave to inform the public, that he makes and repairs all sorts of clocks and watches. He has now ready for sale, a number of the most fashionable and ornamental clocks after the French and English taste, which he will warrant, and dispose of at a very reasonable rate. Any order for any kind of clock, will be thankfully received and punctually executed. (*Pennsylvania Packet*, February 12, 1791)

Nicholas LeHuray was consistently listed in directories as a clock- and watch-maker from 1809 through 1836; a man with that same name was also noted to be a Delaware clockmaker. The commonly accepted explanation is that one Nicholas Le-Huray worked in Philadelphia until perhaps 1820 or 1821 and then moved to Ogle-town, Delaware, leaving a son to carry on his business. Although Nicholas, Jr. was independently listed in directories from 1825 through 1846, it is possible that he maintained his father's listing for some reason. One clock bearing his name and place is known.

William Lemist and W.B. Tappan had unique listings in the 1819 and 1820 directories as clock and patent timepiece makers. Simon Willard of Massachusetts had produced in 1802 his patent timepiece, which today is universally called the banjo clock; perhaps Lemist and Tappan were constructing a copy of this. If so, they might have been the first in Pennsylvania to do so.

Robert Leslie's dates and location are unknown, and even information about him, recorded by three accomplished horological historians, is at variance. Carl W. Drepperd made these simple entries in his *American Clocks and Clockmakers*:

> Leslie, Robert (Sr.?); Philadelphia, 1740's–1790's.
> Leslie, Robert: Baltimore (agent for Leslie & Price) 1790's.
> Leslie & Price: Philadelphia, 1790's–1800's.

The supplement to Drepperd's book has this additional entry:

> Leslie, Robert: Philadelphia, from 1745. Father of Major Leslie, Miss E. Leslie, an authoress, and C.R. Leslie, artist. Granted a patent in 1789 for an improvement in the mechanisms of clocks and watches. Characterized as an ingenious workman.

Brooks Palmer wrote the following in his *Book of American Clocks*:

> Leslie, Robert & Co.; Baltimore, 19 Baltimore St. 1796.
> Leslie & Parry: Phila. Dir. 1803.
> Leslie & Price: Phila. 1793–1800. Tall clock, 8-day brass movt. and tall clocks painted metal dial owned by Mrs. Robert Heyl, Pelham, N.Y.; another by Mrs. McKay, Lykens, Pa. Mahogany case, domed hood, bracket feet, decorated dial, brass capped corner reeding. Price d. 1799, Leslie d. 1803. Leslie & Price, Baltimore adv. 1795 as branches of the Phila. firm at 119 Market St., Abraham Patton, representative.

In his *Pennsylvania Clocks and Clockmakers* George H. Eckhardt made these entries:

> Leslie, Robert A. Scotsman, as a clock and watchmaker he pursued a very busy life. In 1789 he was granted a patent for certain improvements in the mechanism of clocks. The first patent was from the Assembly and run afterwards by the laws of Congress. Powerful combinations were found in the trade to oppose his innovations. He had many other patents. In 1789 he proposed a museum but in 1793 advertised the return of the subscriptions.

It is hard to comprehend how the findings of these contemporaries differed to the degree they did; the men agreed, actually, only that Leslie was an ingenious craftsman who obtained one or more patents. It appears that Leslie was at 167 High Street in 1791 and at 144 High Street in 1803. Leslie, Robert, & Price, Isaac C. & W. Ms. were at 167 High Street in 1793 and at 79 High Street from 1794 to 1800. However, on March 13, 1799, the administrators of the estate of Isaac Price advertised that they wished to settle the affairs of Leslie & Price. Leslie & Parry C. & W. Ms. were at 245 High Street in 1803. In addition, it seems that in November 1795, Robert Leslie was also in partnership with Abraham Patton, under the name of Robert Leslie & Company, 119 Market Street, Baltimore, Maryland.

Was Leslie a maker, an assembler, or simply an importer? If actually a watchmaker, he would predate Luther Goddard, who is generally accepted as America's first watchmaker. Perhaps an examination of some of his advertisements and related items can help us find some answers.

> Leslie, Robert, Clock Maker. A Time-Piece on a new and improved plan, which is not subject to any visible variation from the different changes of weather, is now in possession of the Inventor and Maker, and may be seen at his shop on the west side of Front Street, seven doors above Market Street, where all kinds of Watch and Clock Works are performed in the best and neatest manner and with punctuality and dispatch, by the Public's humble servant. Robert Leslie.
>
> N.B. Any person having Clocks or Time-Pieces of any kind, going with either weight or spring, pendulum or balance, may have the above additional improvement annexed to them at a small expense, by applying to said Leslie. (*Pennsylvania Packet*, April 11, 1787)

It is interesting that Leslie sometimes referred to himself as a clockmaker and sometimes as a watch- and clockmaker. While we have no description of exactly what his invention entailed, we find it could be added to a clock or timepiece and not just incorporated in a new object. Curiously, his invention was touted two years before it was patented.

Leslie, Robert, Clock and Watch Maker. At the north-east corner of Second and Market-streets, makes and repairs all kinds of Timepieces, musical, chimney, quarter and chamber clocks, on an improved plan, entirely new, which prevents the different changes of weather from affecting the swing of the pendulum, and thereby prevents any variations which can arise from that cause, and annexes the said improvement to any old clock or time-piece; he repairs, with the greatest accuracy all kinds of un-common watches and those made upon watches, which he hopes will be thought of great utility, by every person acquainted with the principles.

N. B. Any person wishing to have movable Dialwork to serve any particular purpose, or pieces of fancy, may have them made either with new clocks or time pieces or annexed to those already made, and any gentlemen wanting small machines or models, ei-ther for trying philosophical or mechanical experiments, may have them executed according to their particular direction, by ap-plying to said Leslie. (*Pennsylvania Gazette*, August 27, 1788)

Leslie, Robert, Clock and Watch Maker, Philadelphia. General Assembly, Feb. 13, the bill entitled "An Act to grant and secure to Robert Leslie, for a limited time, the sole and exclusive right and benefit of constructing, making and selling within this com-monwealth, the improvements by him lately invented on clocks and watches," was read the second time, and debated by para-graphs. (*Independent Gazetteer*, February 18, 1799)

Leslie, Robert, Clock and Watch Maker, the north side of Mar-ket—Between Fourth and Fifth Streets, Philadelphia, Having obtained patents for several improvements on Clocks and Watches, begs leave to inform his friends and the Public, that he is now ready to execute any work on the said Constructions, which, on trial, have been found superior to any heretofore brought into common use, and likewise proposes, to furnish those who please to employ him, with any of the aforesaid Clocks and Watches, at the same prices for which the common ones can be made of [sic] imported. He therefore hopes to receive the patronage of those who prefer a superior article to an inferior one, when both are at the same price. He also repairs, at the lowest prices, horizontal, repeating, plain and other watches, musical, chiming and plain clocks, with punctuality and dispatch, and warrants all the work done in his shop. N. B. One or two Journeymen and an Apprentice wanted.

At this juncture, Leslie put his advertising into the plural, mentioning patents and improvements.

In the late nineteenth century and early twentieth century, it was considered good form in advertising to include testimonial letters, or excerpts therefrom, from satisfied customers. Indeed, American watch manufacturing of the period used this technique extensively. Here is an example.

In the year 1774, I gave seven guineas for a watch which, for the space of ten years, fully answered my expectations; but after that period, she began to move irregularly, and at least to stop, without having received any injury from falls or other untoward treatment. Upon this, I applied to some of the most respectable watchmakers, in this city, requesting that they would find out and cure the defect, let the expence be what it would, one gentleman examined her three times in the space of five months, but could not discover the fault. Mortified with the disappointments and hearing of Mr. Robert Leslie's improvements I determined to make trial of his abilities also; and to my great satisfaction, since he applied his Cylindrical Verge, the watch moves every hour with the regularity of a clock, not gaining or losing above two minutes in a week; this I can testify after the experience of nine months, and therefore think it a happy improvement in that branch of business, adequate to the author's designs, and a high gratification to those who may experience its utility. James Davidson. (*Federal Gazette*, March 12, 1791)

What a magnificent antecedent of Madison Avenue advertising at its last turn-of-the-century best—a satisfied customer's testimonial! Whether it was voluntary or induced makes little difference.

Leslie, Robert, Clock and Watch Maker, No. 167, Market street, After returning his sincere thanks to his friends, and the public in

general, for the great encouragement he has experienced since the
commencement of his business in this city, takes this opportunity
of informing them, that, in consequence of his intention of going
to London in April next, he is selling off, at very reduced prices,
his stock in trade, consisting of a very large and general assortment of enamelled and plain gold, gilt and silver, capt and capt
and jewelled Warranted Watches, Most of which are of the latest
importation and newest fashion, . . . Also a variety of the highest
finished cut steel, and gilt, ladies, and gentlemen's Watch Chains,
Keys, and Trinkets, together with a few Gold Chains, Keys and
Seals. (*National Gazette*, Philadelphia, January 23, 1793)

This public notice raises two interesting questions: why did he decide to go to England? and why did he mention that most of his watches were imported? This entry,
of course, confuses Leslie collectors and students because he continued to advertise
himself as a maker.

The most fascinating of Leslie's news releases hints at a partnership, tells of his
move to London, and describes new inventions.

Leslie & Price, Clock and Watch Makers, Market street, No. 79,
Respectfully inform their friends and the public, that R. Leslie is
now resident of London, where he is enabled to put in execution
the various improvements which he made in clocks and watches
previous to his leaving Philadelphia, as also some valuable additions since his residence in England. Nautical Watch No. 1, is
just imported in the ship George Barclay, and now lays at their
works for the inspection of the public, and such in particular as
are acquainted with the true principles of clock and watch work.
R. Leslie has the satisfaction to assure the public, from the authority of several scientific men in London that this watch exceeds every other kind for convenience, utility and simplicity of
construction, as it shows at one view, the time at place sailed
from, and the time of the present place, the time of the tide, & c.
and the bad effects of heat and cold, friction & c. are remedied at
much less expence than any other. R. Leslie has other watches
and clocks on new and improved principles, which he will forward to Philadelphia, in the course of a few months for the whole
of which he has obtained patents in England; and he begs leave
to inform the public that he has disposed of a share of his patents
to Joseph Dodds, goldsmith and watch-maker, No. 12, Alders-

Fig. 31. Leslie & Price's illustrated directory advertisement.

gate street, London . . . where orders for any of these articles will meet due attention. Also, just received in the ships Delaware, William Penn and George Barclay, a complete assortment of warranted watches, selected by R. Leslie. They trust their present assortment will merit the attention of purchasers, either wholesale, or by the single watch. (*Pennsylvania Packet*, May 7, 1794)

This first reference to the partnership of Leslie & Price is interesting, as the partners operated 3,000 miles apart. Leslie's advertisement leaves us with several unanswered questions concerning the improvements made in Philadelphia, the additions realized during his stay in England, the sale of patents to Joseph Dodds, and the mention of inventions such as "Nautical Watch No. 1." This illustrated directory advertisement (fig. 31) yields no answers to these questions. Against a background indicating various phases of Leslie & Price activities, it may show a symbolic handing over of the Nautical Watch from Father Time to King Neptune.

In the twilight of his career, Leslie again advertised himself as a clockmaker who sold only imported items. No reference was made to any of his own handiwork.

> Leslie Robert, Clock Maker, Just imported, in a ship Washington, Captain Williamson from London—a large assortment of Clocks and Watches, and Clock and Watch-maker Tools and Materials, All of which are offered for sale by the subscriber—Who earnestly requests all persons indebted to the late firm of Leslie and Price (whose debts were contracted previous to the decease of the late Isaac Price) to come forward and settle their accounts; likewise that all who have claims against said late firm will exhibit them for payment, at No. 181 Arch-street, Robert Leslie. (*Pennsylvania Packet*, May 17, 1800)

So the mystery continues: was Robert Leslie a maker, an assembler, or just an importer? Surely he was more than an importer; indeed, the well-known *Horology Americana* illustrates a Leslie & Parry, Philadelphia, tall case clock. It is mahogany, Hepplewhite style, with moon phase, calendar, and seconds dial. The case is 97 inches high and 19 inches wide. It is worth noting that John Parry inherited the clock tools belonging to David Rittenhouse, though Leslie also appears to have been an inventor of considerable ingenuity and skill.

Although there is no proof, it seems likely that George Levely was clockmaking in Philadelphia from 1770 to 1774. That he did work there is confirmed by this advertisement, published after he had moved to Baltimore.

> George Levely, Watch and Clock Maker, from the City of Philadelphia begs leave to acquaint the public and his friends in general, that he hath just opened shop opposite the Fountain Inn, Market Street, where he accurately makes and repairs all kinds of clocks and watches, with care and expedition, on the most reasonable terms. (*The Maryland Journal*, July 2–9, 1774)

Michael and Isaac Levy, evidently brothers, were originally clock- and watchmakers in England. At some point they moved to Baltimore.

Michael and Isaac Levy, Watch and Clock Makers, Late from London, Have for Sale, a large assortment of the most elegant and fashionable Clocks and Watches, which they dispose of for cash on the lowest terms; they likewise repair and make Clocks and Watches in the neatest and most fashionable manner, and have also for sale, a large quantity of well assorted Plate and Jewellery. Those gentlemen and ladies, who chose to favour them with their custom will be pleased to call on them at the store lately occupied by Mr. Christopher Johnston, in Market Street. (*Maryland Journal* and *Baltimore Advertiser*, October 21, 1785)

This advertisement reports that Isaac Levy moved to Philadelphia.

ISAAC LEVY, Watch-Maker, lately from London, Takes the liberty to inform the public, that he has just opened shop on Front-street, next door but one to the Coffee-house, where he repairs all kinds of watches and clocks. . . . (*Pennsylvania Journal*, November, 1790)

Michael joined him somewhat later, and the two appeared regularly in directories from 1802 to 1816.

John Lind's name was listed in directories up to 1801.

JOHN LIND, Watch and Clock Maker, Begs leave to inform the Public, and his Friends in particular, that he has opened shop at the corner of Arch and Second-streets, in the house lately occupied by Mr. Edward Duffield, Watch-maker, where he carries on the said business in all its various branches, and at the most reasonable rates. (*Pennsylvania Packet*, April 24, 1775)

Thomas Lindsay was listed as a clockmaker in Frankford in 1810 (Frankford was not incorporated into Philadelphia until 1854). Several clocks bearing his name are known to exist. The most celebrated one is housed in the Historical Society of Pennsylvania. The pedigree of this particular clock, however, held by the society, casts some doubt on Lindsay as a maker.

The dial clearly is signed "Thoˢ Lindsay Frankford"; however, the pedigree attests that the brass movement was imported from England for £ 20, presumably around 1763. It also states that the mahogany case was made in Frankford. It is believed that for the first forty or forty-five years of its life, the clock hung as a wag-on-the-wall (which is not likely for a brass movement) or was otherwise cased until it was installed in the Frankford case, presumably by Lindsay. Although Lindsay could simply have added his name to the original dial, he more likely substituted a new one to assure a good fit between dial and case. Also, the unusual mixed flowers and fruit spandrels and painted decorations in the center portion of the dial are more typical of the American style of 1810 than of the English style of 1763. Lindsay might have been a joiner, a cabinet maker, or even a furniture maker.

The Philadelphia city directory for the years 1823 to 1824 reads: "ISAIAH LUKENS, town clockmaker and machinist, back of 171 High street." This description epitomizes the life and work of one of Pennsylvania's most ingenious craftsmen. Lukens built a great timepiece for Independence Hall, an instrument still in existence; he invented the first practical forerunner of the speedometer long before the automobile was even dreamed of; he achieved membership in the most famous learned society in the new world, the American Philosophical Society; he served as the first vice president of the Franklin Institute; he exposed one of the greatest perpetual-motion hoaxes in history by duplicating the device after seeing it once; he constructed, as early as 1834, two magneto-electric machines from written descriptions; and he continued to produce, after all these high attainments and the subsequent recognition, simple household clocks, which today are the cherished possessions of a few fortunate collectors.

It is presumed that Independence Hall in Philadelphia generally presents the same architectural lines prescribed in the original plans; however, for almost a half-century before 1828, the State House had no steeple. This feature had been removed in 1781 because of decaying timbers.

The original State House clock, made in 1759 by Thomas Stretch, was not located in the steeple. The works were housed in the main building under the roof, and from here rods extended to operate the hands on two dials on the outer walls, the dials sitting at opposite ends of the building. No striking arrangement was provided.

In 1828 the Thomas Stretch clock was declared decrepit, so the city council finally arranged the building of a steeple at a cost of $8,000. Isaiah Lukens agreed to supply a steeple clock, for which he was to receive $2,000. John Wilbank cast a new bell for $1,923.75.

The old Thomas Stretch clock was given to St. Augustine's Catholic Church, Philadelphia, where it was destroyed when a mob burned the edifice in 1844. On January 1, 1829, the Lukens clock began to strike the hours regularly on the new Wilbank bell. Later, when gas was introduced, the faces of the clock were illuminated at night.

32

In the centennial year of 1876 a public-spirited citizen, Henry Seybert, provided Independence Hall with a new clock and bell, each costing $10,000. The Lukens clock and the Wilbank bell were taken to the Town Hall in Germantown, and the citizens of that section raised funds for an adequate tower to accommodate them. The new Municipal Building of Germantown was erected in 1924, and the already much-traveled clock and its companion bell were moved into their tower. Unfortunately, the clock mechanism is now badly worn and is no longer entirely reliable.

Lukens's first tower clock, built in 1812, can be found in the tower of the Loller Academy building, in Hatboro, Pennsylvania. It has not been running for many years.

At a stated meeting of the Franklin Institute, April 20, 1921, Henry R. Towne of New York presented an apparatus for measuring the distance traveled by vehicles, an odometer, made by Isaiah Lukens. Mr. Towne said: "The Odometer, which it is my pleasure to present to The Franklin Institute this evening, is an excellent example of Mr. Lukens' skill, both as a designer and a mechanic."

Lukens became known to the public through his exposure of the so-called Redhoeffer perpetual-motion machine. In 1812 Charles Redhoeffer constructed a machine which he claimed would run without any application of power. The Pennsylvania legislature appointed a commission to investigate the inventor's claims; because the commission was not permitted to examine the device minutely, it could find no flaw in it. Isaiah Lukens, however, proceeded to make a model similar to the Redhoeffer machine, and discovered that it was operated by a concealed spring. The Lukens model is still a prized possession of the Franklin Institute.

Lukens's great interest in scientific matters led him to construct from a written description two magneto-electric machines, one of which is lodged in the Franklin Institute. The original apparatus, invented and built by Joseph Saxton, was exhibited and described at a meeting of the British Association for the Advancement of Science in 1833. The next year it was brought to the attention of the institute by Professor Alexander D. Bache, at which time one of Lukens's machines was used to illustrate the subject.

Actually, Isaiah Lukens was not only a highly skilled craftsman; he was also a scientific man of considerable ability and wide versatility. Like David Rittenhouse, this versatile genius was born in the country and later came to Philadelphia. His family was of old German stock, descendants of Jan Lucken, one of the followers of Pastorius who, coming from Crefeld in lower Germany, landed in Philadelphia in October 1683. Isaiah's father, Seneca Lukens, was a farmer at Horsham, Montgomery

Fig. 32. Signed "Tho⁵ Lindsay Frankford," clock of good proportions and pleasing appearance. Permission from the Historical Society of Pennsylvania.

Fig. 33. Dial of the clock in fig. 32. Permission from the Historical Society of Pennsylvania.

County, but he also carried on the business of clock- and watchmaking. He taught Isaiah, born in 1779, the art and science of clockmaking. After the death of his parent, the thirty-one-year-old Lukens moved to Philadelphia. Here he participated whole-heartedly in the scientific activities of that city until his death in 1846.

Lukens again resembles David Rittenhouse in that, no matter what other business demanded his attention or what honors came to him, he always remained a clockmaker. He visited Europe as a young man, having made improvements in certain surgical instruments that had been invented by a surgeon in Paris. Securing employment as a clock- and watchmaker, Lukens gained recognition for his methods of tempering steel. He remained in England and France for about three years, and then returned to Philadelphia. In 1828 he was once more firmly established as "town clock maker and machinist," and, besides the Independence Hall clock, he made timepieces for the Bank of the United States and for the Philadelphia Bank. His ability as a mathematician brought him employment making the necessary observations for correcting the city time.

Lukens established a firm friendship with Charles J. Wister of Grumblethorpe, Germantown, and this association is accountable for two excellent specimens of his workmanship. The two men had kindred tastes; Wister also enjoyed experimenting with clocks and other scientific instruments in his workshop. Several handsome Lukens clocks are still in the possession of the Wister family. A tall clock which still stands in Germantown Academy was purchased from Lukens for fifty dollars in 1825 while Wister was one of the academy's trustees.

Isaiah Lukens occupies a peculiar position in the industrial history of America. Born in the late 1770s, having learned his art from his father, he may properly be regarded as a colonial craftsman. On the other hand, since he lived and worked until the mid-nineteenth century and was thoroughly cognizant of current progress in the sciences, he may be recognized as a creative investigator of the modern school of science. He was one of the early members of the Academy of Natural Sciences in Philadelphia, the oldest institution of its type in America. A handsome tall clock still standing in the library of the academy proclaims Lukens's devotion to his association. Likewise, a list of scientific material purchased by the High School Committee of Philadelphia tells that in 1837 an astronomical clock was purchased from Lukens for $300. This timepiece was destroyed when a fire gutted the observatory in 1905.

The previously referred to Wister clock is one of the finest mechanisms of its kind made in America. Its sensitive accuracy is such that if thrown off-balance (by changes in temperature, for example) even so minute a distance as would measure the thickness of tissue paper, it requires careful adjustment. It carries no striking apparatus, but is geared for an eight-day run on a single winding.

The outstanding feature of this clock is the tremendous mercury pendulum, which alone weighs sixteen pounds. To sustain this heavy mass, the clock itself had to be reinforced with an iron plate; this device is found in many other clocks by Isaiah, who was fond of heavy, but delicately balanced, pendulums. Curiously enough, the weight that actuates this great pendulum amounts to only three pounds. The main dial is divided into twenty-four hours, instead of the usual twelve. A smaller dial for ticking off the seconds is an additional feature of interest.

Jeweled throughout (Lukens was also a watchmaker) and housed in an appropriate mahogany case, this timepiece represents a lavish expenditure of skill and knowledge. It bears the date 1834.

The Athenaeum of Philadelphia houses a huge Isaiah Lukens clock; that this piece was originally made for a bank attests to its designer's versatility. Being very tall, it required a mechanism comparable to that of a tower clock, yet, at the same time, sufficiently compact to fit within a disproportionately narrow case. For Lukens, as for Rittenhouse, each clock represented an individual effort. Neither man was a commercial standardizer. The story of the Athenaeum clock is told by a yellowing card found in its case which reads: "This Clock was made by Isaiah Lukens . . . for the Philadelphia Bank, where it remained until the Bank removed June 30, 1859 from the old Building . . . to its present Quarters, when it was exposed at Public Sale, W. Thomas & Sons, Auctioneers, and bought by Henry Bird, Librarian of the Athenaeum, for twenty-three dollars."

Since each Lukens clock was of special design and some of his mechanisms were of unusual dimensions, the ingenuity of the cabinetmaker who fashioned the cases must often have been sorely taxed. Still, whether planning a monumental housing for a bank clock or a graceful shrine for a domestic timekeeper, the craftsman was usually equal to his task. All in all, the cases and clocks made by this man represent the best in the colonial tradition, carried over almost into the middle of the nineteenth century and modified along the way.

At some point during his career in Philadelphia, Lukens took a young man named Saxton into his employ and later into partnership. The firm was called Saxton & Lukens. Joseph Saxton became important in his own right.

No watches made by Matthew Mahve are known and there is nothing but this advertisement to establish his trade.

Matthew Mahve. This is to inform the Publick that Mathew Mahve, Watch finisher, from London, now living next shop to

Mr. Edmond Milne, Gold-Smith in Second-street, next door but
one to the corner of Market-street, makes and repairs all sorts of
Watches. And as said Mahve has wrought from some of the most
eminent Watch-makers of both London and Dublin, those who
shall favour him with their Custom, may depend upon having
their work done with Dispatch, and in the most exact manner.
(*Pennsylvania Journal and The Weekly Advertiser,* November 19,
1761)

White Matlack advertised in January 1777 as a clockmaker who had just arrived
from New York. White and William Matlack advertised in July 1780. William then
moved to Charleston, South Carolina, where he advertised in 1787 as a watchmaker
late of Philadelphia. By 1794 he was back in Philadelphia at the old address, ready to
make or repair all kinds of clocks or watches and also prepared to buy and sell old or
new clocks or watches. The Matlacks were listed in the directories until at least 1797.

Frederick Maus advertised in 1782 and was found in the directories from 1785 to
1793 as a clockmaker in Brewer's Alley between Third and Fourth streets. One of his
tall clocks has a prophetic motto on the dial: "Time Shews the Way of Life's Decay."

John Menzies (1777–1860), born in Scotland, was a well-known and prosperous
watch- and clockmaker who was thoroughly established in Philadelphia by 1832. He
was something of a mechanical genius who tried to build a perpetual motion machine, and his name appeared in directories from 1804 to 1851.

Records pertaining to George Miller are somewhat confusing: apparently there
were two of them, both without middle initials, living about two decades apart. We
are concerned here with the George Miller who worked in Germantown about the
last quarter of the eighteenth century. Figures 34, 35, and 36 display one of his
clocks, owned by the Historical Society of Pennsylvania. It is certain that this clock
was built by Germantown Miller because it was formerly owned by the Nice family
of Germantown.

The clock's walnut case is 92 inches tall, 18 inches wide, and 10 inches deep. Notice the splendid rosettes in the broken arch and the elaborate finials combining two
decorative features, urn and oriflamme, ordinarily used separately. Some collectors
claim that the thirty-hour pull-up time and strike movement shows the influence on
Miller of Dr. Christopher Witt and the Pietist religious movement in general.

Thomas Morgan appears to have been clockmaking in Philadelphia before 1772;
his work then shifted to Baltimore for seven years, and he was back in Philadelphia in
1779, laboring until the end of his career in 1793.

Fig. 34. Unusually handsome case for a one-day clock by
George Miller. Permission from the Historical Society of
Pennsylvania.

Fig. 35. Dial of the clock in fig. 34; picture also shows the
endless weight chain. Permission from the Historical Society of Pennsylvania.

Fig. 36. Movement of the clock in fig. 34. Permission from
the Historical Society of Pennsylvania.

34

35

36

THOMAS MORGAN, Watch and Clock-Maker, informs the Public that he hath opened shop, in Arch-street the fourth door above the New-building, where he intends carrying on the business, in all its various branches, having a tolerable supply of materials, is in hopes to give satisfaction; those ladies and gentlemen who please to favour him with their custom, may depend on the greatest care and punctuality. Said Morgan informs his former kind customers in the Southern States, that their commands shall be duly adhered to. (*Pennsylvania Gazette*, July 7, 1779)

Augustine Neisser, an exemplary Moravian clockmaker, was born in Schlen, Moravia, in 1717. He came to Savannah, Georgia, with the first migration of Moravians in February 1736. More immigrants arrived, and some moved on to what is now Old Salem, North Carolina, while others ventured farther north to Pennsylvania to found what is now Bethlehem. Neisser went with the latter group in 1739 but was charmed by Germantown and so settled there to carry on his trade. His professional reputation was so outstanding that he was engaged in 1746 to construct the tower clock for the great Moravian Church in Bethlehem. When his project was completed the following year, he was paid £ 8—a small return for a clock that is still there.

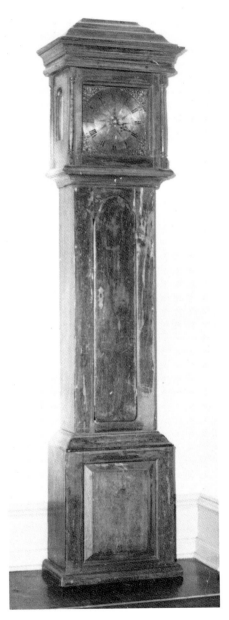

AUGUSTINE NEISSER, watchmaker, living at the lower end of Germantown, in the second house above the graveyard, desires all those who are indebted to him by bond, note, book account, or in whatsoever way it may be, especially those of many years' standing, to pay their respective debts before the 28th of next May. And those who are not able to pay by that time shall give sufficient assurance for their debts, in order that he in the future will not suffer such loss as has hitherto taken place; if they do not give assurance he will be under the necessity to give the account of his debtors to someone who will force payment. Persons for whom he is bondsman are reminded to pay their debts and release him from his security, which he can no longer hold. He continues to make all kinds of new watches, and repairs old clocks and watches with care and punctuality at low prices. (*Staatsbote*, April 17, 1770)

AUGUSTINE NEISSER, watchmaker in Germantown, finds it advisable to make known to those who wish to find him, that last summer he moved from his former dwelling to Mr. George Hittner's house, directly opposite the inn, the White Horse, kept by Mr. Adam Haas and two houses above Mr. Baltes Roser, the tanner. He makes as before, all kinds of new clocks, also repairs clocks and watches in the most careful manner cheaply. He seeks all who are indebted to him, in whatever kind or way it may be, that they come and pay him. Also those for whom he is bondsman must likewise pay their debts and release him from his bond, for he will no longer be bound for them. If perchance parents or guardians have a boy willing and clever to learn the profession of watchmaking, he shall have sufficient instruction to become a good worker. Further information given at above named place.

   The motive, beginning and issue of the judicial procedure between Mr. Johann Wister and Augustine Neisser will soon be

37

38

laid for examination before the impartial public. (*Staatsbote*, April 7, 1772)

Augustine Neisser. Eight Dollars Reward. Was taken out of the house of the subscriber, in the Northern Liberties, between Germantown and the Rising Sun, on the Philadelphia road, by some of the British troops, on the 25th or 26th of September, 1777, a repeating 30 hour clock, with an alarum, minute hand, and day of the month, the maker's name, Augustine Neisser, engraved on the circle, the face eleven inches square; It was taken without the pendulum and weight. . . . Philip Wagner. Captain of the fifth Penna battalion of the Philadelphia Militia. (*Pennsylvania Packet*, October 10, 1778)

One wonders why apparently so many persons owed money to Neisser and why he sought an apprentice for watchmaking rather than clockmaking. No watches bearing his name are known to exist, and it is doubtful—despite the wording of his advertisements—that he made watches, although it is likely he could and did repair them. Figures 37 and 38 show an early Neisser clock standing in the Mercer Museum of the Bucks County Historical Society; note the severity and plainness of the case and the relatively small square brass dial. Figure 39 displays a Neisser clock belonging to a Neisser descendant who lives in Florida. Although the case is still plain and severe, the dial has been enlarged and the arch and moon phase have been included. Figure 40 shows one of his clocks which is an intermediary mixture of styles—the dial remains small and square, but the case has acquired some flare, and even two thin finials have been added.

Griffith Owen was previously mentioned as the stepson and apprentice of Jacob Godshalk. By 1780 the apprenticeship ended and he was then a full-fledged clockmaker. From 1781 to 1789 he attended the State House (now Independence Hall) Clock. This had been made in 1753 by Thomas Stretch, who looked after it for a while. Owen was succeeded by such giants as Edward Duffield, David Rittenhouse, and Thomas Parker—which is an indication of his ability.

Perhaps not as much attention would have been given to the Stretch clock after the Revolution had a lively controversy not arisen between two rather cantankerous local clockmakers, Griffith Owen and Robert Leslie. Owen had taken care of the clock for at least one year when the *Minutes of the Supreme Executive Council* for March 22, 1784, contained these blunt statements:

An order was drawn on the Treasurer in favor of Mr. Griffith Owen, for twenty-

Fig. 37. Plain-cased clock by Augustine Neisser. From the collection of the Mercer Museum of the Bucks County Historical Society.

Fig. 38. Dial of the clock in fig. 37, showing fine spandrels, calendar, and wind rose and punch mark decoration that was also used by Godshalk. From the collection of the Mercer Museum of the Bucks County Historical Society.

seven pounds seventeen shillings and six pence specie, in full for his services in taking care of the State House clock for one year, ending the fourth day of March, 1784, and cash paid for a new pair of lines.

ORDERED, That the Secretary inform Griffith Owen that he is now discharged from any further care of said clock, and that he deliver up the key of the same to the Door-keeper of this Board.

Owen's reply to this action explains some of the difficulties under which the clock and its caretaker had to operate. His letter, endorsed March 25, 1784, was addressed "To His Excellency the President & Council."

Gentlemen:

Mr. Trimble inform'd me that you had concluded that my employment should cease in taking care of the Clock, the reasons were that she had stopt sundry times & had not kept the true time—the reasons why she stopt I shall point out—the first time she was stopt two days whil I was cleaning of her, the second time the frost broke the arbour that swings the hammer, the third time was occasioned by the breaking of the old lines & the new ones being considerably thicker took me some time in freeing them. The severity of the weather I believe stopt her once & it was the occasion of her going irregular the sudden changes of the weather is all the way that it can be ac-counted for, those accidents happening in the most part, & I being obliged to work in the Clock room delay'd me longer than I should have been had it been otherwise; the Clock is now in good order & keeps good time, & is I think effectually guarded against the like accidents for the future. If you will be pleased to continue me to take care of her & she should not perform to yours and the publicks satisfaction I will give up my charge at any time without demanding any thing for my future trouble.

With the most perfect respect
I remain Gentlemen your
most humble Servant
GRIFFITH OWEN[4]

Owen was successful in his plea, and for the next three years operations seemed to have gone quite smoothly. At its meeting on February 1, 1788, however, the council performed an action which foreshadowed new difficulties for him: "The petition of Robert Leslie, stating that the hammer of the State House Clock is not properly

4. *Pennsylvania Archives*, First Series X, p. 563.

39

Fig. 39. Another plain-cased clock by Augustine Neisser, with the addition of a moon phase arch to the dial. Courtesy of Colonel Charles J. Seibert, II.

Fig. 40. Perhaps the finest cased clock by Augustine Neisser. The topmost part of the hood can be slid off, leaving it a flat-top case. From the collections of the Historical Society of York County, Pennsylvania.

Fig. 41. The earliest of the Augustine Neisser clocks illustrated, featuring a flat top, a severe case, a small square brass dial, no feet, a one-day movement, original rat tail hinges, and pegged case construction. Notice that the spandrels are missing. Private collection.

40

41

fixed, and that for a trifling expence it could be made to answer the purpose much better than at present: Ordered, That he be employed to make the alteration in the hammer, mentioned in his petition."[5] The job must have been done promptly, because within two weeks, on February 13, 1788, the council approved the payment to Leslie of sixteen pounds.

Griffith Owen was apparently not favorably impressed by Leslie's innovation. According to the council minutes for December 9, 1788, he removed the hammer before it had been in operation for even a year: "A memorial from Robert Leslie of the City, clock and watch maker, containing a complaint against Griffith Owen for removing from the State House clock, the newly constructed hammer which the memorialist had invented and placed there by direction of the late President and Council was read and referred to Colonel (Richard) Willing, Colonel (Abraham) Smith, and Christopher Kucher, who were instructed to make inquiry into the necessary annual expence of keeping the said clock in repair, and report to Council."[6]

There is no record of the committee's report. Owen, however, continued to hold his job for almost a year thereafter, until October 3, 1789, when it was taken over, at least until October 11, 1790, by his rival, Leslie.[7]

One of Owen's advertisements displays an early record of a clockmaker producing a few units for stock, rather than waiting to be "bespoken."

> OWEN, GRIFFITH, Clock Maker, No. 73, North side of Mulberry-street, between Second-street and Moravian Alley, Respectfully informs the Public in general and his Friends in particular, that he still continues to carry on the Clock making business in all its various branches; those who please to favour him with their custom may depend on having their commands executed with the utmost neatness and dispatch; he has now on hand, ready finished, three or four Clocks with cases, which he will dispose of reasonably for cash; and as he is determined to keep a constant supply of those articles, he flatters himself that it will always be in his power, to comply with any orders he may receive. The neatness of his work, and the promptitude of the execution, he hopes will merit the attention of the Public.

5. *Colonial Records* XV, p. 380.
6. Ibid, pp. 618–19.
7. Ibid XVI, p. 180.

42

43

N.B. Mr. Jacob Carver carries on the Watch-making business at
the same place. (*Pennsylvania Gazette*, May 15, 1793)

Owen maintained the shop on Mulberry Street until about 1811. At some point
soon thereafter he reversed his step-father's actions by moving out to Towamencin
Township, Montgomery County. Curiously, he then signed his clocks "Griffith
Owen in Towamencin."

John Owen is simply mentioned by historians as being listed in directories from
1818 to 1820. One of his clocks, described as being of the Chippendale style, mahogany case with fluted corners, and ogee feet, fine scroll top, having urn-oriflamme
finials, carved rosettes on the broken arch, moon dial, and painted women's faces as
spandrels, was sold at Pennypacker's Auction Gallery some years ago.

Fig. 42. Simple but massive clock by Solomon Park & Co.
Courtesy of Harmon Yerkes.

Fig. 43. Close-up of the hood of the clock in fig. 42. The
handsome hands are an enhancement to any clock. Courtesy of Harmon Yerkes.

Fig. 44. Not all Solomon Park clocks were plain and massive, for here is a decorative, well-proportioned example.
This also has ornate hour and minute hands. From the collections of the Historical Society of York County, Pennsylvania.

44

Solomon Park settled in Newtown, Bucks County, in colonial days and continued as a clockmaker for many years. Listed in Southampton Township in 1782, he first appeared in Philadelphia directories in 1791 and remained there until 1796. He was again listed from 1802 to 1822. Earlier reference books maintain that Park operated a clock factory from 1814 until 1822. It reportedly was a large operation which employed many foreign workmen, such as the French, Swiss, and Germans. A diligent search in several libraries and the city archives, however, failed to unearth a single shred of confirmation that the factory existed. Conversely, we have the story of a fine Lancaster County clock mechanic, William Fraser, who, it is maintained, obtained his excellent training as an apprentice and journeyman at the Solomon Park Clock Manufactury of Philadelphia. To compound the mystery, figures 42 and 43 display a clock made expressly for Harmon Yerkes, which has descended through many generations to its present owner, also a Harmon Yerkes. The dial is signed "Solomon Park & Co"; inside the case there is a small label that reads, "Solomon Park & Co. Philadelphia Clock Guild." Of course, there is also no information on the guild. It is interesting that this clock was once repaired by Seneca Lukens. Figure 44 shows another, more ornate Solomon Park clock, owned by the York County Historical Society.

Thomas Parker (1761–1842) was a descendant of the Quaker Parkers who settled in Philadelphia in 1684. After receiving a liberal education (for the period), he was placed first with David Rittenhouse to learn the art of clock and philosophical instrumentmaking, and then with John Wood to acquire a knowledge of watchmaking. He became very eminent in this latter branch, commencing business about 1783 and continuing for nearly fifty years. Curiously, his earlier advertisement, circa 1786–92, described him as a clock- and watchmaker, while those of 1793 and later styled him only as a clockmaker. He was proverbial for the correctness of his timekeeping, and his regulator was regarded as the standard on all occasions where precision was deemed important. He had charge of the State House clock for a period.

Aside from his trade, Parker was active in an antislavery society and was president of the Mechanics' Bank from 1814 to 1830, president of the Board of Managers of the Almhouse, and a member of both Select and Common Council. He was active in a group of concerned citizens who were responsible for Philadelphia's first reservoir for pure water, besides being very attentive to his religious duties.

Parker is perhaps best remembered by collectors for his bracket clocks. He employed both the arch and round dial and both brass and painted iron dials.

John J. Parry (1773–1835) was listed in Philadelphia directories from 1794 to 1835. A nephew of Mrs. David Rittenhouse, Parry inherited his uncle's tools upon

45   46   47

the death of the great clockmaker. This suggests he possessed some skill as a clock-maker, an idea supported by his advertisements in December 1793 and again in November 1798 for an apprentice in clock and watch work.

Thomas Perkins, clock- and watchmaker, advertised in June 1785 that he carried on the business in all its branches on the most reasonable terms. He also "wanted as an apprentice to said business a lad of about fourteen or fifteen years of age of reputable connexions." In May 1793 he advertised that he was discontinuing that business to become a nail manufacturer, but in 1799 he returned to his former trade.

The Philadelphia Watch Company, incorrectly described as existing as early as 1889, remains an enigma today. It has been the subject of extensive research, many notes, and several articles, but there is still no satisfactory answer as to whether it produced an American watch, imported a Swiss movement, or assembled Swiss

Fig. 45. Thomas Parker arch top bracket clock with painted iron dial. Private collection.

Fig. 46. Rear view of the clock in fig. 45. Some collectors feel that the movement is an English import. Private collection.

Fig. 47. Thomas Parker round top bracket clock with painted iron dial. Courtesy of Frank S. Schwarz & Son, Philadelphia.

Fig. 48. Ladies' hunting case watch signed "Philada. Watch Co., E. Paulus." Private collection.

Fig. 49. Movement of the watch in fig. 48. Private collection.

parts. As its founding date moves farther into the past, it becomes less likely that the puzzle will ever be solved.

Nevertheless, Ernest A. Cramer, first president of Chapter I of the National Association of Watch and Clock Collectors, spent years investigating and finally summed up his findings in a paper entitled, "The Philadelphia Watch Company, 1867–1887." William Muir also broached the topic in his article, "The Problem of Chestnut Street." By extraction from these two works, a discussion of the evidence in condensed form shall be attempted.

The Philadelphia Watch Company appeared in directories from 1875 until 1887, earlier at 618 Chestnut Street and later at 806 Chestnut. Eugene Paulus was president; his obituary notice in the *Jeweler's Circular* of June 22, 1892 read:

> Eugene Paulus, well-known expert watchmaker, died at Geneva, May 29, 1892. He was a native of Paris. After serving in the French Army for a number of years he came to America about 1852, worked at his trade in New York and some other large cities, finally locating in Philadelphia. In 1868 he organized the Philadelphia Watch Company and carried on the manufacture of watches to which he applied several very ingenious and meritorious parts. [He] invented and patented by himself a compound duplex chronometer escapement and many other inventions of the art of watchmaking. These were the result of his great mechanical skill and life-long close application and love of his profession.

Such a company was duly incorporated in Pennsylvania on October 23, 1868 for the manufacture of a new style of improved watch movement, under the Paulus patents issued by the United States Patent Office and in harmony with a system invented and practiced by Eugene Paulus in Philadelphia for years. It appears that both gilt and nickle movements in 15 and 16 sizes for ladies and 19 and 20 sizes for gentlemen were made.

Cramer's paper presents the cornucopia of opinions of various experts, who rank the origin of the company's watches from "absolutely American" to "absolutely Swiss." Cramer did include two relatively unrecognized items that enhance the Paulus stature. In the 1876 Centennial, Paulus exhibited an escapement of his invention to be used in what were called "traveling clocks." It was the ordinary chronometer escapement, modified first by placing the locking spring at right angles to the passing spring, and then a'scape wheel to communicate the impulse at right angles to the direction of the ordinary form. This avoided the use of a change wheel to alter the direction of motion, as is done in the usual form of construction and in that of

48

49

the cylinder watch escapement. Paulus also submitted a handmade model of a marine chronometer escapement. There was a fork like that in the lever escapement, while the other extremity of the lever was geared into a pinion. The arbor of this pinion had a notch on the upper side in which the teeth of the escape wheel rest. The impulse was given by a pin on the roller acted upon directly by the escape wheel. The fork and balance moved in the same direction when the impulse was given. Paulus patents were obtained: one on November 5, 1867 for a watch key; two on April 25, 1868 for watch top plates; one on August 25, 1868; and one on November 3, 1868 for a watch winding click.

In "The Problem of Chestnut Street" Muir quoted various early printed references to the Philadelphia Watch Company, neatly pinned down the errors and discrepancies, and finally concluded that there was little originality in the work of Paulus. He suggests that the French horological training and tendency to borrow from—but not infringe upon—other patents renders difficult the pinpointing of the location of the actual manufacturing.

Even if the true story of the Philadelphia Watch Company is never known, American watch collectors can accept in good conscience these practical and elegant watches because they *were* patented in the United States and designed and marketed in Philadelphia.

Benjamin Rittenhouse was born in 1740 in Norriton, where he grew up and was educated. Around 1760 he was working with his famous older brother, David, making mathematical and surveying instruments in addition to tall clocks, some of which still exist and are variously marked "Worcester Twp." and "Phila. Co." Rittenhouse served in the Revolution and was wounded at Brandywine. In 1778 he was appointed superintendent of the government gun lock factory in Philadelphia. In 1785 he advertised for an apprentice to learn the art and mystery of the clock. In 1791 he became a judge in the Common Pleas Court of Montgomery County, but his name appeared in Philadelphia directories periodically from 1807 to 1820.

Benjamin's brother, David Rittenhouse, was such a multifaceted, great man that a separate chapter will be devoted to him.

Christopher Sauer was born in Westphalia, Germany, in 1693 and studied medicine at the University of Marburg. He immigrated to Pennsylvania in 1724 and settled in Germantown, where he felt comfortable with fellow Germans of special religious beliefs. He was either a Dunkard—that is, an early member of the Church of the Brethern—or a Pietist (he enjoyed a close association with Dr. Witt, the last great Pietist in Germantown). Because it was tedious and expensive to bring clocks from Europe, he established himself as a clockmaker, doubling as an oculist, a cabi-

50

51

Fig. 50. Beautiful clock by Christopher Sauer of Germantown. Permission from the Library Company of Philadelphia.

Fig. 51. Dial of the clock in fig. 50. Permission from the Library Company of Philadelphia.

netmaker, a bookmaker, and a medical practitioner—he spent considerable time in Lancaster County seeking medicinal herbs. Upon his return to Germantown he became a devotee to Dr. Witt, dividing his time between serving as a clock- and watchmaker, an oculist, and an apothecary. Finally, in 1738, he set up a printing press and directed his efforts to defending the interests of German immigrants. He printed the first German newspaper and bibles in America. Both his bibles and clocks are much sought after, though the bibles are far more scarce.

Joseph Saxton, born in 1799 in Huntingdon, Pennsylvania, worked first in his father's nail factory and then was apprenticed to an unknown watchmaker. At the age of eighteen he struck out for himself by moving to Philadelphia and setting up as a watchmaker. From then on, his career was multifarious. He took up engraving and later became associated with Isaiah Lukens. The 1823 and 1824 directories listed Joseph Saxton as a clock- and watchmaker at 94 Chestnut Street. In October 1824 Saxton exhibited a clock with a new escapement at the Franklin Institute. The friction of this ingenious clock was so slight that it required no oil for the pallets. He later associated himself with the Adelaide Gallery of Practical Science in England; in 1837 he became the balancemaker of the United States Mint; and he went with the Coast Survey in Washington in 1843. From that point until his death in 1873 his activities are not known, but the late J.E. Coleman thought so highly of Saxton that he wrote this memorandum:

SAXTON—UNKNOWN INVENTOR by J.E. COLEMAN

Merely because we did not produce a Tompion, Breguet, Harrison, Kulberg or Jurgenson does not necessarily mean that each and every movement and/or method of making timepieces came from without the United States.

For a long time, I've considered Philadelphia the real seat of all things horological, even before the Rittenhouse brothers. Even when the great Breguet was considering coming to America, he planned to come to Philadelphia, as correspondence with his friends there indicates.

Recently I ran across this little-known fact. For years horologists used a "rounding up" tool. It was considered English in origin. In fact, many old timers referred to it as the English rounding up tool.

In a little, 180-page volume, titled, "A Treatise on the Teeth of Wheels," translated from the French of "M. Camus" by John Isaac Hawkins, London, 1837, I find this comment by Hawkins, page 178: "Mr. Saxton of Philadelphia, now in London who is justly celebrated for his excessive acute feeling of the nature and value of accuracy in mechanism; and who is reputed to be not excelled by any man in Europe or America for exquisite nicety of workmanship; made in Philadelphia, an instrument for cutting the teeth of watch wheels, truly epicycloidal; or rather curving them after they were cut down in the ordinary manner, with radial faces. The following is his verbal description of this instrument. The wheel to be rounded being put on a vertical arbor, another arbor stood parallel to the first, carrying, on a third but horizontal arbor, a steel wheel file-cut on the plane side, which plane side lies in a vertical plane passing through the axis of its vertical arbor. On the arbor of the wheel to be rounded is a circular plate, equal in diameter to the primitive circle of that wheel; the edge of the wheel is milled into teeth as fine as possible: This plate forms the basis of the epicycloidal. On the other vertical arbor is a similar plate, but equal in diameter to the radius of the primitive circle of the wheel to be engaged with that about to be rounded; this plate is the generating circle." It goes further into details, but this is sufficient to see that it is practically identical to what we know as the "English" rounding up tool, and, to me, is PROOF it was invented by a Philadelphian. It had to be darned good for an Englishman to admit (and publish) it.

It is thought that Robert Shearman worked in Wilmington, Delaware, as early as 1768 and for probably thirty years before moving to Philadelphia, where his name appeared in directories from 1799 to 1804. He may have labored as late as 1808, but that would have been a *long* career. An illustration of a tall clock signed "R. Shearman" appears in the Chippendale section of Edgar G. Miller's *American Antique Furniture*, volume 2. The clock's decoration includes a painted dial, floral design spandrels, and a pastoral scene of a girl and sheep in the lunette. The hood has two fluted columns, an elaborately carved broken arch top, and three oriflamme finials.

Actually, Shearman's long career seems confirmed by the fair number of his clocks which appear for sale, all signed "Philadelphia"; there are almost too many for the previously noted short period of 1799 to 1804.

The finely cased shelf clock in figure 52 contains the label of James S. Smith. The paper proclaims Smith the maker, yet the only bits of evidence available about him are the listings in directories from 1839 through 1850. One suspects that he was a dealer who bought Connecticut clocks and pasted in his own labels.

Daniel H. Solliday, a member of the prolific Solliday family of clockmakers, was born in Sumneytown, Montgomery County, where he worked as a clockmaker until 1823. He then moved his trade to Evansburg in the same county and labored from 1824 to 1828. From there he moved into Philadelphia, where he was listed in the directories until 1850.

John Sprogell's name appeared in Philadelphia directories and newspapers, both English and German, for nearly thirty years.

52

Fig. 52. Fine cornice and column shelf clock attributed to James S. Smith. Private collection.

Fig. 53. Label of the clock in fig. 52 is alone insufficient evidence to prove Smith was actually the maker. Private collection.

53

JOHN SPROGELL, Has lately opened Shop in Front-Street next Door to the Corner of Market-Street; where he makes and Repairs all kinds of Clocks and Watches in the best and neatest manner: Those Gentlemen that please to favour him with their Custom, may depend on the utmost Dispatch in his Power.

Said Sprogell has worked with general Satisfaction for several Maryland Gentlemen, and takes this public Method to inform them, that by sending their Watches to the Post Office at Annapolis, they may meet with a very ready Conveyance, by the Post-Rider to Philadelphia, and may depend on their being returned with Punctuality and Dispatch. (*The Maryland Gazette*, January 4, 1764)

JOHN SPROGELL, clock and watchmaker, has recently begun business in his own store. . . . Said Sprogell has worked for John Wood, the watchmaker, to the complete satisfaction of his customers. (*Staatsbote*, March 26, 1764)

JOHN SPROGELL, JR.—Watches made in Philadelphia. The Subscriber having employed Journeymen from London, proposes making the best of plain, horizontal, second and stop Watches, that he can insure for three or four years free from all Expence to the purchaser, unless cleaning. The Public may be assured, as the character of the Maker lies at stake, that he will make his work perform, and will endeavour to give general satisfaction. He likewise cleans, and repairs all kinds of Clocks and Watches, at the most reasonable rates, at the north corner of Market and Front streets, opposite the London Coffee House, John Sprogell, jun. (*Pennsylvania Chronical*, December 9, 1771)

Sprogell continued advertising for twenty years and his name appeared in directories as late as 1791. His emphasis was on watches, yet none are reported existing, although several tall clocks bearing his name are extant.

Early compilations dismiss Peter Spurch (also spelled Spruck or Spurck) after noting that he was listed as a clock- and watchmaker at different locations, found in Philadelphia between 1794 and 1806. For the history-minded reader, there is an interesting accomplishment attached to this man. On the east wall of the entrance hall at Monticello, Thomas Jefferson's home, there is a contrivance known as the great clock. The official description reads: "The big clock above the door is a seven-day calendar clock, thought to have been made to Jefferson's design by Peter Sprenk of Philadelphia, circa 1801. It is run by Revolutionary War cannon ball weights. Friday afternoon the weights pass into the basement through holes cut into the floor and they remain there until Sunday morning when the clock receives its weekly winding." The only mistakes in this passage are the date and the name "Sprenk." As will be seen, Jefferson spelled it "Spurck" and, because the order was undoubtedly personally placed, this spelling is accepted as correct. Actually, it was Robert Leslie who designed the clock from Jefferson's specifications, but the timepiece was constructed and installed by Peter Spurck, one of Leslie's journeymen clockmakers.

That all was not originally satisfactory with this clock and that Jefferson had an uncommon grasp of horological mechanisms is attested by this letter to Robert Leslie, the prominent practical clockmaker of Philadelphia and London.

Sir   Philadelphia Dec. 12, 1793
I have received with great satisfaction your two letters of July 10. & Sep. 26. and particularly the last stating your present situation. I have no doubt that the public will be benefited as well as yourself by your leisure & opportunity of pursuing your inventions. I wish this may reach you in time to make a little change in wach you were to make for my daughter, but which I now destine for myself, that is, to put a second hand on the wheel which stands nearly between the 6 aclock mark & the center of the watch. I do not know its name. I prefer this method because it does not add a single wheel to the works, it only enlarges a pivot.

My large clock could not be made to go by Spurck. I ascribed it to the bungling manner in which he made it. I was obliged to let him make the striking moment anew on the common plan, after which it went pretty well, the time part with three fifty sixes, & the striking part with a fifty six & a twenty eight. . . . The little balance clock he could not make go at all. He told me so before hand, so that I did not receive it. It was no disappointment, as the great clock renders all chamber clocks unnecessary.

No directions can yet be given to make experiments on the pendulum rod, because Congress have as yet come to no decision—direct to me in the future at Monticello Virginia & by way of Richmond, because I leave my office the last day of this month, and become a farmer at home.

wishing you every profitable success   I am with esteem   Sir
                                        Your most obed't. sevt.
                                        Th. Jefferson

Mr. Robert Leslie
Watchmaker, No. 12, Aldersgate Street[8]

---

8. Edgehill-Randolph Papers, University of Virginia Library, Charlottesville, Va.

SPURCK, PETER, Watch and Clock Maker, Has opened shop, at No. 2, North Front-street, where he has for sale, an excellent assortment of Watches capped and jewelled, with seconds; and plain ditto of the latest importation. He has also an assortment of the most fashionable plain Silver Watches, which are all warranted to be of the best quality, which he will dispose of on the most reasonable terms. Also makes and repairs every kind of Clocks and Watches in the neatest manner, at the shortest notice, and with the greatest satisfaction to his customer. (*Aurora*, October 27, 1795)

Peter Stretch was the second fully corroborated, but possibly the third clockmaker in Philadelphia, hence also in the colony of Pennsylvania. His predecessor, Abel Cottey, arrived in Philadelphia before 1700. His contemporaries, Benjamin Bagnall and William Claggett, came to Boston about 1712 and 1714 respectively. Stretch was born in 1670 in Leek, Staffordshire, England, where he was apprenticed to his uncle Samuel, a maker of lantern clocks. Peter emigrated to Philadelphia in 1702 with his wife and sons, Daniel, Thomas, and William. Like Cottey and Bagnall, Stretch belonged to the Society of Friends. Many of the first settlers of Philadelphia were artisans who came from the gentry of England, having sold their property and migrated to America to escape religious persecution. With pride, the descendants of Peter Stretch assert that he belonged to that class and point to the fact that his work was acceptable to and has been found in the possession of cultured families with English backgrounds. It appears also that he rapidly acquired substance and became a power in the social and political life of Philadelphia, having served as a Common Councilman from 1708 to 1746. His youngest son, Joseph, born in Philadelphia in 1704, was a member of the Provincial Assembly for many years and was a founder of the Philadelphia Library, which was established through Franklin's influence in the year 1741. Peter's son Thomas was one of the founders of the Pennsylvania Hospital.

The Historical Society of Pennsylvania owns a brass dial tall clock made by Peter Stretch. Its one-day brass movement is wound with a chain and it has only an hour hand, which suggests, as do the plain, flat top case and bull's-eye glass in the door, that this clock was constructed soon after his arrival in Philadelphia. One other one-day clock by Peter Stretch is known, but no other one-hand American-made clock has been reported. Altogether, it is a fair example of an English country clock.

At least two dozen of Stretch's tall clocks have been found. The earlier ones had one hand. Minute and second hands were added to clocks made later. Earlier clocks

55

Fig. 54. Peter Stretch clock with door open to show endless chain, single driving weight, and original hinges and door clasp. The pendulum may not be original, as the bob does not exactly coincide with the bulls eye window. Permission from the Historical Society of Pennsylvania.

Fig. 55. Dial of the clock in fig. 54. Permission from the Historical Society of Pennsylvania.

were cased in walnut, later ones in mahogany. For the most part, the lines of the earlier cases were simple, reflecting the temperament of the contemporary members of the Society of Friends. As Peter had no peer in Pennsylvania, we do not know how he acquired the knowledge to graduate to sophisticated eight-day movements. Also the addition of feet and sarcophagus type tops lent more style to his cases. Several even more sophisticated styles are known to have been adopted. The clock owned by the State in Schuylkill (the famous fishing club founded in 1732 in Philadelphia) has a domed dial with moon phases, a broken arch bonnet with graceful turned decorations, and ogee bracket feet. Peter's son Thomas was a founder and the first governor of this club.

The identity of Stretch's casemaker is unknown. William Savery, the renowned furniture maker and a fellow Quaker, kept shop only a block away as early as 1737. Possibly he supplied some of the later, more sophisticated cases, but several bits of evidence suggest the majority were made by some Stretch family member. For the half-hour markers, which were used on clock dials long after the minute hand appeared regularly, Peter employed a variation of the arrow head, instead of the fleur-de-lys used by many makers. As a rule, he signed his clocks on the lower side of the hour ring—although after the arched dial was used and when that space was not occupied by a moon dial, his name appeared on a cartouche in the arch, always accompanied by the name of the city.

Peter reportedly also learned to build tower clocks, and, indeed, he did build the town clock, probably in 1716.

> PETER STRETCH. Feb. 26, 1717. Peter Stretch Exhibited on account of Work done, & several Disbursements on the town clock, which was read, & the Sum of Eight pounds Eighteen shillings & ten pence is allow'd him. (*Minutes of Common Council of Philadelphia*, p. 143)

On the balance, from among the half-dozen earliest clockmakers, Peter Stretch appears to have produced the finest clocks. Perhaps the advantage of the Quakers, as the first citizens and persons of substance in Philadelphia, gave Stretch a boost over his colleagues: marketing his products among people of similar temperaments and tastes to his own, Stretch, unlike his confreres, was free to build as he liked. Occasionally he produced a surprise, as is seen in the clock in figure 56. All of its features are readily discernible, except one. The sarcophagus top with two finials is removable, leaving the old flat top and, of course, significantly reducing the height if the owner has a low ceiling.

56

57

Stretch also sold clock movements to Henry Flower, Francis Richardson, and Frederick Domenic. For a long time after his death in 1746 the southeast corner of Front and Chestnut streets was known as Peter Stretch's Corner.

As has been noted, Thomas Stretch was born in Leek, England, and as a young lad was brought to Philadelphia. He also made tower clocks—one of which was the State House clock, famous throughout the land—and tall clocks, quite a few of which are extant. His tall clocks are shorter, more graceful, and much more elaborate than those of his father; therefore, they are considered even more desirable than the earlier, rarer ones by his father. One of Stretch's clocks stands in the Governor's Palace in Williamsburg.

Peter and Thomas most probably obtained their ornamental brass on-laid spandrels from the same source. After his father's death, Thomas sold that shop and opened his own one block farther west at the southwest corner of Second and Chestnut Streets.

We know that the watches signed by Thomas Stretch were also greatly treasured by their owners. The following advertisement appeared in the *New Jersey Gazette* of April 17, 1782: "A robbery! The house of a subscriber in Hopewell Township, Hunterdon County was entered on the night of the 12th instance by eight or more armed men who robbed it between eleven and one o'clock. Among the articles taken was a very good plain silver watch, engraved Thos. Stretch-Philadelphia no. 25." This hints that he was also a watchmaker, but since no other such claims exist on record, a more reasonable supposition is that he imported these for resale. His firmest claim to fame is indeed that he built the first clock for the Pennsylvania State House, now known as Independence Hall.

During his prime years, Stretch was probably the most competent clockmaker in Philadelphia. In 1752, therefore, when Isaac Norris was selecting a man to build the first tower clock for the State House, he chose Thomas, the son of his old friend and fellow council member, to do the job.

The original steeple plans for the State House located the clock and the bell in the uppermost stories; the bell, recast by Pass and Stow, was installed there as soon as the appropriate frame was ready. The remaining part of that plan, however, was disregarded: the clock was not installed in the tower, but rather at the center of the attic floor in the main building; the second of the two British bells was mounted immediately—and conveniently—overhead in a little cupola on what was then a flat platform on the building's roof.

The clock was provided with two long, slender rods supported within tubes. The rods extended to the east and west ends of the building, where they operated the

Fig. 56. Premier example of the happy marriage of Peter Stretch's genius and that of his casemaker, whoever he was. Private collection.

Fig. 57. Splendid Thomas Stretch clock with amusing moon phase face—a perfect caricature of former Soviet premier Leonid Brezhnev.

hands on the clock dials. No masonry clock case was provided on the eastern wall; a circular window now occupies the place where that dial had been located. The masonry case on the west wall was obviously intended to create an impression of a gigantic grandfather's clock, but it also served an important operational function. Within it were long vertical slots extending downward to below ground level, which were meant to accommodate the heavy weights that activated both the clock and the clapper of the clock bell. The weights were suspended from ropes which passed over pulleys near the top of the case and onto the large drums within the clock works. (In the recently installed replica of the clock, an electric motor operates the clock hands; thus, the slots are not needed.)

There can be little doubt that Isaac Norris and his fellow superintendents of the State House were directly involved with this change of plans. Norris's personal influence is suggested in the "Historical Structures Report on Independence Hall": "The intention at first was to put the clock in the tower. Perhaps the availability of a second bell after the decision to place the Liberty Bell in the tower influenced the builders to place the clock elsewhere. Norris himself may have had something to do with it, for in the Norris of Fairhill manuscripts at the Historical Society of Pennsylvania is a diagram of a clock on an account dated August 5, 1755, which is a fair, if plain, prototype for the one eventually placed on the west wall of the State House." Several eighteenth-century views of the building show the westerly facing clock dial with its huge masonry case. The well-known 1799 sketch by William Birch also shows a portion of the little cupola on the roof, close to the tower, and the outline of the bell hanging within it.

Master carpenter Edmund Wooley completed his work on the tower in June 1753. Included in his account is an item for "Time Spent in attending the Clock makers while fixing ye Clock first time." By mid-1753, therefore, the clock had been installed in the State House attic, but six years elapsed before Stretch received any payment for it. Among the incidental expenses reported to the assembly on September 30, 1759, was one "To Mr. Stretch for making the State-house Clock, and for his Care in cleaning and repairing the same for six Years, £ 494, 5, 5½."

There is evidence, however, that the clock may not have performed as reliably as it should have. In 1756, for example, when the Friendly Association for Regaining and Preserving Peace with the Indians by Pacific Measures was organized, its rules stipulated that members were to be fined two shillings "for not attending punctually at the time appointed, which is to be determined by the State House clock, if it does; if not by the watch of the oldest member present." The next year, however, right or wrong, "Thomas Stretch's Standard Clock" was to fix the time of meeting.

On January 13, 1762, just over two years after Stretch ceased his maintenance work on the clock, the assembly took the following action: "The House being acquainted that the State-House Clock is found to be much out of Repair, and the Public likely to be deprived of the Use thereof, Ordered, That the Superintendents of the State-House do agree with Mr. Duffield, to repair the said Clock, and take Care of the same for the future." A list of "Incidental Charges," dated September 30, 1763, shows that Edward Duffield was paid £ 76,14 s. 1 d. for his "Account of Services done." Whether these services included anything more than the care of the clock is not known, there being no indication that the assembly had authorized him to perform any other work. Considering that Duffield received only £20 in both 1764 and 1765 for maintaining the clock, it would appear that he had done a considerable amount of extra work in 1762 to make it run satisfactorily. Some problem requiring the maker's particular knowledge and attention must also have turned up in 1764, for, in addition to a maintenance fee to Duffield, the assembly paid Thomas Stretch £33, 4 s. for his services. Stretch's death in 1765 ended, of course, any further attention he might have given his clock; for the next thirteen years Duffield performed the maintenance work on the Stretch clock.

William Stretch, another son of Peter, was also a clockmaker, but he survived his father by only two years. Two of his clocks are known.

Samuel Stretch, generally believed to be Peter's uncle, also left Leek for Philadelphia in 1711. The *Minutes of Common Council of Philadelphia* carry this entry on page 131: "Samuel Stretch, watchmaker, on May 27, 1717 was admitted freeman of Phila. and paid 15 s. 6 d." Assuredly, he made no watches and it cannot be verified that he made clocks in Penn's "Green Countrie Towne."

Samuel S. and Isaac Stretch, Peter's nephew and grandson respectively, were clockmakers who apparently labored at the old shop on Peter Stretch's Corner. No examples of their products have been reported.

Philip Syng was born in 1703 in Cork, Ireland, and came to Philadelphia about 1720, where he engaged in watchmaking and silversmithing. Syng made the silver writing paraphernalia used to sign the Declaration of Independence. A friend of Benjamin Franklin, he was also one of the founders of what is now the University of Pennsylvania and he served a term as treasurer of the county of Philadelphia. Despite his prominence, his association with watches continued until his death in 1789.

Of the six important previous clockmaker compilations, only one listed Henry Taylor (d. 1763) as being at work in Philadelphia. One clock in a prominent local collection was described; another, circa 1750, appeared in a local antique shop in April, 1976. However, ANTIQUES magazine in December 1982 included an illustrated article on Wright's Ferry Mansion in Columbia, Pennsylvania, in which there is a fine tall clock by Henry Taylor. The mansion's curator dates the clock circa 1750.

David Vaughan presents a provoking vignette. He traveled from London to Philadelphia in 1695 and was supposedly mentioned by William Penn, although the context of this comment is unclear. However, Penn's illustrious secretary, James Logan, made the entry in his 1702 account book, "D. Vaughan, note for Work done to Clock and Watch." Vaughan was most likely a repairman, for there is no evidence that he was a maker—had he been one, he might have edged out Abel Cottey as the first in the colony.

Henry Voight (1738–1814) appeared in Philadelphia directories for only eight years, 1785 to 1793, but his varied career stretched over a longer span. In 1780 he was taxed as a clockmaker in Reading, where he was also operating a wire mill. By 1785 he was definitely in Philadelphia. As noted in the Bucks County chapter, he was sometimes associated with John Fitch between 1786 and 1792, and he actually helped make the first American steam boat.

> VOIGHT, HENRY, In Second-street, nearly opposite the Buck Tavern above Race-street, Respectfully informs his friends in particular and the public in general that he carries on the watch making business in all its branches. Such as making all sorts of new watches, upon all the principles which they can be made on in Europe, & c. He flatters himself, from his past experience, he shall be able to convince all those who may be pleased to employ him, that he has made some improvements on watches, which will be of great utility. He likewise carries on the watch case and watch hand making business in all sorts of metal. Watch-makers in the country or in any other part, may be supplied on the shortest notice, Watches and watch cases gilt, Clocks, watches, and watch cases repaired at the most reasonable rates. (*Freeman's Journal*, April 29, 1789)

Voight is the only man who claimed that he not only made improved watches but also cases and hands. Despite this positive statement, however, we know of no Henry Voight watches. If his claim is true, he was a contemporary of Thomas Harland of Norwich, Connecticut, reputedly the first maker (or assembler) of watches in the American colonies.

58

59

60

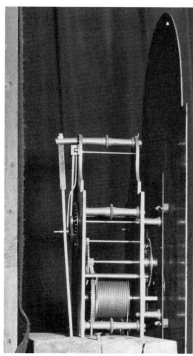

61

Fig. 58. Handsome timepiece made by Thomas Voight. It would be interesting to know if Jefferson suggested the design to Voight. Permission from the Historical Society of Pennsylvania.

Fig. 59. The timepiece in fig. 58 with door open to show the markers inserted by Jefferson, indicating the daily fall of the weight. Permission from the Historical Society of Pennsylvania.

Fig. 60. Close-up of the clock's hood (fig. 58) to show the imaginative treatment of the columns and the almost geometrical floral design of the dial decorations. Permission from the Historical Society of Pennsylvania.

Fig. 61. Utter simplicity of the movement, which was designed solely to provide accurate time. Collectors will especially note the unusual escapement. Permission from the Historical Society of Pennsylvania.

The following public announcement attests that 1793 was an important year for Voight.

> VOIGHT, HENRY, watchmaker of this city, is appointed by the President, with the advice and consent of the Senate, principal corner to the Mint of the United States. (*Federal Gazette*, February 15, 1793)

Sebastian Voight, Henry's brother, was registered in the Philadelphia directories from 1793 to 1800 as a clockmaker. Perhaps his activities are best described by his advertisement.

> VOIGHT, Sebastian, Clock and Watchmaker, Informs his friends and the public in general, that he has removed from No. 149, North Second street, to Market, between Fourth and Fifth streets, No. 173, where he carries on the above business in all its various branches. He keeps as usual a general assortment of warranted watches. (*Gazette of the United States*, June 25, 1798)

Thomas Voight, son of Henry, maintained his clock shop at 44 North Seventh Street from 1811 to 1836. Most collectors agree that his claim to fame rests primarily on one item: a tall clock of his make stood in Monticello. It is quite likely that this was specially ordered by Thomas Jefferson because the striking mechanism was omitted. This timepiece must have been special to Jefferson, for on the inside of the case he marked a scale showing the fall of the weight for each day of the week. After Jefferson's death, the clock was presented by his daughter, Martha Randolph, to Dr. Robley Dunglison, whom Jefferson had brought from England to serve as professor of medicine at the University of Virginia, an institution which Jefferson was instrumental in establishing. The tradition persists that the gift of the timepiece was payment for medical services rendered during Jefferson's final illness. Later, when Dr. Dunglison was called to what is now Jefferson Medical College in Philadelphia, he brought the timepiece with him and in 1894 it was presented to the Historical Society of Pennsylvania.

Few know that Thomas Voight has another claim to fame: an unusual and handsome clock of his stands proudly in the Capitol Building in Washington. For some unknown reason, this timepiece is called the "Ohio Clock." In 1963 the late George Eckhardt, Congressman Fred Schwengel, and I tried to unravel the mystery but had no success.

62

Anthony Ward is briefly mentioned by earlier compilers as being from England and working first in Philadelphia, then in New York City. Britten's *Old Clocks and Watches and Their Makers* (seventh edition) lists Anthony Ward, Truro, England, "Long-case clock, about 1700," and places him in New York from 1724 to 1750. H. Miles Brown in his *Cornish Clocks and Clockmakers* also mentions Anthony Ward, Truro, "long-case month movement, brass square dial, herring bone border, etc. ca. 1705"; Ward was "reported in Philadelphia in 1717 and six clocks [are] still extant with his name in handsome walnut cases. [He is] supposed to have died in New York about 1731." The clockmaker may have arrived in Philadelphia a bit earlier, because on May 27, 1717 he was admitted freeman of Philadelphia as a clockmaker and was paid 15 s. 6 d., according to the *Minutes of the Common Council*, page 131. (By coincidence, this was the same day that Samuel Stretch was accorded the same privilege.) It is fairly certain that he moved to New York in 1724. Anthony Ward has not been properly recognized for his fine clocks, though he indeed ranks among the earliest clockmakers in the American colonies.

David Weatherly's name appeared in the Philadelphia directories over the long period of 1805 to 1850, always as a clock- and watchmaker. He was a prolific maker of tall clocks, a large number of which are still in existence. Like his contemporary, Thomas Parker, Weatherly also produced bracket clocks. A particularly handsome example is seen in figure 63.

The entire clock design is faithful to its English counterpart. It is not known if Weatherly merely imported, finished, and assembled parts or whether he actually made the movement using only imported springs, as good steel for coil clock springs was not then available in America.

The maker of the exceptional dial of this clock signed his name as "Nolen." A well-known dial and sign painter, and a son-in-law of Aaron Willard, Jr., he spent most of his working period in Boston but did work in Philadelphia around 1809.

John Wilbank first appeared in the 1814 Philadelphia directory as a bell founder. In 1839 he advertised as having the largest assortment of tavern, auction, and church bells in the United States. His connection with Independence Hall makes his story worth telling.

The year 1952 marked the 200th anniversary of the arrival of the original Liberty Bell from England. This bell was ordered by the General Assembly of Pennsylvania in 1751, with its now famous inscription: "Proclaim Liberty throughout all the land unto all the inhabitants thereof" (Lev. XXV, V, X). It arrived in 1752, was recast twice by Pass and Stow in Philadelphia, and was finally hung in 1753. While this was happening a second bell arrived from the English founders. The Thomas Stretch

63

Fig. 62. Handsome, massive Thomas Voight clock that stands in the United States Capitol Building. Courtesy of the Architect of the Capitol.

Fig. 63. Extremely fine David Weatherly bracket clock, the dial of which represents industrial mechanics. Courtesy of Edward Railsback and John Sweisford.

clock was attached to this second bell while the "Liberty Bell" was used to call together meetings and sound alarms. In 1828 it was decided that Independence Hall needed a new clock and bell. Isaiah Lukens made the new clock and John Wilbank cast the new bell. However, Wilbank was forced to recast this bell after the first essay cracked. The old Thomas Stretch clock and its bell were then given to St. Augustine's Church. This church was burned by a mob in 1844, the clock was destroyed, and the bell crashed into the ruins. From the fragments a new bell was cast, which is still to be found at Villanova College in Villanova, Pennsylvania. The Liberty Bell itself became a national symbol of freedom. In 1876 the Isaiah Lukens clock and Wilbank bell were given to the town hall in Germantown, when a new clock and bell were obtained for Independence Hall. When Germantown built a new municipal building in the 1920s the Lukens clock and Wilbank bell were installed where they are still giving service. In 1836 he cast the bell for the West Chester town clock.

Joseph Wills (1700?–1759) was a well-known clockmaker and many of his products are extant. He built both thirty-hour and eight-day tall clocks, both varieties with brass movements and dials, some as small as 10½ inches square. Some of his clocks have sweep second hands and/or a moon phase; most of his clocks, however, are plain and severe, as seen in this specimen (fig. 64) that was in the Bake House at Valley Forge State Park.

At the same time, that he could produce more ornate clocks is attested by the specimen in figure 65, a clock cased in rare red walnut and bearing the date 1748, cut into the inside of the case.

Wills apparently was important enough to have had an apprentice:

> THOMAS WINTERBOTTOM. Run away the 10th Inst. from the subscriber in the city of Philadelphia, a servant named Thomas Winterbottom, a clock maker by trade. . . . whoever secures him for me so that I may have him again, shall have Ten Pounds Reward paid by Joseph Wills. (*Pennsylvania journal or weekly advertiser*, June 14, 1750)

In June 1694 a religious sect of Germans called the Pietests arrived in Germantown under the leadership of Johann Kelpius, Ph.D. Some of them, including Kelpius, lived in caves along the Wissahickon Creek, where they created an atmosphere of learning. Into this group came Dr. Christopher Witt of Wiltshire, England. Before joining Kelpius in 1704, Dr. Witt had practiced occult and practical astronomy. In 1706 Witt painted a portrait of Kelpius, probably the earliest oil painting done in

Fig. 64. Early, plain thirty-hour clock by Joseph Wills. Courtesy of the Valley Forge State Park Superintendent.

Fig. 65. More ornate eight-day clock by Joseph Wills. Courtesy of Edward Railsback and John Sweisford.

the colonies, which still exists and is in the possession of the Historical Society of Pennsylvania. A clock shown in the background of the painting is undoubtedly the first representation of a clock in an American painting. Witt quite probably built the clock, which is a type then called "Wand-uhren"—that is, a clock regulated by a long pendulum and powered by fifteen- to twenty-pound weights hung on chains. These were the forerunners of conventional tall clocks and tower clocks, later also made by Witt. As noted, the physician taught the clockmaking trade to Christopher Sauer. He also taught the art to his mulatto slave, Robert Claymen, whom he manumitted in his will and to whom he bequeathed all his "tools, instruments and utinsels [sic] belonging to or apportaining [sic] to the making of clocks, his great clock which strikes the quarters, and many other things." Claymen labored as a clockmaker in Philadelphia between 1765 and 1780.

Witt apparently built clocks during the winter and cultivated medicinal herbs during the summer. Furthermore, he built a telescope to pursue astronomy and practical horoscopy to the degree that he earned the nickname "Hexmeister." His one known tower clock, constructed in 1735 for what today is called the "Ephrata Cloister," deserves mention. Julius Sachse, author of several books concerning German religious sects in Pennsylvania, maintained that this may have been the first tower clock made in America; however, there were actually at least two earlier ones, both in Guilford, Connecticut. After the demolition of buildings on Zion Hill during the Revolution, the Witt tower clock and its bell were removed to a smaller building near the Saal (the house of prayer). After 1837 it was installed in the cupola of the New Academy building. That it was apparently still operable is attributable to Witt's skill. It is believed to be currently stored in a building called "Saron."

Little is known about John Wood, Sr. (d. 1761). In his earlier days he must have made clocks, for it is stated that Francis Richardson, the noted silversmith, engraved fine clock faces for John Wood in 1734. A later advertisement tells the maker's story:

JOHN WOOD, Clock and Watch-Maker, at the corner of Front and Chestnut streets, has for sale, A Parcel of best Silver Watches; a variety of clock and watch tools; also watch main springs, fusee chains, glasses, enamel'd dial plates, pendants, pinion and pendulum wire, steel and brass keys, silk strings, steel chains and seals, small square steel, cast clock-work, ditto faces, finish'd and unfinished, heads, bells, clock and watch hands, case-string, catgut, & c. All kinds of Clock and Watch-Work done in the best manner, at reasonable rates. (Pennsylvania Chronicle, May 9, 1768)

The reader may recall that the location of the shop was at Peter Stretch's Corner. One of his clocks is pictured in *The American Heritage History of Colonial Antiques*.

Much more is known about John Wood, Jr. (1736–93), perhaps because he advertised so extensively between 1760 and 1793, though in only six of those years did his name appear in directories. The story of his successful career as a clockmaker and a merchant is told in part by his advertisements.

> JOHN WOOD. Philadelphia-Made Watches. The subscriber, having engaged in his employ some capital workmen from London, in the different branches of watch-making, can furnish any gentlemen with repeating, horizontal, seconds, or plain watches, warranted good. . . . The advantage of having the maker of such machines on the spot, is obvious to every purchaser, as reputation and interest will engage him to put out of his hands such work only as will give satisfaction; which will be the constant endeavour of the public's humble servant, John Wood. (*Pennsylvania Journal*, October 24, 1771)

Wood advertised a long and diverse selection of gadgets and tools: "corner and arch pieces, crucibles, clock-wheels and pinions, turned and cut, clock and watch plyers, screw dividers, beam and wind compasses, hand and tail vises, sliding tongs, cutting nippers, beak irons, spring-saw frames, hammers, spring blewers, screw plates, broaches, turn-benches, pivot turns, bench vises, pinion and frame gauges, double and steel tweesers, braces, and bitts, calipers, clock freesing tools, watch-rivetting tools, screw-keys, screw-drivers, spring tools, clock and watch turning arbors, barrel arbors, and ratchets, verge rivetting stocks, wire drawing plates, clock and watch main springs, watch glasses, fusee, watch chains, gold, silver, and pinchbeck pendants, clock & watch hands, case springs and buttons, chain hooks, steel and brass watch keys, pinion wire, gravers, clock-bells, sheet brass, catgut, turkey oyl stones, polishing stones, gliding wax, fine scratch brushes, borax, rotten and pumice stones, emery, black wax"—and the list goes on.

> JOHN WOOD. Watch main springs, made in Philadelphia, are sold by the Manufacturer, Matthias Eyre, Spring-maker from London, at his house in Third-street, below South-street, and by John Wood, Watch maker, in Front-street, at the corner of Chestnut-street Philadelphia, where watch-makers and others may be supplied with any quantity of springs much cheaper than

66

67

can be afforded when imported from England; from which circumstance, and the quality of the springs, the maker hopes for the encouragement of the watch-makers in this and the neighbouring provinces, whose orders will be gratefully received and faithfully executed. N.B. Thirty shillings by the dozen, and three shillings the single spring. (*Pennsylvania Packet*, January 30, 1775)

In one of the Diplomatic Reception rooms of the State Department in Washington stands a Philadelphia Chippendale tall case clock, circa 1775, built by John Wood. This highly styled clock has its three original flame finials, a superb shell, and other carvings on the bonnet. The dial is in perfect condition and shows not only the time but the day of the month. Above the dial is an unusual blue sky with gold stars.

Wood's tall clocks generally seem to have been of the Chippendale style.

The clock shown in figure 67 was once, and probably originally, owned by Samuel Cooper of Cooper's Ferry (now Camden). Overhaul dates of 1829, 1837, and 1845 are chalked inside. Wood also sold bracket clocks bearing his name, but, considering the date, they probably were imported from England in whole or in part.

John Wood made clocks and watches for his fellow townsmen, but he also catered to the country trade, supplying all parts of both watches and clocks to those who wished to assemble their own timepieces. This distinguished member of the Grand Lodge of Free Masons and officer under the Washington Continental Army died in 1793 of yellow fever and was buried at St. Paul's Church. His finest clock remains in the Metropolitan Museum of Art in New York.

Directory List of Names

As stated at the beginning of the chapter, our history-minded predecessors endowed Philadelphia with an overabundance of clock- and watchmakers. There are critics who feel strongly that a book of this nature should not list any name that is of doubtful merit; however, I believe that every name which has any connection to the field ought to be recorded as a possible aid to future researchers. If nothing else, such procedure at least reflects "the state of the art" at the time of publication.

This list, then, is of names that have appeared in one or more publications but are

Fig. 66. High style clock by John Wood. From the collections of the Historical Society of York County, Pennsylvania.

Fig. 67. Another high style clock by John Wood, very similar to the clock in figure 66. Courtesy of Edward Railsback and John Sweisford.

in no way embellished or authenticated. "D." after a date indicates a directory listing; "Adv." means advertisement.

Abel, Robert K., 1840–41
Aherns, Adolph, 1837 D.
Alexander, Samuel, 1787–1808
Allebach, Jacob, 1825–40
Alsop, Thomas, 1842–50 D.
Altmore, Marshall, 1819–32
Amant, Peter, 1794 D.
Antrim, Charles, 1837–39; 1844–47 D.
App, Samuel, 1850 D.
Arbuckle, Joseph, 1847–48 D.
Arnold, Jacob, 1848 D.
Ashton, C.W. & C., 1762–97 D.
Atherton, Mathew, 1837–40 D.
Atherton, Nathan, 1825 D.
Atherton, Nathan, Jr., 1841–60 D.
Attmore, Marshall, 1821–37 D.
Austin, Isaac, 1781 Adv.; 1785–1801 D.
Bailey, Gamaliel, 1828–33 D.
Bailey, William, Jr., 1816–22; 1829–36 D.
Baker, Benjamin H., 1823–25 D.
Baker, James M., 1842 D.
Banks, Joseph, 1819–20 D.
Banstein, John, 1791 D.
Barbeck, C.G., 1835–36 D.
Barber, George, 1844 D.
Barger, George, 1844 D.
Barnhill, Robert, 1776–78 Adv.
Bassett, George F., 1791–98 D.
Bayley, Simeon C., 1794 D.
Beatly, Albert L., 1833 D.
Bechtel, Henry, 1817 D.
Beck, Henry, 1837–39 D.
Beigel, Henry, 1816–17 D.
Belk, William, 1797–99 D.
Bell, S.W., 1837 D.
Bell, Thomas, 1837
Berrgant, Peter, 1829–33 D.
Bevins, William, 1810–13 D.
Biersen, Thomas, 1839–42 D.

Billon, Charles, 1798–1820 D.
Bingham & Bricerly, 1778–99
Black, John, 1839–49 D.
Bland, Samuel, 1837; 1845–50 D.
Blane, Lewis, 1810 D.
Blowe, George, 1837; 1845–50 D.
Bode, William, 1796–1806 D.
Bond, William, 1829–33 D., clock dial manufacturer
Bonnard, M., 1799 D.
Borhek, Edward, 1829–40 D.
Borkek, Charles G., 1830–40 D.
Boute, Lewis C., 1839 D.
Bower, Michael, 1799 D.
Boyd, Thomas, 1807–9 D.
Bradier, John, 1802–5 D.
Brady, John, 1835–36 D.
Brearly (also Breacky), James, 1795–1822 D.
Breiderbauch, L., 1807 D.
Brennan, Barnabas, 1843 D.
Brewer, Thomas A., 1830–47 D.
Brewer, William, 1791 D.
Bringhurst, Joseph, 1813 D.
Brintzinghoffer, F., 1804 D.
Broomall, Lewis R., 1846 D.
Brown, Brant, 1796
Brown, John, 1819–22 D.
Brown, William, 1823–24; 1837 D.
Buard, Charles W., 1849 D.
Buffet, G.F., ca. 1796
Bunting, Daniel, 1844 D.
Burk, Charles, 1848 D.
Burkhart, Trudpert, 1839–46 D., musical clock maker
Burkloe, Samuel, 1791–1813 D.
Burns, Hugh, 1809–11 D.
Burrows, Dowdney, ca. 1768
Butler, Franklin, 1846 D.
Calderwood, Andrew, 1800–1822 D.

Campbell, Alexander, 1798–99 D.
Capper, Michael, 1798–1800 D.
Carter, Jacob, 1806–8 D.
Carter, Thomas, 1823–24 D.
Carvalks, D.N., 1846 D.
Carver, Jacob, 1785–1833 D.
Charles, Lewis, 1837 D.
Castan, Stephen, 1818 D., watch case maker
Cave, Joseph, 1837–47 D.
Cecil, Charles, 1808–11 D., clocksmith
Chamberlain, Charles, 1833–39 D.
Chamberlain, Lewis, 1829–42 D.
Child, Henry T., 1840–42 D.
Child, Samuel T., 1843–48 D.
Child, Thomas T., 1845 D.
Chollot, John B., 1816–20 D.
Chrystter, William, 1828–36 D.
Clark, Charles, 1809 D.
Clark, Charles, & Clark, Ephraim, 1806–10
Clark, Edward, 1797 D.
Clark, Elias, 1802 D.
Clark, Ellis, 1813–48 D.
Clark, Ellis, Jr., 1842–47 D.
Clark, Jesse, 1809–14 D.
Clark, Thomas W., 1839–41 D.
Clark & Hartley, 1839–41 D.
Clayton, Elias B., 1848–50 D.
Clein, John, 1831–33 D.
Coates, Isaac, 1835–39 D.
Coleman, James, 1833 D.
Coleman, John, 1848 D.
Collom, David W., 1846 D.
Conrad, Osborn, 1841–50 D.
Cooper, Joseph B., 1842–46 D.
Cooper, Robert H., 1850 D.
Cooper, Samuel B., 1840 D.
Corgee, Arthur, 1823–24 D.
Corvazier, Edward, 1846 D.
Cox, Benjamin, 1809–13 D.
Cozens, Josiah B., 1818–24 D.
Craven, Alfred, 1843 D.
Curtis, Solomon, 1793 D.
Crowley, E., 1833 D.

Crowley & Farr, 1823–25 D.
Cure, Jule F., 1839–40 D.
Cure, Louis, 1813–20 D.
Curtis, Solomon, 1793 D.
Daff, Thomas, 1775 Adv.
Dawson, Jonas, 1813–24 D.
De Benneville, N., 1820–22 D.
Deschamps, Francis, 1846–49 D.
Deuconer, G., 1817 D.
Dix, Joseph, 1769 Adv.
Domment, John, 1736–37
Douty, Henrick, 1774 Adv.
Droz, Charles, 1813–14 D.
Droz, Charles A., 1816–41 D.
Droz, Hannah, 1842–50 D.
Droz, Humbert, 1793–1811 D.
Drysdale, William, 1816–50 D.
Drysdale, William, Jr., 1842–45 D.
Ducommun, A.L., 1795–98 D., watch case
    maker
Ducommun, Henry, 1843–50 D.
Dupey, Odran, ca. 1735, watch case finisher
Earp, Robert, 1811
Elliot, Benjamin P., 1843–50 D.
Ellis, Benjamin, 1829–33 D.
Elson, Hermann, 1843–48 D.
Elson, Julius, 1842–44 D.
Endt, Theodore, 1740s
Engard, Samuel, 1837–42 D.
Erwin, Henry, 1817–29; 1837–42 D.
Evans, William M., 1813–48
Faff, Augustus, 1835–37 D.
Farr, John C., 1824–50 D.
Fulton, Frederick, 1830–39 D.
Favre, John J., 1797 D.
Ferris, Benjamin, 1806–11 D.
Ferris & McElwee, 1813 D.
Ferris, Edward, 1846–48 D.
Fertig, Benjamin, 1811
Fertig, Jacob W., 1810–11 D.
Feton, J., 1828–40
Fling, Daniel, 1809–22 D.
Fraser, Jacob, ca. 1822–60

Fries, John, 1830–50 D.
Fries, P., 1839–50 D.
Galbraith, Patrick, 1794–1817 D.
Garrett, Philip, & Sons, 1828–35 D.
Garrett, Thomas C., 1829–40 D.
Garrett & Haydock, 1837–40 D., watch case
    makers
Gaw, William, 1816–22 D.
Goodfellow, William, 1793–1818 D.
Govette, George, 1811–19 D.
Graham, William, 1733 Adv.
Green, John, 1794–96 D.
Groff, J.R., 1844–50 D.
Guile, John, 1818–24 D.
Hahn, C.G., 1789–98 D.
Hall, John, 1804–40 D.
Hall, Peter, 1818–24 D.
Halliday, Elias H., 1828–33 D.
Hamilton, James, 1848 D.
Hamilton, R.J., 1837–46 D.
Hamilton, Samuel, 1837 D.
Hansell, James, 1816–50 D.
Harrington, William, 1849–50 D.
Hartley, Jeremiah, 1837–50 D.
Haydock, Edward, 1839–50 D., watch case
    maker
Heineman, G., 1847–49 D.
Heineman, L.G., 1849–50 D.
Heiss, James P., 1849–50 D.
Helm, Christian, 1802–4 D.
Helm, Thomas, 1839–50 D., watch case maker
Hemphill, T.J., 1836–41 D.
Hepton, Frederick, 1785 D.
Hight, Christian, 1819–22 D.
Hildebum, Samuel, 1810–44 D.
Hildeburn, Woodworth, 1816–20 D.
Hillworth, Frederick, 1794–1849 D.
Hodgson, William, 1785 D.
Hoffner, Henry, 1791 D.
Holms, J., 1842 D.
Hooper, B.C., 1848 D.
Hopkins, H.P., 1831–32 D.
Hopkins, Robert, 1833 D.

Hopper, Joseph M., 1816–22 D.
Houguet, Augustus, 1819–22
Huckel, Jacob, 1824 D.
Huckel, Samuel, 1818–29 D.
Hughes, George W., 1829–33 D.
Hugenin, Charles F., 1797–1802 D.
Hutchinson, Samuel, 1828–39 D.
Hutchinson, Thomas, 1816–24 D.
Jacks, James, 1797–1800
Jackson, Joseph A., 1802–10
James, Edward, 1797–98 D.
Jeanes, Thomas, 1835–37 D.
Job, John, 1819–20 D.
Johnson, Robert, 1831–50 D.
Johnson & Crowley, 1832–33 D.
Johnson & Lewis, 1837–42 D.
Jonas, Joseph, 1817 D.
Joyce, Thomas, 1821–25 D.
Karn, A.L., 1809–10 D.
Kennedy, Hugh, 1845–50 D.
Kennedy, Patrick, 1795–1801 D.
Kessler, John, Jr., 1806–8 D.
Keyser, Joseph, 1828–33 D.
Kinkead, James, 1765 Adv.
Kirchoff, J.H., 1805 D.
Klein, John, 1828–50 D.
Kleiser, Jacob, 1822–24 D.
Klingle, Joseph, 1823–25 D.
Knowles, John, 1784 Adv.
Lacey, John, 1819–25 D.
Lackey, Henry, 1808–11 D.
Ladomus, Jacob, 1843–50 D.
Ladomus, Lewis, 1845–50 D.
Lamoine, Augustus, 1811–17 D.
Lane, James, 1803–18 D.
Laquaine, Francis, 1794 D.
Latimer, James, 1813–22 D.
Law, William, 1849–50 D.
Leeds, Gideon, 1841–42 D.
Lefferts, Charles, 1818–22 D.
LeHuray, Theodore, 1844–50 D.
Lemoine, A., 1810–17 D.
Levi, Garretsen, 1840–43 D.

Levy, H.A., 1846–50 D.
Levy, Lewis B., 1845 D.
Levy, M., & Co., 1816–17 D.
Levy, Martin, 1814–17 D., watch case maker
Lewis, John, 1845–50 D.
Limeburner, John, 1791 D.
Linn, John, 1794–1805 D.
Loew, John J., 1846–48 D.
Long, Samuel, 1842–46
Lownes, David, 1785–1807 D.
Ludwig, John, 1791 D.
McCormick, Henry, 1833 D.
McCoy, George W., 1837–50 D.
McCully, William, 1841 D.
McDowell, James, 1794–1808 D.
McDowell, James, Jr., 1805–25
McDowell, William H., 1818–36 D.
MacFarlane, William, 1805 D.
McIlhenney, Joseph E., 1823–25 D.
McIlhenney & West, 1818–22 D.
McKeen, Henry, 1823–50 D.
McKinley, Edward, 1830–37 D.
McManus, John, 1840 D.
McMasters, Hugh A., 1839 D.
McMullen, Edward, 1846–48 D.
McPherson, Robert, 1837–50 D.
McStocker, Francis, 1831–51 D.
Martin, John, 1849–50 D.
Martin, Patrick, 1821–50 D.
Mason, Samuel, Jr., 1820–30 D.
Massey, Charles R., 1837–39 D.
Mathey, Lewis, 1797–1803 D.
Maxwell, A., 1805–10 D.
Mears, Charles, 1828–35 D.
Mecke, John, 1837–50 D.
Mends, Benjamin, 1796–97 D.
Mends, James, 1795 D.
Menzies, James, ca. 1800
Menzies, John, Jr., 1835–? D.
Menzies, Thomas, 1806–25
Merry, F., 1799 D.
Miller, George, 1829–33 D.
Miller, Thomas, 1819–40 D.

Miller, William, 1847 D.
Miller, William S., 1843–48 D.
Milner, Robert, 1817 D.
Mollinger, Henry, 1794–1804 D.
Montieth, Benjamin, 1818 D.
Montieth, Charles, 1818 D.
Moonlinger, Henry, 1741–1804 D.
Morin, Augustus, 1833 D.
Morris, William, 1837 D.
Morris, William, Jr., 1844 D.
Morrissey, C.R., 1837 D.
Mountain, S.P., 1842 D.
Murphy, Robert E., 1848–49 D.
Neal, Daniel, 1823–33 D.
Newberry, James W., 1819–50 D.
Nicollett, Joseph W., 1797–98 D.
Nicollett, Mary, 1793–99 D.
Nolen, Spencer, 1816–24 D., clock dial maker
    and painter
Northern, Elijah, 1844–50 D.
Norton, Thomas, 1794 Adv.; 1800–1811 D.
Nowland, Thomas, 1806–8 D.
O'Brien, John, 1844–49 D.
O'Daniel, Perry, 1837–50 D.
Oertelt, Charles E., 1844–50 D.
O'Hara, Charles, 1799–1800 D.
Oliver, Griffith, 1785 D.
Olewine, Henry, 1845–49 D.
Orr, Thomas, 1809–17 D.
Palmer, John, 1795–96 D.
Parke, Augustus, 1817–22 D.
Parke, Charles, 1806–10 D.
Parker, Isaac, 1819–50 D.
Parker, Thomas, Jr., 1817–22 D.
Parker, Thomas, & Co., 1818–20 D.
Parker, T.H., 1833 D.
Parks, Augustus W., 1819–33 D.
Parmier, John P., 1793 D.
Parrott, F.W., 1847–50 D.
Parrott, Joseph, 1835–43 D.
Parsons, Henry R., 1849–50 D.
Patton, Abraham, 1799–1817 D.
Patton & Jones, 1804–14 D.

Pavey, John, 1803–20 D.

Peale, James, 1814–17 D.

Perpignann, Peter, 1809–25 D.

Peters, James, 1821–50 D.

Petty, Henry, 1829–33 D.

Pfaff, August, 1831–50 D.

Pfluefer, Hermann, 1849–50 D.

Pickering, Henry, 1816–49 D.

Pierret, Mathew, 1795–96 D.

Platt, John, 1843 D.

Ponson, Peter, 1796 D.

Praefelt, John, 1797–98 D.

Price, Benjamin, 1828 D., also a copperplate printer

Price, Isaac, 1791–97 D.

Price, Philip, 1824 D.

Price, Philip, Jr., 1813–44, also a copperplate printer

Probasco, Jacob, 1822 D.

Purse, John, 1803 D.

Quandale, Lewis, 1813–45 D.

Rankin, Alexander, 1829–33 D.

Rapp, William, 1828–ca. 1850 D.

Read, Daniel I., 1798 D.

Read, W.H.J., 1831–50 D.

Reed, Frederick, 1818–22 D.

Reed, G.W., 1839–50 D.

Reed, Isaac, 1819–46 D.

Reed, Isaac, & Son, 1837–50 D.

Reed, John W., 1846–47 D.

Reed, Osman, 1831–50 D.

Reed, Osman, & Co., 1841–43 D.

Reeve, George, 1804–5 D.

Reeve, Richard, 1803–7 D.

Reeves, David S., 1831–36 D.

Richardson, Francis, ca. 1736, clock dial engraver

Riehl, George, 1805 D.

Riggs, W.H.C., 1819–61 D., furnished timepieces for railroads, steamships, and banks and commercial firms and serviced ship chronometers

Riggs, W.H.C., & Son (Daniel), 1863 D., furnished timepieces for railroads, steamships, and banks and commercial firms and serviced ship chronometers

Riggs, Daniel, & Co., 1864–65 D., furnished timepieces for railroads, steamships, and banks and commercial firms and serviced ship chronometers

Riggs & Brothers, 1866–70 D.

Riggs Brothers, 1872–1972

Riley, John, 1785–1813 D., advertised for an apprentice in 1783; repairer of equation clocks and watches of unusual construction

Riley, Robert, 1806–8 D.

Ritchie, George, 1785–1811 D.

Robbins, George, 1833–51 D.

Roberts, F., 1828–29 D., manufacturer of patent mantel clocks

Roberts, John, 1797–99 D., cabinet- and chairmaker

Roberts, William, 1821 D.

Robeson, Isaac, 1843–46

Robinson, Anthony, 1796–1802

Rode, William, 1795 D.

Rohr, John A., 1807–13 D.

Rouse, Emanual, 1747–68 Adv.

Rudolph, Samuel, 1803 D.

Rue, Henry, 1835–36 D.

Russell, George, 1833–50 D.

Sailor, Washington, 1825–33 D.

Sampson, William, 1802–3 D.

Sandoz, Charles H., 1800–1802 D.

Sandoz, Louis, 1845

Schell, Samuel F., 1829–36 D.

Schreiner, Charles W., 1813–39 D.

Schuller, J., 1845–46 D.

Schultz, Gottlieb, 1821–44 D.

Schume, Thomas, 1823–25 D.

Seddinger, Margaret, 1840 D.

Servas, Charles, 1849 D.

Shermer, John, 1803–13 D.

Shermes, Robert, 1803–13 D.

Shields, Thomas, 1785–94 D.

Shippen, William A., 1818–24 D.

Shoemaker, Abraham, 1846 D.
Shuler, John, 1848–49 D.
Simpson, Alexander, 1848 D., watch case maker
Smart, John, 1847–50 D.
Smeck, Peter, 1848 D., watch case maker
Smelten, R.T., 1846–47 D.
Smith, Charles N., 1835–50 D.
Smith, Ernest, 1830–33 D.
Smith, Frederick, 1843–50 D., watch case maker
Smith, Hezekiah, 1845 D.
Smith, Isschar (Isaac), 1842–43 D.
Smith, James, 1839–50 D.
Smith, Philip, 1847–50 D., watch case maker
Smith, Robert, 1821–31 D.
Smith, William, 1818–25 D.
Somerdike, William, 1849–50 D., watch case maker
Somers & Crowley, 1828–33 D.
Souza, Samuel, 1819–20 D.
Sperry, William, 1843–48 D.
Speyers, Moses, 1830 D.
Statzell, P.M., 1845–50 D.
Stellwagen, Charles R., 1840–48 D. Watches bearing his name are known but look quite English.
Stewart, George, 1837 D.
Stilles, John, 1786–93 Adv.
Stoltenwerk, P.M., 1813–14 D.
Stuart, James, 1837–50 D.
Sturgis, Joseph, 1813–17 D.
Syderman, Philip, 1785–94 D.
Taf, John J., 1794 D.
Tappan, W.B., 1818–20 D.
Taylor, Luther, 1823–35 D.
Taylor, Samuel, 1798–99 D.
Thomas, Joseph, 1805–8 D.
Thompson, John P., 1819–24 D.
Thornton, Andrew, 1811 D.
Thornton, Joseph, 1819–20 D.
Thum, Charles, 1828–33 D.
Townsend, Charles, 1799–1849 D.
Townsend, Charles, Jr., 1829–50 D.

Townsend, Elisha, 1828–29 D.
Townsend, John, 1811–33 D.
Townsend, John, Jr., 1849 D.
Tracy, Charles, 1843–50 D., watch case maker
Tracy, Charles, & Tracy, Elizabeth, 1846–50 D., watch case maker
Tracy, William, 1844–50 D.
Trahn, Peter C., 1843–49 D.
Treadwell, Oren B., 1846–49 D.
Vantine, John L., 1829–47 D.
Waage & Norton, 1798 D.
Waples, Nathaniel, 1816–20 D.
Ward & Govelt, 1813–14 D.
Ward, Jehu, 1808–48 D., took over the shop of Abraham Patton in 1819.
Ward, William L., 1831–50 D.
Ward, Edward H., 1840–42 D.
Ward, Isaac, 1811–18 D.
Wark, William, 1848–50 D.
Warner, Cuthbert, 1837–50 D., watch case maker
Warner, John S., 1833–45 D., watch case maker
Warner, Joseph P., 1837–39 D., watch case maker
Warner, Robert P., 1839–50 D., watch case and gold dial maker
Warner, William, 1839–50 D., watch case maker
Warner & Keating, 1840–43 D., watch case maker
Warner & Newlen, 1848–50 D., gold dial makers
Warrington, John, 1811–33 D.
Warrington, Samuel, 1828–50 D.
Watson, James, 1821–50 D.
Weller, Francis, 1777 Adv.
West, Josiah (Joseph), 1798–1808 D.
West, Thomas G., 1819–22 D.
Westphall, Charles W., 1822, watch case maker
Westphall, Ferdinand, 1814–24 D., watch case maker
White, Joseph, 1808–18 D.
White, Joseph, Jr., 1811–17 D.

White, Sebastian, 1795–96 D.
White, Thomas, 1810 D.
Whitehead, John, 1831–49 D.
Whitehead, William G., 1850 D.
Widdefield, William, Jr., 1821–22 D.
Widdefield & Gaw, 1821–22 D.
Widdifield, William, 1816–17 D.

Wiggins, Thomas, & Co., 1831–46 D.
Wilson, Robert, 1835–36 D.
Winters, Isaac, 1844–48 D.
Yeager, William, 1837 D.
Young, Francis, 1777 Adv.
Young, William J., ca. 1857, sun dial maker
Zeissler, G.A., 1848 D.

Dr. David Rittenhouse

We usually think of David Rittenhouse in superlative terms. His amazing mechanical genius, his extensive knowledge of astronomy and science, his inventions and discoveries—all still impress us as extraordinary accomplishments in an age when an academic education was not a usual feature of our civilization.

Rittenhouse was born on April 18, 1732 in a little stone house in Germantown on the bank of the Wissahickon Creek, the site of a former paper mill.

His early interest in mechanics was stimulated by his uncle, David Williams, from whom he inherited at age twelve a chest of tools and some books pertaining to science and mathematics. One volume in particular, a copy of the First Book of Newton's *Principia*, had a profound influence on his future. That he apparently acquired a firm grasp of the principles is surprising because Newton's teaching at Harvard and Yale had barely begun at that time. As a result, when the family moved to a farm in Norriton, Montgomery County, young David often neglected his farm chores in favor of making his own calculations and solving mathematical problems.

By 1749 David's father despaired of thinking of his son as a farmer and assisted him in building a small shop. David soon had the shop well equipped—and even made some of the tools himself to meet special needs. Before the year was out he had built, without instruction, his first clock. It was a thirty-hour, wood movement timepiece, accurate enough to amaze the neighbors. Soon afterwards he was able to construct thirty-hour tall clocks with brass movements. Figure 68 shows one of these which comes quite close to being completely original. The actual work was done by hand; the train of wheels and the escapement were cut from brass and the weight was cast from lead. Possibly Rittenhouse made the cases himself while living in Norriton, as many of his inherited tools were for the joiner's trade, suitable wood was available, and he had ability and time. It is reasonable to believe that the dial spandrels were imported because they are very similar to those used by Peter and Thomas Stretch and Edward Duffield. Few of the existing Rittenhouse clocks have been authentically dated, so it is difficult to trace the development of his skill; however, he was quick in producing eight-day, brass movement tall clocks equal to or better than those constructed by his contemporaries. His astronomical clocks far surpassed theirs.

Long before Rittenhouse became famous as a clockmaker he made a friend who strongly influenced his career. Thomas Barton, twenty-one years old and educated at the University of Dublin, arrived in Norriton in 1751 to establish a school. Barton met the young student and was surprised by his grasp of mathematics. Recognizing untapped genius, Barton encouraged David to study disciplines such as philosophy and languages. The prescribed long hours of work and study, however, brought on a painful ailment, which most likely was gastric ulcers. This became so severe that in 1753 he went to Yellow Springs (now Chester Springs) to drink the chalybeate spring water, which he found beneficial. Unfortunately, the water acted as a palliative, not a cure, and poor Rittenhouse was plagued by this debilitating ailment throughout his lifetime.

In 1756 Barton, now a minister of the Church of England, established a mission near Sulphur Springs (now York Springs) in Adams County. Despite the threat of indians in the area, Rittenhouse spent some time at Sulphur Springs for his health. While there, he built a clock for the Bartons, and inscribed the phrases "Tempus Fugit" ("Time Flies") and "Mind Your Business" on the dial. This proved to be prophetic, since Barton joined the Forbes expedition to capture Fort Duquesne, later accepted a call to an itinerant mission in Lancaster County, and with the outbreak of the Revolution, found himself and his brother-in-law on opposite sides of the political fence. Meanwhile, at Sulphur Springs David considered his situation. True, there was a fairly constant demand for his clocks at low prices and he had learned to make telescopes and had done a prodigious amount of scientific study. This, however, was not enough.

Like his contemporary, George Washington, Rittenhouse was a competent, even renowned, surveyor. He settled the boundary between the provinces of New York and New Jersey; helped establish the boundary between the New York and Massachusetts provinces; and fixed the circle with the 12-mile radius around New Castle that still constitutes the border between Delaware and Pennsylvania.

While still at Norriton, he performed in 1769 his most celebrated astronomical observation—the transit of Venus over the sun. The American Philosophical Society

Fig. 68. Rather short, unadorned, thirty-hour brass movement clock, with brass dial and calendar. Made by David Rittenhouse, circa 1750s. The case is wood pegged. Private collection.

arranged this project at the Rittenhouse observatory. For the occasion Rittenhouse constructed an astronomical quadrant, an equal altitude instrument, a transit telescope and, naturally, a fine timepiece. The pendulum rod of this timepiece was a flat steel bar with a bob weighing about twelve pounds and vibrating in a small arc. It had a dead beat escapement and was powered by a five-pound weight. This particular timepiece is now the property of the American Philosophical Society. Earlier writers have judged it so accurate as to deserve the title of pendulum chronometer. Mentioning that more than one was built during Rittenhouse's lifetime, they have ascertained that these pendulum chronometers were either made by the master himself or by his brother Benjamin, under David's immediate supervision. An assistant in the observation was Owen Biddle, a competent Philadelphian clockmaker.

In the summer of 1770, before moving to Philadelphia, Rittenhouse completed one of his greatest inventions—his first orrery. Tradition says that such an instrument was named for Richard Boyle, Earl of Orrery. This orrery was sold to the antecedent of Princeton University, but it subsequently disappeared. The next year he completed his second orrery for the University of Pennsylvania (at that time called the College of the City of Philadelphia), in whose possession the orrery proudly remains. By manipulating the hands on the dials of this amazing mechanical device, it is possible to observe the movements of the celestial bodies over a period of ten thousand years—five thousand both before and after the year 1770. For example, complete data regarding eclipses of the sun and the moon during these many millenia are obtainable to the precise hour and minute of occurrence. The inventor described the invention thus:

> This machine is intended to have three faces standing perpendicular to the horizon; that in the front to be four feet square, made of sheet brass, curiously polished, silvered, and painted in proper places, and otherwise ornamented. From the center arises an axis to support a gilded brass ball, intended to represent the sun. Round this ball move others, made of brass or iron, to represent the planets. They are to move in elliptical orbits, having the central ball in focus; and their motions to be sometimes swifter and sometimes slower, as nearly according to the true law of an equable description of areas as possible, without too great a complication of wheel work. The orbit of each planet is likewise to be properly inclined to those of the others, and their aphelia and nodes justly placed, and their velocity so accurately adjusted as not to differ sensibly from the tables of astronomy in some thousands of years.
>
> For the greater beauty of the instrument, the balls representing planets are to be of a considerable lightness, but so constructed that they may be taken off at pleasure and

others much smaller and fitted for some other purposes put in their places.

When the machine is put in motion by the turning of a winch, there are three indexes which point out the hour of the day, the day of the month, and the year (according to the Julian account) answering to the situation of the heavenly bodies which is then represented—and so continually for a period of five thousand years, either forward or backward.

In order to know the true situation of a planet at any particular time, the small set of balls are to be put each upon its respective axis, then the winch is to be turned round until each index points to the given time. Then a small telescope made for the purpose is to be applied to the central ball, and directing it to the planet its longitude and inclination will be seen on a large brass circle, silvered and properly graduated, representing the zodiac, and having a motion of one degree in 172 years, agreeable to the procession of equinoxes. So, likewise, by applying the telescope to the ball representing the earth, and directing it to any planet, then will both the longitude of the planet be pointed out (by an index and graduated circle) as seen from earth.

The lesser faces are four feet in height, and two feet three inches in breadth. One of them will exhibit all the appearance of Jupiter and his satellites—their eclipses, transits, and inclinations; likewise all the appearances of Saturn, with his ring and satellites. And the other will represent all the phenomena of the moon, particularly the exact time, quantity, and duration of her eclipses, and those of the sun occasioned by her interposition; with a most curious contrivance for exhibiting the appearance of a solar eclipse at any particular place on earth; likewise the true place of the moon in the signs, with her latitude, and the place of her apogee in the nodes; the sun's declination, equation of time, etc. It must be understood that all these motions are to correspond to exactly with the celestial motions, and not to differ several degrees in truth in a few revolutions, as is common with orreries.

If it is thought proper the whole is to be adapted to and kept in motion by a strong pendulum clock—nevertheless at liberty to be turned by the winch and adjusted at any time, past or future.

N.B.—The diurnal motions of such planets as have been discovered to revolve on their own axis are likewise to be properly represented, both with regard to the times and situation of their poles.

This machine, absolutely prodigious for its time, even captured the fancy of the State Assembly, as revealed by this newspaper clipping.

DAVID RITTENHOUSE. The Members of Assembly having viewed the Orrery, constructed by Mr. David Rittenhouse, a native of this Province, and being of opinion, that it greatly exceeds all others, hitherto invented, in demonstrating the true situation of the Coelestial Bodies, their magnitudes, motions, distances, periods, eclipses and order, upon the principles of the Newtonian System.

Resolved, That the Sum of Three Hundred Pounds be given to Mr. Rittenhouse, as a testimony of the high sense which this House entertains of his Mathematical Genius and Mechanical Abilities, in constructing the said Orrery . . .

That this curious Machine deserves the commendations which the Assembly have bestowed upon it, will never be doubted by those who are capable of forming any judgment concerning it, and will attend to the following particulars.

1. In the main part of this Orrery, all the primary planets are represented in their true proportional distances from each other, and from the Sun, likewise in their proportional magnitudes.

2. Each Planet moves in its own plane different from that of any other and all of them intersecting each other in the Sun's center, the several angles of their inclination are truly adjusted and preserved.

3. Each Planet varies its distance from the Sun in its revolutions, according to the quality of its eccentricity, and the velocities likewise vary with the distances, so as to describe equal Areas in equal Times, agreeable to the true Laws of the Newtonian System; and the numbers of the wheel-work are such, as to give the mean Motions not sensibly different from the tables of Astronomy in many hundred years.

4. The axes of Jupiter, Mars, the Earth and Venus, are truly posited, on which they revolve in the same time and manner as they do respectively in the Heavens, and the Poles of the Earth also revolve about the Poles of the Ecliptic, contrary to the order of the signs, with such a motion as would carry them one entire revolution in 25,921 Solar, or 25,920 Siderial years; so that through that long period, by looking at the several indices, the places of the different Planets, in the Signs, and also of their aphelia, perihelia and nodes may be known to the given time. The little Globes, representing Saturn and Mercury, have no revolutions on their axes, because it is not yet discovered whether they have any in the Heavens; and the axes of Jupiter, Mars and Venus, are continued parallel to themselves, as no observations have yet shewn that they change their direction.

5. All the Transits of Venus and Mercury are accurately shewn, and at every apparent conjunction of any two Planets, may be seen how near they approach to each other, and which

will pass to the Northward or Southward, in respect to Latitude.

6. The Lunar part of this Orrery represents most of the irregularities of the Moon's motions, according to Sir Isaac Newton's theory; particularly her eccentricity, ever varying in quantity; her apogee sometimes moving forwards, sometimes backwards, and sometimes becoming stationary, and at all other times moving retrograde; and the inclination of her orbit varying from 5° to 5° 18′, according to the situation of her nodes with respect to the Sun. The annual equation of the Moon, and the variation, are also allowed their proper effect.

7. Moreover, the accuracy of this Lunar part is such, as makes it capable of shewing all Eclipses of the Moon in their precise quantity, and not only the day, but the hour of the day, on which they will happen. And though Eclipses of the Sun be of such a nature, on account of the Moon's parallax, that what may be a total eclipse at one place, may, at the same time, be no eclipse at all at another place; yet this Orrery can, in a minute or two, without any calculation, be set to the latitude and longitude of any particular place upon Earth, and will then truly represent eclipses of the Sun, as they will be seen at that place. It can also be set, to shew any eclipse, as it would be seen from the center of the Earth; all which is effected by a very singular and curious, though simple contrivance, for including in the motions of the machine, the various intricate effects of the Moon's parallax, which so much diversify the phases of Solar eclipses, and the construction of any other Orrery, and are entirely new; and where it agrees with other Orreries, it is so much improved in every article, that it can hardly be considered as a machine of the same kind with them.

The very ingenious Mr. Ferguson speaks of a contrivance of his, the most perfect of any that I have read of, for shewing the motions of the Earth and Moon, somewhat similar to the Lunar part of this Orrery of ours; but he says, "it would be difficult to make it intelligible by a description, and that he keeps the position of the wheels, and the number of teeth, &c. a secret, as he proposes to instruct his son how to make it, for his own benefit." The accuracy, Mr. Ferguson proposes in this machine, is only this, "that it will not vary above one degree from the truth in 304 years." But this is only about the twentieth part of the accuracy of our Pennsylvania Orrery; for it will not vary a degree from the truth in less than six thousand years, if the present order of Nature subsists. (*Pennsylvania Journal*, March 28, 1771)

In the autumn of 1770, Rittenhouse moved his family to Philadelphia, taking resi-

69

70

71

72

Fig. 69. The George W. Childs clock, a magnificent masterpiece by David Rittenhouse. Permission from Drexel University.

Fig. 70. Superb dial and adjacent portions of the hood of the clock in fig. 69. Permission from Drexel University.

Fig. 71. Complicated gearing behind the dial of the clock in fig. 69. Permission from Drexel University.

Fig. 72. Complete movement, minus pendulum, of the clock in fig. 69. Permission from Drexel University.

dence at Arch and Seventh Streets. In January 1771 he was elected one of the secretaries of the American Philosophical Society.

Rittenhouse built another small private observatory. In 1775 the American Philosophical Society honored him by petitioning the Pennsylvania Assembly to create a government-subsidized observatory, similar to the Royal Observatory at Greenwich, England. Rittenhouse was to be made chief astronomer, a position undoubtedly patterned after that of Dr. Maskelyne, the Astronomer Royal of England. Unfortunately, the impending Revolution took precedence.

Rittenhouse's contributions to the patriot cause were considerable. He experimented in rifling cannons and served as engineer to the Committee of Safety, as vice president of the Council of Safety, and, ultimately, as president of the Board of War for the Commonwealth of Pennsylvania. In addition, he was elected to the Pennsylvania House of Representatives in 1776; he was a member of the first Constitutional Convention of the State; and he presided as state treasurer of Pennsylvania from 1776 to 1789.

He was equally as useful in the academic world. He became first professor of astronomy at the University of Pennsylvania and later was voted its first vice provost. He resigned as professor in 1782, but was immediately elected a trustee and the university seal was designed to picture the famed orrery. In 1791 Rittenhouse succeeded his friend Benjamin Franklin as the second president of the American Philosophical Society. He was appointed director of the first United States Mint in 1792. Academic honors continued to be bestowed upon him until just before his death on June 26, 1796, by cholera.

It is interesting to recall that in the years between 1792 and 1796, he and Thomas Jefferson worked out a scheme for making a standard foot a definite part of the length of a second-ticking pendulum in the latitude of Philadelphia. They also devised a new system of weights and measures, preserving most adequately the common measures known and used by all. These were almost adopted by Congress.

To celebrate the two-hundredth anniversary of Rittenhouse's birth, six prestigious Philadelphian organizations joined forces to organize a Rittenhouse exhibition. The master's claims to fame were many and his contributions to knowledge were great, but his reputation remains most closely allied with his clocks. In 1932 approximately forty were known to exist, sixteen of which were on exhibit. The George W. Childs clock (fig. 69), now the property of Drexel University, is almost universally accepted as the David Rittenhouse horological masterpiece. This remarkable instrument indicates the time of the day, the day of the week and of the month, the month of the year, and the equation of time. It strikes the hours, halves, and quarters, and any one of ten tunes may be played at the hour on a nest of bells. A small orrery above the face shows the position of the sun and the other units of the solar system, and a smaller lunarian shows the position of the earth and moon. The phases of the moon are shown in the usual way.

This fabulous clock was made for Joseph Potts, a wealthy Philadelphian Quaker, who reportedly refused to pay the $640 which Rittenhouse asked; therefore, it was purchased in 1774 by Thomas Prior. Potts then commissioned Rittenhouse to construct a simple wall clock, the only one of this type he is known to have made. This

73

74

Fig. 73. Complicated clock by David Rittenhouse, housed in a smaller, more symmetrical case. Permission from the Pennsylvania Hospital.

Fig. 74. Fine dial and adjacent portions of the hood of the clock in fig. 73. Permission from the Pennsylvania Hospital.

timepiece was also in the exhibition, and at that time it still belonged to a Potts descendant. Finally, one of a series of owners gave the big clock to Drexel University in 1898.

The Pennsylvania Hospital clock, a timepiece nearly as elaborate as the Childs clock, was also exhibited. It, too, demonstrates the position of the planets and plays one of six tunes on the hour. This clock, constructed about 1780, is so large that it requires winding only twelve times a year. It was given to the hospital by Miss Sarah Zane in 1819. After a severe accident to the movement, J.T. Gropengiesser repaired the timepiece and later supplied this description of it:

The clock is provided with a planetarium, showing the motion around the sun of the heavenly bodies—Uranus, Jupiter, Saturn, Mars, Venus and the Earth. It has a zodiac circle telling the daily equation of the sun and the length of the day. It shows the passage of the moon and its equation.

It has two chiming bells, sounding the quarter hours, and ten musical bells playing a tune every hour. When the clock was put in order by Mr. Gropengiesser he introduced a new musical barrel, playing six different airs, vis. Old Folks At Home, Home Sweet Home, Auld Lang Syne, Star Spangled Banner, The Last Rose of Summer, and Then You'll Remember Me. There is no record telling what airs were formerly played by this instrument. The clock was originally made with a Cirhell (circular) or Graham escapement, which has no maintaining power, such as now is commonly used in these clocks. It also has a peculiar system of calculating fractional numbers, which early in the present century was abandoned by clockmakers, for a better mode of dividing equal numbers by higher number of cogs in the calculation. The clock has a wooden pendulum, beating seconds. The dial is of metal, engraved, the numbers being in Roman characters. The upper central portion above the dial exhibits the planetarium, on the left hand upper corner of the dial is a small dial giving the tonic position of the moon, the right upper corner shows the sun equation, by a hand indicating the daily differences between the mean and the apparent time. In the left lower corner is an arrangement to control the mechanism for striking; on the right side is a dial indicating the succession of six tunes. On the inner hour circle of the dial is the moon with a special visage of the position of the same. It also shows the movement of the earth independently of the moon.

When the musical portion of the clock was renewed by Mr. Gropengiesser, new connections with the planetarium were also introduced. Previously to repairing, it had only been used for several years as a silent timepiece, but since the restoration, the chimes are now regularly heard; the musical airs, however, are generally kept in reserve, in order to obviate annoyance by their constant repetition.

The Hospital clock was made under the personal direction of Rittenhouse and cost at that time considerably more than one thousand dollars, but its intrinsic value is greatly increased by its historical association with the development of the institution, of which it has been an inmate for the greater part of a century. (*History of the Pennsylvania Hospital, 1751–1895*)

The University of Pennsylvania loaned to the exhibition a unique clock that Rittenhouse built for William Smith, the first provost. The clock has no hour hand; instead, the hours are indicated by numbers on a dial that rotates behind a rectangular orifice. Reverend Smith customarily used this to time his classes.

Whether the Rittenhouse clock made for the Hamilton family of West Philadelphia appeared in the 1932 exhibition is uncertain. It stood for more than a century in their mansion, "The Woodlands," at Hamilton Village and is presently found in the Atwater Kent Museum.

Most of the Rittenhouse clocks exhibited had eight-day movements, but two one-day specimens were also present. The plainest yet scientifically more interesting one was that previously described which he had built for observing the transit of Venus. The University of Pennsylvania orrery was, of course, also on exhibit, as were various surveyor's instruments attributed to the great inventor.

These words, written by a prominent contemporary of David Rittenhouse, provide a fitting close to his story: "Yesterday I attended the funeral rites of the celebrated Dr. Rittenhouse, American astronomer, whose loss this country most justly mourns. He was buried in the floor of the Observatory which he had constructed in his own Garden. What a philosophical union, perishable ashes with an edifice consecrated to the observation of the most sublime marvels of nature! What a rapprochement between the genius of man and his nothingness!"

Watch Case Makers

In the annals of American watchmaking enterprises, one of the highlight events was the marketing and legal fight between the twenty-seven members of the American Watch Trust and John C. Dueber. By innovative selling methods and with the aid of the Sherman Antitrust Act, Dueber eventually broke the watch case trust, thus freeing the industry to open competition.

Fig. 75. Hamilton family clock by Rittenhouse. Courtesy of the Atwater Kent Museum.

Fig. 76. Dial of the clock in fig. 75, dated 1769. Courtesy of the Atwater Kent Museum.

To be sure, Pennsylvania had a great multiplicity of watch case makers.

A.L. Ducommun was in business from 1796 to 1799 in Philadelphia.

Charles W. Westphall was in business from 1801 to 1820 in Philadelphia.

William Warner made gold cases in Philadelphia from 1811 to 1839; William Warner & Company, a firm founded by Warner and his sons, operated from 1839 to 1849, when Mr. Warner left. His sons, C. and C.P. Warner continued operations until 1861, when Pequignot & Brothers bought the business; they carried on until 1889 as C. and A. Pequignot.

John Warner was in business from 1829 to 1837 in Philadelphia.

David L. Huguenin ran his firm in Philadelphia until 1832, when his sons succeeded him.

Jules and Edward Huguenin stayed in business one year; they were bought by the Paul brothers, who in turn sold to Celestine Jacot in 1839.

Working in Philadelphia as casemakers in the early to mid-1800s were: Thomas A. Garrett, who labored from 1834 to 1844; William McNeir, 1834 to 1846; Constant Gigon, 1837 to 1840; Z. and G. Gigon, 1840 to 1855; and G. Gigon, 1855 to 1859.

Gigon, Pequignot & Brothers, who were in business from 1859 until 1863, achieved production of about 250 gold cases a week.

Casemakers of Philadelphia from the 1860s through the 1880s were: Gigon & Williams, 1863 to 1867; G. Gigon, 1867 to 1869; Gigon & Company, 1869 to 1876, with Alfred Humbert; and Gigon & Company, 1876 to 1881, composed of Humbert and Mrs. Gigon.

The National Watch Case Company, operating in the 1880s and the 1890s, was formed of a combination of Gigon & Company and Booz & Company.

Hagstoz & Thorpe, 1876, acquired the watch case division of Appleton, Tracy Company, which subsequently became the American Waltham Watch Company.

Celestine Jacot, a Swiss casemaker, bought the P & S Paul business in 1839.

C. Jacot & Brother formed in 1852 to make cases of both less and more than 14K gold. At its zenith, the firm employed about fifty persons, but financial troubles brought a closure in 1871.

Harper, McClelland & Gill operated from 1850 until 1857, when McClelland left, and then until 1859, when Harper left. Gill began again with five employees in 1864; by 1875 he employed fifteen persons and the business produced about seventy-five cases per week. About then he branched into machinery and discontinued the silver cases, but he continued making gold cases.

R.S. Peters & Brother started operations in 1851. Reese dropped out sometime in 1853, leaving Randolf and an employee, James Boss, to carry on; they formed Randolf Peters & Company, which lasted until 1856. Randolf then tried it alone, but he soon failed. Meanwhile Reese and Boss had become partners; Boss won everlasting fame by obtaining in May of 1859 a patent, #23,820, for a gold-filled watch case.

Low & Courvoisier started business in 1853, but sold to Deecret & Leichty in 1855, who remained together until 1860.

Crowell & Dunkerly began business in 1855, but they sold to George L. Wait the next year. From 1858 to 1862, Wait & Crocker employed some thirty to forty people, making only gold cases.

John Henry had worked for four years when he sold to Jacob & Brother in 1860.

Booz & Hagstone entered into business in 1869. Hagstone left in 1874, when they had some twenty-five employees turning out about thirty-five cases weekly—an unusually high employee-product ratio.

Booz & Company, 1882 to 1888, gained Frederich Schober as a new partner. In 1888 they merged with Humbert & Company and became the National Watch Case Company, which manufactured three grades of gold cases.

Lungren & Bell, 1864 to 1867, made only silver cases.

Mackle & Zesinger operated from 1865 to 1872.

Theophilus Zurbrugg bought Leichty & LeBouba in 1884. In 1888 the firm became the Philadelphia Watch Case Company, producers of various kinds of cases. The company moved to Riverside, New Jersey in 1902. Zurbrugg eventually put together quite a watch case combine by merging his firm with Bates & Bacon, Crescent, and the Keystone Watch Case Company, which lasted until 1956.

Interestingly, all the foregoing watch case manufacturers were located in Philadelphia. Considering the size of Pennsylvania and the number of substantial communities, it is indeed strange that watch case establishments appeared in only one other community—Milford boasted two such firms, both staffed largely by foreign workers.

The one firm, known either as Berthoud & Courvoisier or as the Gold Watch Case Factory, was founded by Ferdinand Berthoud and J.W. Courvoisier, both Swiss, in 1877. At its zenith the company employed about thirty workers, many of whom were also Swiss. Their products were high quality gold cases in two grades. Courvoisier left in 1883, but operations continued until 1894.

The other firm, the Silver Watch Case Factory, was founded in 1863 by a French-

Fig. A. Development of Pennsylvania watch case making.

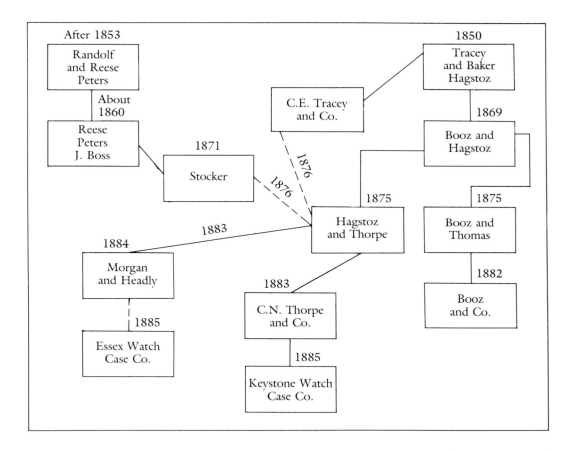

man, Desire Bournique. Blossoming to some sixty or seventy employees, many of whom were French, it ran until 1885 and produced only cases of silver.

This brief survey of watch case production in the Keystone State is made possible through the courtesy and generosity of Mr. Warren H. Niebling. For further reading and information, including illustrations of trademarks, patents, etc., see his outstanding and authoritative book, *History of the American Watch Case*.

The development of some of the Connecticut clockmaking firms is hard to trace even today. Likewise, the story of Pennsylvania watch case making is difficult to follow (see figure A).

Sometime after 1853, Randolf and Reese Peters were manufacturing watch cases in a small shop located in an area which is now the center of the Society Hill redevelopment in Philadelphia. Their operation faced a dilemma: low gold content watch cases tarnished easily, while those containing more gold were too expensive for a volume-business. Luckily, Peters employed James Boss, who eventually solved the problem (though some believe that Reese Peters unconsciously suggested the solution). They produced a three-sheet combination, bearing an outer layer with a high gold content, a base metal center, and an inner layer containing little gold—all bonded together to permit pressure rolling to desired thickness. Boss experimented until he perfected the process to the point of receiving a patent, #23,820, dated May 3, 1859.

Reese Peters quickly made Boss his partner and "J. Boss" gold-filled cases were soon on the market. Regarded as a revolutionary milestone by the trade, they were thus an important success. A twenty-year, money back guarantee against wear was of course a big inducement for sales.

In 1871 Boss sold his patent rights to John Strecker, who continued producing these phenomenally successful cases until his death in 1875. It is thought that Strecker's death might partly have been caused by inhaling fumes from an acid used in the process.

Thomas B. Hagstoz of Tullytown, Pennsylvania, took employment in 1854 with the small, four-year-old watch case firm of Tracey & Baker. By working in different departments, Hagstoz became a top mechanic, and in 1869 he and his fellow employee, Albert Booz, formed their own watch case operation. This continued until 1874 and was successful, although Hagstoz left the firm the following year. Booz then took one of his employees, Thomas, as his partner, and they continued making both gold and silver watchcases.

Hagstoz established a new firm with Charles N. Thorpe, an ex-employee of Clark & Biddle. The partners bought the factory of the just-deceased John Strecker, along with the J. Boss patent rights. In 1886 they also purchased E. Tracey & Son, the descendant of the Tracey & Baker Company, including all their tools and inventory. Now Hagstoz & Thorpe owned good machinery, took larger quarters, and extended the J. Boss line to include cases for ladies' watches. The Centennial Exposition helped spread their fame and enriched sales across the country and overseas.

By 1880 Hagstoz & Thorpe had moved to a six-story factory and had expanded to employ about 175 persons. Not long afterward, they developed a new method of producing silver watch cases out of a solid piece of metal, so again they could boast a superior product. Additional factory space was acquired in 1882, in 1886, and again in 1891. This was indeed a large enterprise.

Hagstoz retired in 1883, when he was less than forty years old. This idea soon palled, and in 1884 he bought Morgan I. Headly, a diamond specialty company. This, however, was not his line, so the next year he accepted the presidency of the Essex Watch Case Company of Newark, New Jersey, and soon production was booming.

Hagstoz & Thorpe became the C.N. Thorpe Company after Hagstoz's departure, but expansion made it desirable to reorganize in 1885 into a stock company called the Keystone Watch Case Company. With over a thousand employees, production soared to approximately 1,500 watch cases per day; a variety of cases was now available, from solid gold to J. Boss gold-filled in two grades, to silver, to a nickel called "Silveroid." In addition to these basic cases, Keystone could also produce ones with raised gold ornamentation and with fancy stone and diamond settings, enameled gold cases, and Niello silver cases. Of course, engraved decorations displaying a wide variety of subjects were available. Variety of cases prevailed over standardization because it was customary at that time for watch movements and cases to be sold separately. Thus, the product was married to the customer's taste.

At the time of Thorpe's death, Keystone production was up to about 2,000 cases per day, even with a small reduction in employment to 1,300. Obviously, Keystone was aggressive and made great use of testimonial letters, the great advertising ploy of the time. Perhaps they sometimes "doctored" these a bit, for once they were challenged by the pugnacious John C. Dueber, president of the large Dueber Watch Case Company, on the veracity of an advertising claim. In 1899 the Boss gold-filled cases provided sixty percent of Keystone's revenue and no competitor, including the ingenious Dueber, had a product to seriously challenge theirs. Continuing on its successful course, Keystone eventually became part of a new combination in Riverside, New Jersey.

Bucks County

Bucks County, named for Buckinghamshire, England, organized as early as 1682, was one of the three original counties in Pennsylvania. Bucks figured strongly throughout the colonial period and the Revolutionary War, but managed to maintain a pleasant, bucolic setting until well into the twentieth century. Early settlers were English Quakers, Dutch, Swedes, Scotch, Irish, Welsh, and French Huguenots. A population with such variety of national backgrounds would almost have to host its full share of artisans, including clockmakers. In fact, Bucks County was home to probably the most prolific family of clockmakers anywhere in America. The Ellicotts were the county's best-known clock tradesmen; they and the large Solliday family will be dealt with in well-deserved separate chapters.

Hugh Ely was at work in New Hope from 1799 to 1803 before moving to Trenton. He is known to have made at least four clocks, one of which was built for the county almshouse. He also constructed for his brother a musical clock which played Yankee Doodle, Nancy Dawson, and Beggar Girl.

Septimus Evans was a clockmaker in Doylestown about 1807; in Warwick Township about 1810; in Jenkintown, Montgomery County in 1821; and finally in Delaware. Several of his clocks are known.

John Fitch is so important a figure in the inventive annals of the county that a brief resume is warranted. Fitch (1742–98), born in Connecticut, was first apprenticed to Benjamin Cheney for a year in East Hartford and then to Timothy Cheney in

78

Fig. 77. Typical early Pennsylvania clock by Henry Got-shalk, which has the hingeless door in the trunk. Case appears to be pegged together. From the collections of the Historical Society of York County, Pennsylvania.

Fig. 78. The unusually ornate hood and dial and rocking ship feature of this James Heron clock make it somewhat unique for its estimated date. Courtesy of *The Magazine* ANTIQUES.

Windsor for another year to learn the trade of brass worker and clockmaker. In 1764 he opened his own brass shop in East Windsor, but he also cleaned and repaired clocks. Never a good businessman, he tried many endeavors and moved innumerable times, settling finally in Bucks County, Pennsylvania, in 1783. Until his death, he devoted his efforts to the invention of the steamboat. He succeeded in obtaining exclusive rights from New Jersey, Pennsylvania, New York, Delaware, and Virginia for fourteen years in which to build and operate steamboats on all waters in those states. He also secured both a U.S. and a French patent, but never met with success in the accepted sense of the word. Assisted by Henry Voight, a Philadelphian watchmaker, in the construction of the engine, he built and launched his first steamboat (a forty-five footer propelled by twelve paddles) on the Delaware River at Philadelphia, August 22, 1787, in the presence of the delegates to the Constitutional Convention.

Altogether Fitch produced four successful steamboats, including one with steam paddles and another with a screw propeller. However, he failed to realize any financial gain from his genius. He defended a claim of priority by James Rumsey and certainly anticipated Robert Fulton, whose "Claremont" was not seen until after Fitch's death in Kentucky. The occurrence of misplaced credit for important milestone inventions is curious and common.

Henry Gotshalk made several clocks in New Britain about 1760. They were apparently of the thirty-hour, pull-up variety. Figure 77 shows a unique specimen. Ordinarily the door would be hinged so that it could be opened daily to pull up the weight; instead, this door is completely removable by lifting out a wooden pin. Other clocks of his making exist, the dials of which are signed "Allen Twp." and "Northampton." These areas would be present-day Allentown.

The famous Hagey family of clockmakers is ordinarily identified with Montgomery County, but one of them, Jacob Hagey (1775–1834), became a resident of Bucks. Born in Franconia Township, Montgomery County, Jacob, like his father, was a noted clockmaker. Various accounts of his life and work testify that he produced more than a hundred superb tall case clocks. On April 7, 1828 he moved to Hilltown Township, Bucks, where he died on September 11, 1834. This Hagey seems to have been highly regarded because of his occupation, for on all deeds where his name appears, it is followed by the designation "Clock Maker."

James Heron is mentioned as a clockmaker in Newtown from 1760 to around 1780. The earlier date is probably more accurate because his known clocks have brass dials. At least one was sufficiently sophisticated to have the rocking ship feature.

Job Hollinshead, one of a family of clockmakers mostly associated with New Jersey, advertised as a clockmaker in 1821 in Newtown; Jacob Kneedler was a Horsham clockmaker around 1790; and Jacob Krout was a maker in Plumsteadville in the 1830s.

The illustrious father and son team of Seneca and Isaiah Lukens is described in some detail elsewhere in this book; Seneca (1751–1829), because he was associated with Bucks County, will receive attention here. He was born and lived his entire life in Horsham. He was an excellent clockmaker, largely self-taught, who also farmed. A good father, he made a special clock for each of his four daughters. His clock #41 can be identified as having been made in 1795.

William J. Maus, identified with both Hilltown and Quakertown, made some clocks around 1819.

Benjamin Morris (1748–1833), a descendant of English Friends, was a prolific producer of clocks, having constructed perhaps as many as three hundred. Although his working period in Hilltown and New Britain has been said to cover approximately sixty years, it is more plausible that he worked through a shorter period, probably from 1760 to 1780. His clocks, while quite handsome, are sometimes a bit awesome, surmounted as they are with unusually tall, thin finials. Morris often attached a little brass plate plainly engraved "B.M." to his painted dial clocks.

Enos Morris, Benjamin's son, learned his trade from his father but chose instead to go into law.

Seth Park(e) (fl. 1790s) worked in Newtown.

Solomon Parke, another famous maker, began manufacturing clocks at Newtown, the county seat in colonial days, and continued producing them for many years thereafter. He moved into Southampton about 1780 and into Philadelphia about 1790 or 1791, where it is averred that he later operated a clock factory. Judging by the number of clocks bearing his name, he must have been a popular artisan. Parke's name on the dial testifies to the quality of the movement.

Paul Preston, a great mathematician and an associate of Benjamin Franklin, is recorded as a sun dial and clock maker in Buckingham in the 1750s and 1760s.

Modern horological historians have not given one of Buck's great scientists their well-deserved recognition. In 1869 two young German immigrants, Louis H. Spellier and Abraham Yeakel, came to Doylestown and opened a watch and clock factory on the northeast corner of Main and State Streets. Yeakel subsequently moved to Perkasie and there established himself in business. Spellier, possessing an aptitude for invention, remained in Doylestown and built what he called a "time clock,"

79

Fig. 79. A fine example of Seneca Lukens's craftsmanship. Courtesy of John O. Sweisford.

Fig. 80. This Chippendale walnut tall clock has a broken arch top with carved rosettes and flame finials. The slender waist with arched door and the raised base panel with arched crest are flanked by fluted quarter columns. Beneath the calendar dial is an attached brass plate, engraved "Benj. Morris-Hilltown." Courtesy of Israel Sack, Inc., N.Y.C. catalog.

which was run by a galvanic battery. The battery was set up in one building, and wires were run to another nearby and attached to a timepiece. Thus, Electric-Time-Telegraphy was born to civilization. Spellier's invention surmounted several obstacles in the mechanics of electricity that had heretofore baffled science-minded men. It was perfected at Doylestown in 1876 but was greatly improved some years later.

In 1884 Spellier again added to his list of inventions and discoveries by devising a means by which the electric circuit could be broken at will. His "Electric-Magnetic-Escapement" and "Sparkless Current Breaker" secured a successful future for the electric clock, the former by its remarkably light action and the latter by allowing what had never before been accomplished—namely, "an almost unlimited number of electric dials to be inserted into one circuit." A German magazine of applied mechanics called this invention the "Electro-Magnetic-Escapement" and claimed that it "removes noted defects of electric clocks."[1]

The biography of Spellier provides further insight into the inventor.

> He was born in Germany on January 6, 1841, of German and French parentage, and died in Philadelphia on August 22, 1891. He was, for a time, a tutor in the German Royal Family. To escape military service he came to America and settled in Doylestown about 1871. Where he obtained the training is not known, but he opened a watch, clock and jewelry store near the corner of Main and State Streets. He was a splendid mechanic with an inventive turn of mind. Much of his spare time was devoted to experimentation and development of a new system of electric clocks.
>
> On St. Patrick's Day 1880, he read a paper at the Franklin Institute on his invention which he called Electro-Magnetic Time Telegraph. Two statements, the first entirely prophetic, the second completely erroneous, are worth quoting from that paper.
>
> If we consider that we can control by one correct timepiece just as many time telegraphs to indicate true time, as necessity or fancy requires, provided there is battery power enough to move them, we have reason to believe that they come into general use in hotels and public buildings. . . . Now a few words in conclusion of the utility of the electric clocks before I close. They will hardly ever come into general use, and always a costly novelty for those who desire to have them.
>
> When one considers the tremendous volume of electric clocks in use today, it is difficult to see how Spellier so completely underrated his invention for which the Franklin Institute awarded him the Elliott Crisson Gold Medal. The invention was finally granted a series of patents:

1. Maurice Shoultes, *Invention and Mechanical Progress In Bucks Co.*, vol. 7 of *The Bucks County Historical Society*, p. 560.

#258,818	May 30, 1882	electric motor for clocks
#330,632	Nov. 17, 1885	contact maker for electric clocks
#417,753	Dec. 24, 1889	time distribution for electric clocks

On May 17, 1882, Spellier delivered a second paper at the Franklin Institute on Electric Clocks and Time Telegraphs. The next year he published an illustrated brochure, "Spellier System of Time Telegraphy and the Superiorities." In October 1884, he had an elaborate exhibition of his clocks at the International Exhibition at Philadelphia. In 1886, he published a large brochure "A New System of Electric Clocks." In 1887, while living in Doylestown, he built a clock for the tower of the Courthouse.[2]

William Wilson made clocks in Newtown around 1826.

Henry Wismer appears to have been at work in Plumstead on Durham Road between 1798 and 1828. It is commonly believed that he made many clocks, perhaps more than any other Bucks tradesman, by employing several workmen. If this is true, it is vexing not to learn more about him. Most of his clocks were signed "Henry Wismer, B.C.," meaning Bucks County.

As noted, Abraham Yeakel arrived in Doylestown from Germany either with Louis Spellier or near the time of his arrival. After a short while he moved to Perkasie and set up shop as clockmaker, watchmaker, jeweler, and repairer.

The Ellicotts

The Ellicotts, father and son, were giants in the science of horology and in related fields of endeavor.

Andrew Ellicott (1754–1820) was, like his famous father, originally a mathematical instrument- and clockmaker. Although traditionally associated with Solebury, this peripatetic engineering genius soon became one of the most noted men of his time in this country. In 1792 he was appointed surveyor-general of the United States; he settled the boundary between the United States and Spain in 1796, but he also prepared the plans for Erie, Warren, and Franklin, towns of varying size in

2. Annie M. Fretz, "Louis Spellier and His Electric Clocks" (Paper read before the Bucks County Historical Society, Doylestown, Pa., May 2, 1936), pp. 420–23.

Pennsylvania. The first accurate measurement of Niagara Falls was one of his achievements.

Andrew's most enduring claim to fame, however, was his involvement as a consulting engineer in the laying out of Washington, D.C. according to the general plans of Major Pierre L'Enfant. He was capably aided in this project by Benjamin Banneker, the first black American clockmaker and a great scientist in his own right. Andrew was later the secretary of the Land Office, located in Lancaster, Pennsylvania. In 1812 he was appointed as civilian professor of mechanics at West Point, where he died eight years later. It is somewhat ironic that he taught one of the arts of war after abstaining as a Quaker from fighting in the American Revolution. Even more interesting is the claim of descendants that Andrew was not only George Washington's friend but also did some surveying with him and was given some of Washington's surveying instruments when he went off to war.

One of the earliest and best-known clockmakers in the colony was Andrew's father, Joseph Ellicott (1732–80), of Buckingham. (Both George Washington and David Rittenhouse were also born in 1732.) Joseph's father died before his son was nine; soon thereafter Joseph was placed with his guardian, Samuel Armitage, to learn weaving. When it became obvious that Joseph's total inclination lay in mechanics, he was sent to work for Samuel Bleaker in a grist mill. Before long, young Ellicott was adept at repairing grist mill machinery, which includes great toothed wheels and axeled pinions. On a small scale, these are also the essential parts of a clock movement; indeed, some scholars of the clockmaking science believe that the earliest clockmakers of the thirteenth century and thereabout conceived the idea of a clock movement from rudimentary mills for grinding grain.

Disappointingly, information telling how or when Ellicott entered the clockmaking business has not been found. However, before or during 1766 he acquired a profound knowledge of watchmaking, for he constructed a repeating watch in that period, which may establish him as America's earliest known watchmaker.

On December 18, 1766, he sailed for England to receive his great-grandfather's estate in Cullopton. Not until June 3, 1767 was the sale of the property completed, following considerable trouble in obtaining possession of the title papers. It is said that he realized fifteen hundred pounds sterling—a large sum at that point of time. Fortunately he kept a rather detailed journal of his activities in Ireland and England.

April 6. Enquired for "tools and other materials in Liverpool in the watch way," and was recommended to David Ellison, watch spring maker, who offered to sell [me] watch springs at 15 shillings per dozen, and gave 13 to the dozen. Enquired for a dial plate maker, found William Rimmer, where [I] had made a dial plate for [my] watch. Then went to see tool maker John Wright and came to terms with him.

April 8–11. These days spent cheapening tools with Wright and became acquainted with Edward Gatton, watch finisher.[3]

There are references to visits with various persons named Fox, undoubtedly relatives, and to attending Friends' Meetings, in which Ellicott was a member. His journal lacks details of his four to six week sojourn in London, but he evidently had contact with horologists there, as tradition tells that his repeating watch earned the official praise of Ferguson, the Astronomer Royal, and of other men of science. Joseph makes no mention of visiting a relative or receiving advanced instruction in the art of clockmaking, but there is considerable reason to believe he did these things. It is likely that he spent some time with John Ellicott of London, a Fellow of the Royal Society of Arts and a member of its council. One of the most eminent of British makers, John invented a compensation pendulum and further developed the use of the cylinder escapement for watches. Most importantly, he was clockmaker to the King.

Joseph fell ill and left London on the *Charming Rachel*. After a wretched passage of fifty-two days, he arrived in Philadelphia on September 21, 1767. Shortly thereafter, he and his teenaged son Andrew began the construction of his tour de force, a great four-faced musical clock which played twenty-four tunes and combined marvelous and intricate movements. It was not completed until sometime in 1769. This timepiece is believed by some to be one of the three finest clocks built in Pennsylvania, keeping company with the so-called Pennsylvania Hospital clock and the Drexel University clock, both constructed by David Rittenhouse. Indeed, one descendant of Ellicott's asserts that Rittenhouse called on Joseph for help with some of his more complicated mechanisms.

A detailed description of the Ellicott musical clock was written by Charles W. Evans of Buffalo in 1865.

> The case of this musical clock is of mahogany, in the shape of a four sided pillar, or column, each side of which is neatly though plainly finished, and on the capital of which pillar is the clock, with four faces; it being designed to stand in the center of the

81

3. Edward Gatton is listed by Baillie as at work in Liverpool from 1769 until 1773, but this shows he was at work at least two years earlier.

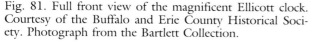

82

83

84

Fig. 81. Full front view of the magnificent Ellicott clock. Courtesy of the Buffalo and Erie County Historical Society. Photograph from the Bartlett Collection.

Fig. 82. Close-up of the hood and the main dial of the clock in fig. 81. Note that Ellicott gave his location as Pennsylvania rather than designate a town or county. Courtesy of the Buffalo and Erie County Historical Society. Photograph from the Bartlett Collection.

Fig. 83. Left side of the dial of the clock in fig. 81, showing the orrery and related features. Courtesy of the Buffalo and Erie County Historical Society. Photograph from the Bartlett Collection.

Fig. 84. Right side of the dial of the clock in fig. 81, showing the musical tune selector, separate winding holes, and a glimpse of the mechanism. The six human figures are each playing some musical instrument. Courtesy of the Buffalo and Erie County Historical Society. Photograph from the Bartlett Collection.

room, or a sufficient distance from the wall to enable the observer to pass around it. Possibly the case was made by a close friend of Joseph's, the famous Philadelphia Chippendale furniture maker, William Savery.

On one face is represented the sun, moon, earth and the planets, all moving in their different motions, as they do in the heavens. On another face are marked the minutes, hours, days, months and years, the years representing one century, all having their different hands pointing to the true time. On the third face are marked the names of twenty-four musical tunes being favorite ones of the times before the American Revolution. In the center of this face is a pointer, which being placed against any named tune, repeats that tune every fifteen minutes, until the pointer is moved. On the fourth face is to be seen, through the glass, the curious mechanism of the clock.

Twenty-one of the original musical tunes are presently playable. They are *The Hemp Dresser, Harvest Home, Balance a Straw, Plague on Those Girls, Captain Read's Minuet, Humors of Wapping, Black Sloven, Freemason's Health, King of Prussia's March,*

The Pilgrim, Come Chloe, Give Me Sweet Kisses, Bellisle's March, Lady Coventry's Minuet, The Hounds Are All Out, The Lass with the Delicate Air, God Save the King, Nancy Dawson, Lads and Lassies, Lovely Nancy, Wellingham's Frolic, and *Come Brave Boys.* The tunes no longer playable were *Address to Sleep, Lady Anthem,* and *Seaman's Hymn.*

The extremely fine and sturdy construction of this clock is attested by its ability to withstand an unusual amount of travel. Joseph carried the timepiece with him to Anne Arundel County, Maryland, in 1774, where it occupied the place of honor in the family mansion. His sons, Joseph and Benjamin, moved in 1803 to Batavia, New York, and took the clock with them. The rough-going of a wagon on those two journeys is easily imagined. The continuing changes of ownership of the Ellicott clock has seen it passed to several locations: from Batavia to Albany to Lockport, New York. In the early 1930s the timepiece was returned to the Philadelphia area, but it has since been moved to an unspecified place.

The keen-eyed reader has noticed the marking of No. 32 on the dial in figure 82. It must not be presumed that Ellicott rested on his laurels after making the timepiece; indeed, he may have built as many as three hundred clocks while in Bucks County, all bearing his name, number, and "Buckingham." An Ellicott descendant who states that all of Joseph's clocks had either brass or silver leaf dials maintains that the silver leaf dial for #32 was done by Richardson, the famous Philadelphia silversmith. One may wonder if Ellicott had some apprentices and/or journeymen assisting him, but there is no evidence of it. Moreover, despite this obviously intense activity, Ellicott found time for other pursuits. In 1768 and 1769 he was both the sheriff of Bucks County and a member of the provincial assembly. He also attained eminence in the arts, sciences, and related mechanical pursuits.

In December of 1774 Ellicott moved to Maryland with his family and two brothers. Together they founded Ellicott's Lower and Upper Mills along the Patapsco River; flour and cotton mills and an iron foundry were also established. Joseph knew the young Benjamin Banneker, who later assisted his son Andrew in the planning of Washington, D.C. He also reportedly created a clock factory of sorts, but an exhaustive research of Maryland clockmakers failed to unearth any substantiation of this. In addition to the clocks on display within his mansion, he also built two plain round-dial timepieces for the gables at each end of the house to benefit those persons passing by.

This great clockmaker died on October 15, 1780, long before his contemporaries, Washington and Rittenhouse. Ellicott City and clock #32 remain as great heritages of a distinguished Bucks countian.

Fig. B. This chart, complicated even for a trained genealogist, has been prepared after a close study of the *Book of American Clocks* by Brooks Palmer, *Pennsylvania Clocks* by George Eckhardt, *History of Bucks County* by William W.H. Davis, various articles, and, most importantly, hitherto unpublished data graciously supplied by Mrs. Dillman C. Sallada, Jr., which was obtained from a direct descendant of Jacob Solliday, Jr. As if the duplication of names was not sufficiently confusing, there is also great divergence on many of the dates on the chart. As the best compromise, we have in those cases used the Sallada dates. Similarly, all the sources do not list all the names on the chart, so all names have been included in the hope that they can be reasonably accounted for, whether these parties were makers or not.

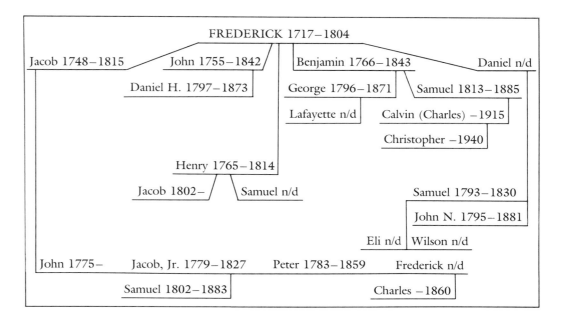

The Solliday Family

The *Book of American Clocks* lists twelve and fourteen members of the Massachusetts Willard and the Connecticut Terry clock families respectively. With twenty-four members, the Pennsylvania Sollidays claim their place as the most prolific clockmaking family in this country, and perhaps in the world. Several of its members are described in the chapters on Berks, Bucks, Montgomery, Northampton, and Philadelphia counties. Such a spread makes it difficult to assimilate chronology and relationship in general, though the purpose of this chapter is to place the whole family into some perspective.

The first difficulty encountered is the variety of spellings of the family name. A collector may find Salede, Solede, Salada, Saleda, Salathe, Solida, Salliday, Saladay, Saladie, Sallada, Salida, Soliday, or Solliday. For simplicity, this chapter will use the last variation listed.

The Solliday family was well established in Europe several centuries ago. Branches of relations spread out in England, Germany, Holland, and Switzerland, and it is believed there were many clockmakers among them. Those who were French Huguenots, driven during the religious persecution of the seventeenth century from France into Germany, eventually immigrated to America. The ship arrivals at either New York or Philadelphia confirm that the migration stretched over a period of nearly thirty years. The first of the family to arrive, Jacob Salathe, came on September 28, 1749 on the *Ann* from Rotterdam. The second arrival was Peter Sallatin, who landed on November 30, 1750 on the *Sandwich*. Frederick Salada came on October 4, 1751 on the *Queen of Denmark* from Rotterdam; Nicholas Salada arrived on October 16, 1752 on the *Snow Ketty* from Rotterdam; and on October 3, 1764 Michael and John Salada landed with the *King of Prussia*.

Frederick and Barbara Solliday emigrated from Basel, Switzerland, most probably in October of 1751. Frederick acquired about 143 acres of land in Bedminster Township on May 6, 1762 from William Allen; his occupation at that time was given as shoemaker, which is odd because he had apprenticed as a clockmaker in Basel in 1740 and later had become an armorer in the German army. Now he rendered a much needed service to his new country by making and repairing guns for the American soldiers. In early tax records he is listed as an armorer and clockmaker.

Frederick and Barbara were early members of the Tohickon Reformed Church. They apparently had eight children; Frederick, the eldest, was born in Europe and died before his father in 1782 (hence he does not appear on the chart). "Old Mr. Solida," responsible for the ensuing generations of clockmakers, expired on June 24, 1804.

Jacob Solliday married Barbara Loux in 1773 and bought a farm next to his father's, where he both farmed and made clocks. Thus, it is entirely possible that father and son sometimes built clocks together. Jacob eventually became an eminent clockmaker; in 1812 he sold his property to his son Peter and moved to Milford Township, where he died on April 15, 1815. He had pursued the trade of clockmaking until eight years before his death; his surviving clocks are marked "Jacob Sallade —Bucks County." Of his four sons, three—John, Jacob, Jr., and Peter—were clockmakers; only his son Frederick was not.

John acquired the farm of his grandfather, Peter Loux, in 1790. This land adjoined the original property of his grandfather, Frederick Solliday. Jacob Jr. moved up to Northampton County, where, like his father, he farmed and produced fine clocks. His ledgers indicate that he made and sold sixteen clocks between 1822 and 1827, and all were signed "Jacob Solliday—North Hampton." He left a son, Samuel. Peter was born in Bedminster Township and remained there all his life. In 1805 he

85

Fig. 85. Dial signed "Benjn. Solliday, B.C." The carved columns on the trunk, base, and feet all match. From the collection of the Mercer Museum of the Bucks County Historical Society.

Fig. 86. Shelf clock with dial signed "Saml. Solliday, Doylstown" [*sic*]. The word *Patent* also appears, though no other reference to it is found.

86

married Magdalena Godshalk, who, considering the spelling variations of the period, *may* have been a daughter or granddaughter of Henry Gotshalk, a clockmaker in New Britain. Peter was an able clockmaker throughout his life, though it is likely he did some farming, too. He bought his father's homestead and 150 acres in 1807, which he later conveyed to his son, Peter, in 1857.

Samuel, the only son of Jacob Jr., lived with his father, learned the trade, and apparently took over the business. His ledger reveals that he built clocks from 1828 to 1834; after that he made no more, probably because by that time tall clocks had become dinosaurs due to the influx of inexpensive Connecticut shelf clocks.

John, third son of the original Frederick Solliday, worked for awhile at clockmaking in Richland Township, according to the Bucks County tax records of about 1782. Shortly thereafter he moved into Montgomery County; the tax records of Marlborough Township reveal that in 1796 he owned forty acres at Maxatawny and Macungie Roads. He died in 1842 and was buried at the Old Goschenhoppen Church of Upper Salford Township, Montgomery County. A grave marker indicates he was a Revolutionary War veteran. John, along with brothers Frederick and Emmanuel, belonged to a company of Bedminster Associators commanded by Captain Robert Robinson.

Daniel Hinckel was the only son of John who engaged in clockmaking, and he became better known than his father. Born in Sumneytown, he lived with his father until 1824 and made clocks with dials signed "D.H. Solliday, Sy.Town." He later married and moved to Evansburg but then relocated to Philadelphia, where his name first appeared in the 1829 directory as a clock- and watchmaker established at 193 N. Third Street. In 1831 he moved to 186 Callowhill Street, and sometime before 1838, Daniel returned to Sumneytown.

Frederick Solliday's fourth son, Henry, also pursued the family trade. He lived in Bedminster and married in 1789, then moved to Towamencin Township in Montgomery County, where he started a family and eventually produced two clockmaking sons, Jacob and Samuel.

The fifth original Solliday son, Benjamin, was undoubtedly taught by his father. It appears that Benjamin was a clockmaker for all his life, living near Sellersville in Rockhill Township. Interestingly, he was the only member of the clan whose name is attached to the manufacture of thirty-hour tall clocks. At an auction sale near Reading in May, 1972, a clock was offered that was described as "Rare Benj. Saleda, Bucks County, Pennsylvania, walnut-cased grandfather clock, circa 1780–90. Fluted corners on case and base, painted dial, broken arch top. Good running condition." The Bucks County Historical Society owns a Benjamin Solliday tall clock.

Benjamin left two sons who were also active in the trade. The elder, George, lived and plied his trade near or in Montgomeryville, Montgomery County. It is interesting that he eventually made shelf clocks.

George's son, Lafayette, helped his father build clocks. None are known, however, which bear only his name.

Benjamin's other son, Samuel, served an apprenticeship and then moved to Doylestown to start his own business. He constructed a few tall case clocks until demand for them ceased; from then on, reportedly, the bulk of his production was shelf clocks. His advertisements show him to be a man of many talents.

87

> The subscriber respectfully informs his friends and the public, that he has just brought up from Philadelphia, and has now opened at his Clock and Watch making establishment; in Doylestown, between Benj. Morris' hotel and Capt. Donaldson's the most extensive and valuable assortment of articles in his line ever before offered for sale in this place. Among the articles may be enumerated: Mantel Clocks, various patterns; 8 day, with brass works; Gold and Silver Lever Watches; Lepine do; Quartier do; Musical boxes; Table and Tea Spoons, Silver and Germando; Spectacles, with silver and steel frames, green and blue glasses; Razors and Penknives of all superior quality; Steel Beads and Silk Twist; Thermometers; Guard Chains, Breast Pins, Lockets, etc.; Silver Pencils and Gold Pens; Chains, Seals and Keys, a variety of patterns; Ear and Finger Rings; Thimbles, Pencil Points, etc. together with a variety of other articles, all of which will be sold very low. The Clocks and Watches will be warranted.
>
> Clocks and Watches cleaned and repaired at the shortest notice at prices to suit the times.
>
> Persons in want of any of the above articles are invited to call and examine for themselves, before purchasing elsewhere.
>
> Cash paid for old Gold and Silver, or taken in exchange for goods.
>
>   SAMUEL SOLLIDAY
> (*Bucks County Intelligencer*, February 13, 1849)

88

Fig. 87. Samuel Solliday, Doylestown, watchpaper. From the collection of the Mercer Museum of the Bucks County Historical Society.

Fig. 88. Samuel Solliday, New Hope, watchpaper. From the collection of the Mercer Museum of the Bucks County Historical Society.

Samuel served for a time as Burgess before moving to New Hope in 1852, where he operated a coal and lumber business in addition to repairing clocks and watches.

89

90

Fig. 89. Calvin Solliday, Doylestown, watchpaper. From the collection of the Mercer Museum of the Bucks County Historical Society.

Fig. 90. Wilson Solliday, Doylestown, watchpaper. From the collection of the Mercer Museum of the Bucks County Historical Society.

Samuel left only one son in the trade; Calvin (whose real name may have been Charles) learned his father's craft, but did not continue his business. *The Democrat* of June 22, 1852 announced that George E. Donaldson would succeed Samuel Solliday and continue the clock, watch, and jewelry store at the old stand. Four years later, Calvin announced in *The Intelligencer* of June 3, 1856 that he had a stock of cheap watches and jewelry at his shop on Main Street opposite Brower's Hotel and that he would not be undersold by any person this side of sundown. In or around 1900 he moved to Lambertville, New Jersey, where he operated a jewelry store and continued repairing.

Apparently his son, Christopher, was involved in this business and maintained it after his father's death and until his own in 1941.

Daniel, the last of original Frederick's sons, was not a clockmaker himself, but his sons, Samuel and John, were.

Almost nothing is known about Samuel other than that he probably made clocks and that he left two sons, Eli and Wilson, who continued in the general trade. It is quite unlikely that they built any clocks—although one signed Eli has been reported but remains to be verified—though they undoubtedly were proficient repairers. They conducted business in Doylestown around 1850 to 1860 as watch repairers.

Daniel's other son was a prominent clockmaker in his own right. John lived in Tinicum Township near the village of Point Pleasant and signed his clocks "John N. Solliday." Being also a musician, he combined these talents in 1830 to make a very fine musical clock. At one time, an editor of the Bucks County *Intelligencer* permitted John N. Solliday to use his office as a depository for repaired watches and may have collected the appropriate charges. John apparently advertised in that newspaper until September 8, 1818, after which he vanished from the public eye for many years. He was listed on the Tinicum Tax Duplicate of 1846, reporting he had been assessed $6.85 for county and $10.83 for state taxes.

It appears there was a firm, perhaps even a small factory, called Solliday & Sons located in Dublin around 1830 with a salesroom in Doylestown. Beginning and ending dates and details of personnel and operations are unknown; no products have been reported. The sole confirmation of the operation's existence is the ownership by the Bucks County Historical Society of a Solliday & Sons receipt, dated 1830, for the sale of a clock.

Chester County

Titled after Cheshire, England, Chester is the oldest of the three original counties of Pennsylvania. The Swedes started settling the area in 1643, and it was organized in 1682. The first American iron works were founded on the French Creek in 1716 and the first rolling mill was established in Coatesville in 1810. This industrial background and a rich mixture of European immigrants foreordained a goodly number of artisans and craftsmen of superior quality to this area.

Withstanding one notable exception, tall case or grandfather clocks were the only kind made in Chester County.

David M. Anderson, born in Waynesburg in the early 1790s, learned his trade in Lebanon County but returned to his hometown to work. In 1833 he advertised that he manufactured clocks and watches of every description and, of course, he also did repairing. At least fourteen of his clocks are known, most housed in cherry or red mahogany cases which may have been made by local cabinetmakers. Inasmuch as he worked long after the Revolutionary War, all his dials are painted iron and some have moon dials. He enjoyed the honor of designing and assembling a fine tower clock in his community.

Fig. 91. Dial signed "Eli Bentley, Taney Town"—obviously one of his later designs. Courtesy of Wesley G. Harding.

This chapter is largely made possible by Dr. Arthur E. James, author of *Chester County Clocks and Their Makers,* the benchmark of local horological history, who graciously permitted me to extract freely from his compilation.

Joel Baily (1732–97) of West Bradford Township was a versatile and distinguished man, serving variously as yeoman, surveyor, gunsmith, clockmaker, astronomer, and mathematician. He aided Charles Mason and Jeremiah Dixon in establishing the Pennsylvania-Maryland boundary and he was a member of the prestigious American Philosophical Society. Although only one of his clocks is known, his talents and accomplishments suggest the possibility that others did or do exist. That one clock is made of walnut and has a brass dial and spandrels; the dial and bonnet are arched. Baily's estate inventory included an eight-day clock and a silver watch, valued at $40 and $16 respectively, as well as tools and materials which indicate his clockmaking ability was more substantial than his skill as an assembler.

George W. Baldwin (1777–1844) was a clockmaker and a farmer in Sadsburyville from 1802 to 1844. About a dozen of his clocks are extant; constructed of either cherry or mahogany, they average about 96 inches in height and usually have a moon dial. George's brother Harlan and Thomas Ogden, both cabinetmakers, most likely constructed for George clock cases with rope carved pillars, an uncommon Chester County feature.

Curiously, none of the standard reference books list Eli Bentley, born on February 16, 1752 in West Marlborough Township. He and his brother Caleb might have learned the clockmaking trade from their cousin, Thomas Shields of Philadelphia. Eli apparently built both thirty-hour and eight-day clocks in Pennsylvania but only eight-day clocks in Maryland. While some of the hoods of his earlier timepieces were plain, the later ones had broken arches and nicely carved finials. Some clocks had brass moon wheels and sweep second hands. Being Baptist he could employ embellishments not usually adopted by the neighboring Quaker clockmakers. His cases were well proportioned and rather tall, usually made of red walnut. He left Chester County after 1778; when he sold his property in 1783, he could be described as a Maryland clockmaker, having purchased his first land in Taneytown in 1779. The records of the Historical Society of Carroll County report: "Bentley made clocks in Taneytown for perhaps twenty years. Some of the clocks reported as not dated were likely dated on the back frame of the works. The most of the dated ranged from 1809 to 1816." However, one earlier timepiece is known because its dial is dated 1797 and signed "E.B." That Bentley was also an artist is proven by the dial of this clock, a half-circle panel above the dial which contains a hand-painted scene of the sun, two buildings, and a background of foliage.

The inventory of Bentley's estate included "1-eight day clock without case, $30; 1 Regulator ditto, $10; 1 clock movement with face $10; clock and watch making tools, including vises, etc. $20; also a long list of accounts due him totaling about $6,500."

Caleb Bentley (b. 1762), Eli's brother, was born near Doe Run, Pennsylvania. Only two sources have been discovered which give facts on Caleb. Dr. James states "he plied his trade in York, Pennsylvania, later at Leesburg, Virginia and finally settled in Sandy Spring, Maryland." According to the history of the Bentley family given by John N. Bentley at a meeting of the Carroll County Historical Society in Taneytown, on October 10, 1946, Caleb was born in 1762, near Doe Run in Chester County, Pennsylvania. He became a great and affluent clockmaker, and eventually settled in Montgomery County, Maryland in 1794. In 1814 he was living in a brick house in Brookeville, Maryland. Here he entertained President Madison for a night, the president believing that Caleb would be more hospitable than the British, who, in fact, burned Washington that very night.

John Boyd (1805–67) was born, lived, and worked in Sadsbury Township, where his father operated a tavern. He may well have learned his trade from George W. Baldwin of Sadsburyville. He was included in 1831 and for several years after on the Sadsbury tax list as a watchmaker, and was still mentioned as such on the 1850 U.S. Census Report. At least seven of his clocks are known.

Joseph Cave (ca. 1799–1846) was probably Chester County's most peripatetic clockmaker, for he worked in West Goshen from about 1817 to 1821, in West Chester from 1821 to about 1824, in Marshallton for a year or two, and then back in West Chester until 1835, when he moved to Philadelphia. His clocks are a bit taller than the average, are usually constructed of walnut or mahogany, and have enamel and moon phase dials. Thomas Ogden, a West Chester cabinetmaker who reportedly made considerable quantities of clock cases between 1820 and 1835, might have supplied Joseph Cave during his two sojourns in West Chester.

By all odds, the most fascinating and versatile clockmakers and craftsmen of allied arts were found in the several generations of Chandlees. Except for Goldsmith Chandlee, who spent his working career in Winchester, Virginia, they all worked in the Nottingham area. However, the completion of the Mason-Dixon Line in 1767 transferred that little community from Chester County to Cecil County, Maryland, so only the first and second generation Chandlees can be considered Pennsylvanian clockmakers.

Benjamin Chandlee, born in Ireland in 1685, came to Philadelphia in 1702, the same year that Peter Stretch arrived. He was apprenticed to Abel Cottey, long considered the first clockmaker in Philadelphia and one of the five or six earliest in the

colonies, married his daughter Sarah, and moved into the inherited Cottey home in Nottingham shortly after the master's death in 1710. The tiny community was only about a decade old, and consequently its people made immediate demands on Chandlee's metal-working ability to provide the needed farm and household implements. It was, therefore, two or three years before he could go back to clockmaking. Until about 1730, his specialty remained clocks which measured less than seven feet tall. The relatively poor town residents built small houses with low ceilings to conserve money and heat. By the time Chandlee received steady assistance from his four sons, and especially from Benjamin, Jr., the residents were more affluent and so the clock cases grew to eight feet or more. They were signed "B," "Benjn," or "Benjamin Chandlee, Nottingham," according to dial design and available space. Benjamin may have made up to, but not more than, forty clocks. It is certain that he made thirty-three, as his number 33, noted for the pair of lovebirds at the apex of the hood, stands in the Brinton 1704 House. His products displayed various designs, including at least one blinking eye constructed approximately 125 years earlier than any by Bradley & Hubbard, the premier manufacturer of blinking eye timepieces in Connecticut. Repetitive features seem limited to lead spandrels and count pins for the striking systems.

Chandlee obviously gave Benjamin, Jr. a most thorough training and quite probably turned his shop, tools, and business over to the youth when he moved to Delaware in about 1741 and became pretty well lost in history, except for an interesting apprenticeship. An entry in the New Castle County Orphan's Court records for May 1749 consents to the binding of Samuel Furniss, the fourteen-year-old orphaned son of William Furniss (who had been a local clockmaker), as apprentice to Benjamin Chandlee, clockmaker of this county, until age twenty-one.

Benjamin Chandlee, Jr. was born in 1723 in Nottingham. He and his three brothers assisted their father in various enterprises, and the firm of Chandlee & Sons was formed to produce articles of brass, iron, and bell metal, as well as to make clocks. Only Benjamin, Jr. continued on to reach the status of expert craftsman, although, oddly, he was not taxed as a clockmaker until 1765. In 1752 he also bought property in Delaware and, like his father's, this next period of twelve or thirteen years are quite obscure. It is known, however, that he neither inherited nor acquired any of his father's Delaware property. He was back in Nottingham in 1765, but the settling of the Mason-Dixon Line made him overnight a resident of Cecil County, Maryland, and he ultimately owned a considerable amount of land in all three states.

Authorities disagree over just how prolific a clockmaker he was, and it is also diffi-

Fig. 92. Flat top, pegged-case clock, signed "B. Chandlee, Nottingham." The silver dial has brass spandrels and lunette decorations. There is a calendar aperture and strike/silent feature. Private collection.

cult to determine which of his products were made in Pennsylvania and which were from Maryland. It is commonly believed, though, that Benjamin, Jr. made most of his own clock parts rather than rely on those imported from England, as did so many of his Pennsylvania confreres. He was listed in the first U.S. Census (1790), and he apparently retired the same year that the old firm became Ellis Chandlee & Brothers, for three of his four sons pursued the trade. Benjamin, Jr. died in 1791.

It is difficult to select repetitive characteristics in Chandlee's work because there is great variation in case and dial design. The cases tended to be tall (between 90 and 110 inches) and were constructed of solid native woods. Like his father, Benjamin favored lead spandrels but did use other metals. His dials, sometimes silvered, are real works of art, sometimes decorated with fleur-de-lys and punch marks. He also made at least one blinking eye; however, he much preferred the rack and snail for the striking system.

George Cochran (d. 1807?) left no authenticating clocks, and therefore his trade is deductively established. Although early West Chester tax lists refer to him as a watchmaker, he taught his nephew, John Hall, both clock- and watchmaking. Subsequent tax lists identify him as a clockmaker. To further complicate matters, in his will he bequeathed his clockmaking tools to his wife and all those for watchmaking to John Hall. It must be borne in mind, however, that at that time the term "watchmaker" did not have the current connotation, as the earliest accepted date for an American watch assembler is about 1812. A beginning for watchmaking akin to the modern interpretation was seen the 1840s. In Cochran's time it must, then, have meant watch repairing.

Abraham Corl (1779–1842), of East Nantmeal and Coventry, left no clue as to where or how he learned his trade, yet he was listed as a watchmaker in 1807 and as a clockmaker in 1808. This last vocation he pursued for about twenty years in East Nantmeal, and the bulk of his production seems to have taken place here. The gradual influx of Connecticut shelf clocks might have gradually reduced him to repairing. His cases, possibly made by others, ranged from curly maple to plain pine. While the majority of them were conventional in design, one remains which is different in concept—it bears a round dial and hood surmounted with the usual broken arch and central finial.

Thomas Crow, like the several Crow clockmakers, is properly connected with Delaware. For some unknown reason, however, Thomas lived and made clocks in West Chester from 1808 to 1810. His clocks are typical for the period, but his West Chester clocks are distinct from those of other Chester County makers in that they use imported Osborne false plates.

Fig. 93. One of the curly maple-cased clocks with sweep second hand, signed "Jacob Fertig, Vincent." Courtesy of John O. Sweisford and Edward F. Railsback.

Benedict Darlington (1786–1864) was a carpenter and a small-time entrepreneur. This enterprising man made and sold washing machines in Westtown Township as early as 1810; merchandised his fans for cleaning grain in 1814; operated a cotton factory in 1820; and was listed as a storekeeper for domestic flannels in 1822. In 1814 or 1815 he joined forces with three veterans of the War of 1812 to establish a clock business. Sketchy records suggest that two of them brought in Connecticut wood movements and mounted them in cases made by Darlington, while the third man made and applied the dials. These seven to eight foot clocks were then peddled by Darlington around the country. One still exists which is made of solid cherry with a broken arch top, a single urn finial, and nice beading—a trifle fancy for Quakers. Darlington, a clock case maker, was the only tradesman to sell wooden movement clocks in the area.

Thomas Dring worked in West Chester for at least a dozen years, 1786 through 1798, as a clock- and barometermaker. His cases were walnut, about 100 inches tall, with brass dials. At least one of his clocks has fretwork in the broken arch which resembles that on some of the clocks of his famous Massachusetts contemporary, Simon Willard.

Jacob Fertig (1778–1823) ranks a close second to Joseph Cave in moving about the land. From 1802 to 1808 he was taxed as a clock- or watchmaker in Vincent Township. In 1810 he was listed in Philadelphia as a clockmaker. Although he moved back to Pikeland of Chester County in 1813 or 1814, he was established in 1815 in Charlestown Township as an innkeeper, with clockmaking as an adjunct. Six of his clocks, three of curly maple and three of walnut, are extant, but two are numbered to suggest a total production of at least twenty-eight pieces. Several are thirty-hour pull-ups; the balance, however, are eight-day. Fertig's estate inventory listed enough clocks, watches, and appropriate tools to confirm him as a clockmaker and as at least a watch repairer.

Benjamin Garrett (1771–1856) of Goshen, a versatile gentleman, was a farmer, a grist and saw mill operator, a fuller and wool spinner, and a cabinet- and clockmaker. His well-proportioned clocks exhibit fine cabinet work—very likely his own—and show that he was adept at inlay decoration. The broken arch tops of his clocks sometimes had delicately carved fretwork terminating in rosettes and sometimes bore the usual curved arches with either single or triple finials, often oriflamme, much like his father's. Walnut seemed to be his favorite wood although one of his finest clock cases is in bird's-eye maple. The period in which Garrett worked saw the twilight of brass dials and the dawn of enameled dials. He generally added the moon phase dial. Showing his dislike of stereotypes, he signed his dials in various ways—"Bn" and

"Benjamin Garrett, Goshen," for example. One suspects that most of the twenty-one or twenty-two of his clocks which are known were purchased by non-Quakers.

Joseph Garrett (1743–92), Benjamin's father, was not as well known as his son. Bits of evidence tell that he was variously a farmer, a gristmill operator, a cabinet-maker, and a clockmaker. Benjamin inherited his father's joiner's and watchmaker's tools. The estate inventory also listed watch keys, glasses, and a quantity of maple and walnut boards. Inasmuch as there is no evidence of watchmaking activity, it may be concluded that those are misnomers in the estate inventory and that, in reality, there were clock items.

That Joseph was out of Meeting during his married life may have influenced his clock design; the description of one piece suggests his preference for a more worldly product. This clock is set in a beautiful solid native wood case with fluted quarter columns on the waist. The waist door is surmounted by a broken arch with a leaf motif in the center. The hood has full, round fluted columns and a broken arch top which ends in rosette scrolls and bears fretwork. The finials are oriflamme, arising out of urns. The dial appears to be enamelled iron with intricately painted spandrels, fancy pierced hands, a small sweep second hand, and a calendar ring. The lunette is decorated with an eagle atop a ribbon in which are written the words "Tempus Fugit." Immediately below this appears the signature, "J. Garrett, Goshen."

In a 1952 addendum to the 1947 edition of *Chester County Clocks and Their Makers,* Dr. James named William Gillespie as a prerevolutionary clockmaker. The appraisal of the goods and effects of William Gillespie, a bachelor, included items indicative of his vocation: an unfinished clock, unfinished clock wheels, patterns, a wheel cutting engine, a screw cutter, a lathe, old brass, etc. One of his tall clocks, signed "Wm. Gillespie, New London," is now located in the Chester County Historical Society.

It has already been mentioned that John Hall (1793–1867) of West Chester learned the trade of clock- and watchmaking (the latter meaning repairing) from his uncle, George Cochran, at an early age. He was in business for himself by 1813. One example of his work, made in 1825, sits in a case constructed by Thomas Ogden. The dial strongly suggests an English origin, which is puzzling because Hall served in the War of 1812 for about three months. He was also the caretaker of the town clock from 1839 to 1862.

Caleb Hibbard, Jr. (1782–1835) lived and worked in Willistown. His grandfather, Isaac Thomas, a prolific clockmaker, and his uncle, clockmaker Mordecai Thomas, were neighbors, so young Caleb naturally learned from them the arts of clock- and cabinetmaking and perhaps of watch repairing. His unusually long apprenticeship of fourteen years must have made him a master craftsman. He, too, most probably produced a fair number of clocks before 1818, as at least eleven known pieces are scattered from New York to California. In 1818 he moved to Ohio where he engaged for a while in clockmaking.

Joshua Humphrey was born in 1743 in Charleston Township, though clock inscriptions confirm that he also resided in the townships of East Whiteland and Tredyffrin. He was taxed in 1770 as a clockmaker in Tredyffrin and from 1771 to 1773 as the operator of a retail and repair shop. All his known clocks appear to predate the Revolutionary War. The Charleston Township clocks are thirty-hour pull-ups housed in somewhat plain, eight foot walnut cases with flat top bonnets, unusual in that they sport two small finials. In 1777 he moved to Staunton, Virginia and later to Richmond. He finally lived in Lexington, Kentucky, where he died in 1810. Whether these moves were dictated by politics or by changes of occupation is not known. That his son David became a noted silversmith in Kentucky might suggest an answer.

Jonathan Hatch was listed on the 1814 tax assessment in Westtown as a clockmaker. Actually, he was one of the three men who helped assemble Connecticut wood movements and dials into the cases made by Benedict Darlington.

The story of Joseph M. Hollis is difficult to interpret. In 1819 he advertised in the *American Republican* as a clock- and watchmaker commencing business in Downingtown, but went on to say that clocks and watches would be carefully repaired and warranted. The next year he advertised in the same newspaper that in addition to repairing watches of every description, he had entered the clockmaking business. He offered eight-day clocks made in the neatest and most permanent manner, warranted for seven years, at a reduced price of $38 and costing as much as $45, according to order. Indeed, a more liberal warranty period would be hard to find. This advertisement confirms that he was not a watchmaker but rather a repairman. It should also place him as a bona fide clockmaker, yet one would feel more comfortable if an example or two of his products were known or even reported.

In the same newspaper early in 1821, he advised the public that he would be leaving Downingtown on April 1 and implored customers who were indebted to him for repairs or otherwise to pay promptly. Notice the lack of reference to repaired or made clocks unless they were covered by "or otherwise." Once in the *American Republican* and more than once in the *Village Record* in 1821, Hollis announced that he was in business in West Chester to execute any work in his line. Former customers from Downingtown were invited to give him work through two agents which would be carefully finished and returned once a month. He also gave final notice to those still indebted to him for repairs, stating that they must pay at once or face legal action. Again, there is no mention of money owed for clocks he had made or any hint that he was still making them. To compound the mystery, he advertised later in 1821 for a journeyman clockmaker. Did Hollis need a qualified maker because he enjoyed a custom he could no longer handle alone or was he personally not a qualified maker?

George Jackson of Unionville was first classified as a clockmaker in 1798 and pursued the trade until 1812. Apparently he did not sign all the clocks he evidently made, as some exist with written notation inside the case that they were made by George Jackson.

Isaac Jackson (1734–1807), of London Grove and New Garden, was originally a blacksmith and silversmith. Gifted mechanically, he learned clockmaking, possibly from Benjamin Chandlee or from Benjamin, Jr. Jackson's graceful clocks are simpler in design and have more uniformity than those of other Chester County makers. There is no evidence that he was a trained cabinetmaker, and, indeed, his clocks are not pretentious. Standing between 7½ and 8 feet tall, they are nearly all walnut, held together with wood pegs. A few of his clocks have only one hand, a feature unique in Chester County and somewhat unusual among American clocks. These pieces, apparently his earliest productions, have thirty-hour movements. His later clocks are eight-day; many tell the date; some contain the strike-silent feature; and a few sport plain finials; but none have the moon dial. Jackson signed his dials in different ways and sometimes added a bit of verse. Other than the Chandlees, he was probably the most complete Chester County maker.

John Jackson, Jr. (1746–95), a cousin of Isaac Jackson's, was the only Chester County clockmaker to turn Tory. Apparently he left his family in East Marlborough Township and fled to Nova Scotia to live with other Loyalist refugees. Consequently, the best-known example of his work has the English style spandrels and wears protecting rings around the winding holes in imitation of earlier English clocks.

Elisha Kirk (1757–90) was an apprentice of and later a partner with Isaac Jackson. He moved from New Garden to York in about 1780 and continued clockmaking until his early death.

An article appearing in the August 4, 1938 issue of the *Honey Brook Herald* reported that Isaac Landis, long in the trade at Coatsville, learned his craft from an au-

Fig. 94. An Isaac Thomas clock in a replacement case, faithfully copied in the best Chester County style. Courtesy of Edward F. Railsback and John O. Sweisford.

thenticated clockmaker, David M. Anderson of Waynesburg.

A. Sidney Logan (1849–1925) was not a true Quaker, although he was of such ancestry. Nor was he a clockmaker in our sense of the word, and yet Logan is worth mentioning. A great student and hobbyist in Goshenville who around 1913 tried his hand at clockmaking, he eventually turned out four timepieces. His tour de force was the famous tower clock known locally as Goshenville's Big Ben, erected around 1920. There is even a clock dial portrayed on the obelisk on his cemetery lot.

Henry Olwine was listed as a watchmaker in Yellow Springs in 1812 and as a clockmaker in 1813; in 1814 he advertised that he made and repaired both kinds of pieces. He probably worked as a clockmaker and watch repairer until 1836. No clocks bearing his name exist, yet some are attributed to him. His brother Abraham, sometimes listed as a watchmaker, may have helped him from time to time.

William Price (1799–1879) advertised in the May 15, 1822 *Village Record* as a clock- and watchmaker and was so listed in the 1823 West Chester tax records—yet there is no substantiating evidence.

Moses A. Regensburg advertised in 1835 and 1838 as a clock- and watchmaker in East Whiteland Township, and three of his clocks are indeed signed "East Whiteland." These timepieces are more ornate, having eight-day movements with moon dials. Their walnut cases, averaging ninety inches in height, are surmounted by rather heavy broken arches and two extra-large finials.

Thomas Scott (1813–79) of Downingtown, supposedly served an apprenticeship under Anthony Wayne Baldwin, the well-known Mennonite clockmaker of Lampeter, Lancaster County, Pennsylvania. This is questionable, however, as Baldwin had only one named apprentice and it was not Scott. Nevertheless, Scott advertised in the *American Spectator* of November 11, 1834 as a clock- and watchmaker, but, again, no substantiating evidence has come to light.

Isaac Thomas (1721–1802) was a master of versatility. In Willistown he was a farmer, a grist and saw mill operator, a surveyor, and a joiner, as well as the most prolific clockmaker of Chester County and perhaps of all the Quaker clockmakers—about forty-four of his products are known. His fine cases were always constructed of solid walnut or cherry, except for one known veneered example. Thomas apparently used brass dials exclusively and never incorporated the moon phase, though he usually applied some sort of date indicator. For non-Quaker customers he seems to have made conventional dials of the period, including spandrels, but for Quakers he used round dials devoid of decoration yet displaying splendid workmanship. Identifying features of his clocks are the spandrels of brass or lead (when these are used at all) and the fancy wooden finials. It is believed that he imported many of his clock parts from England.

Mordecai Thomas (1767–1837), of Willistown, generally followed his father Isaac's vocations, to which he added wool carding. His cases have an even better proportion and symmetry than his father's; the son preferred walnut and mahogany with delicate inlay. His clockmaking may have gradually phased out in favor of his nephew, Caleb Hibbard, Jr., in order to devote more time to his other trades, as he had a large family to support.

John Way (1766–ca. 1848) toiled as a clockmaker in Waggon Town for only a short time, probably from 1796 to 1798, before becoming a tavern keeper first there and then at several localities. Still, clocks signed by him do exist, though set in walnut cases which were very likely made by someone else. His movements are eight-day and his dials are painted iron with moon phase.

These men may be classified as the major clockmakers of Chester County. There were, however, several minor, or peripheral, practitioners of the craft.

Joseph D. Acker appears as a watchmaker on the West Whiteland township assessment for 1850. Likewise, Thomas De Wolf was included on the Westtown tax lists for 1814–15 as a clockmaker, but, actually, like J. Hatch, he was merely a helper to Benedict Darlington. Allen Yarnall advertised in the *Village Record* of May 25, 1825 that he offered second-hand watches for sale, while new clocks and watches would be furnished at the shortest notice—he warranted his work. However, several skilled predecessors in the area had pretty well saturated the market for clocks, so he promoted a lottery to aid his finances. For this he was promptly "disowned" by the Goshen Monthly Meeting. He therefore moved to West Chester and continued as a watchmaker (repairer) until his early death of pulmonary disease—the last clockmaker on record in his former part of Chester County.

Fig. 95. Tall clock by J.D. Custer, Norristown. Private collection.

Montgomery County

Montgomery County, named for General Richard Montgomery, was formed from a part of Philadelphia County and organized in 1784. Containing Valley Forge, Barren Hill, and Crooked Billet (now Hatboro), the county played an active part during the Revolutionary War. The first iron made in Pennsylvania was forged on the Manatawney Creek in 1717. The mixture of early settlers and the diversity of enterprises would suggest an abundance of skilled artisans, and, indeed, there is no disappointment in the area of clockmakers, either quantitatively or qualitatively.

John A. Andre (d. 1880) was a clockmaker and watchmaker, a dentist, and a politician in Pottstown. He may have entered the clock and watch activity by buying the business of David Leigh, and his apparent working years in that trade were 1862 to 1874. The late date, along with the fact that the periods of public office and trade overlap, suggests that his true activities were confined to repairing.

William Bevans (also spelled Bevens and Bevins; 1755–1819) was listed in the Philadelphia directories from 1810 until 1816 and then in Norristown for the next three years. He advertised in 1818: "Clock and watch maker will barter 1 or 2 eight-day clocks for hickory wood."

Adam Brandt (also Brant; b. 1780?), of New Hanover Township, was a prolific clockmaker. Until 1855, all clocks of his which had been found bore painted dials which, generally speaking, replaced brass dials after the Revolutionary War. Brandt's dials are well-executed and his clocks indicate he was a highly skilled craftsman. Several engraved brass dial clocks have recently been reported, one of which went through an auction sale in Lancaster County during the early part of 1974.

Had this county spawned no other clockmakers than Jacob D. Custer (1805–72) it still would have sufficient claim to fame. Indeed, he is important enough to warrant a separate chapter. Jacob's younger brother Isaac, also a clockmaker, joined Jacob in his Norristown clock shop but moved to St. Louis in 1837 or 1838.

Clockmaker Septemus Evans is primarily connected with Bucks County, having labored there for approximately fourteen years, but he did move to Jenkintown in about 1821 and remained there for some time before migrating on down to Delaware.

Information about George Faber is contradictory. One biographer asserts that he was making clocks in Sumneytown in and probably before 1773. That year he moved to Reading, where he continued work for several more years. A later authority states that Faber learned his trade in Reading from his uncle, Daniel Rose, a respected clockmaker, and that he worked in Sumneytown in 1791 and sometime thereafter. Rose (1749–1827) is thought to have done his best work after serving as a lieutenant in the Revolutionary War. This would lend credence to the second interpretation in the absence of vital dates for Faber.

Jacob Godschalk, a native of Towamencin Township and a contemporary of David Rittenhouse, was already a famous clockmaker before the Revolutionary War. His earlier clocks were signed with his name and place. He built both tall case and wag-on-the-wall clocks, some of which had a distinct English flavor because the dials bore cherub and orb applied brass spandrels. In the late 1760s he moved into Philadelphia.

George Govett, son-in-law of William Bevans, came from Philadelphia in 1819 to continue the Bevans business. In 1831, however, he returned to Philadelphia where he appeared in the directories until 1850.

All earlier authors in this field have offered a considerable amount of information about the several generations of Hagey clockmakers. Not all of it has proven completely accurate. Fortunately, a direct descendant of the Hagey family has generously made available the authentic family history and has graciously granted permission to quote extensively from it.

Not all the Hageys stayed in Montgomery County, but they all started there.

HANS JACOB HAGE born near Neustadt, Saxony, Germany, in the year 1749. When eighteen years of age, he, in company with his brother Daniel and sister Catha-

96

97

Fig. 96. Tall clock by Jacob Godshalk. Note the inlay on the door, the vee in the top of the dial door molding, and the unusual ornamentation added to the otherwise flat top bonnet. Permission from the Historical Society of Pennsylvania.

Fig. 97. The dial of the clock in fig. 96 is lacking spandrels but has interesting features, such as the punch mark and wind rose decorations and the plate signed "Jacob Godshalk in Towamencin." Use of the preposition is unique. Courtesy of the Historical Society of Pennsylvania.

rina, boarded the ship "Minerva" bound for America, . . . landing at Philadelphia, October 29, 1767. He settled in Franconia Township, Montgomery County. About the year 1772 he married Elizabeth Stump. . . .

His occupation was clockmaking—his ancestors having been artisans in this field in their native Switzerland. He made upwards of one hundred thirty-four tall clocks, some eight-day. His small shop with several assistants preceded the now famed Eli Terry clock factory at Plymouth, Conn. In 1780 his extensive property and clockmaking enterprise commanded a tax amounting to 93 pounds. During the American Revolution he rendered service in the militia, being a member of the 4th Company, 5th Battalion, Philadelphia County Militia, commanded by Capt. John Cope. His name sometimes appears . . . as Hans Jork Haage. . . .

Earlier publications give a Samuel Hege of Franconia, Pa. who made over one hundred clocks in the "early to mid-eighteenth century." Unsuccessful attempts have been made in establishing his identity, but it is generally believed that he was related to the other Hagey clockmakers, and was probably an uncle of Hans Jacob. In view of the fact that his works preceded Hans Jacob's by a number of years, it is assumed that they were not brothers. Samuel Hege is erroneously identified as the father of Hans Jacob in Fred C. Sweinhart's "Early Pennsylvania Clocks and Their Makers," an essay read before the Historical Society of Montgomery County on April 26, 1941. There is no evidence of when Samuel Hege emigrated to America . . . and no testamentary or church records have disclosed his family connection.

Jacob Hagey, . . . son of Hans Hage and Elizabeth Stump; born April 24, 1775, in Franconia twp., Montgomery county, Pa.; died Sept. 11, 1834, in Hilltown twp., Bucks County, Pa.; married ca. 1797, Catherine Elizabeth Gearhart. . . . Both buried in Blooming Glen Mennonite cemetery in Bucks County.

On the 7th of April 1828 (other authorities, including a grandson, say 1831), he sold his farm and clockmaking establishment in Lower Salford twp., near Harleysville, Montgomery County, and moved to Hilltown twp., Bucks County. He, like his father, was a noted clockmaker. Various accounts of his life and work testify that he produced more than one hundred superb tall-case clocks. Jacob Hagey seems to have been highly regarded because of his occupation for on all deeds where his name appears it is followed by the designation "clock maker."

John Gearhart Hagey, . . . son of Jacob Hagey and Catherine Elizabeth Gearhart; born Oct. 7, 1799, in Lower Salford twp., Montgomery County, Pa.; died in Philadelphia, . . . June 30, 1885; married ca. 1823, Elizabeth Nice . . . in Philadelphia. . . .

At an early age John G. Hagey became engaged in clockmaking. He had a clock shop and store first in Mount Airy, then in Germantown, finally in Philadelphia. The comparatively few clocks produced by him were all of fine workmanship, including both shelf and tall-case types, the latter of which were mostly in Chippendale and

Sheraton styles. It is reputed that he was the inventor of a special type of chimes used in the tall-case clocks. As did his brothers, George and Jonas, he also sold and repaired watches and too, as they, was compelled to discontinue this vocation about the middle of the century, when cheap New England clocks were introduced into Pennsylvania. In 1826 he removed from Lower Salford twp., Montgomery county, and purchased from his parents a house and lot in Germantown on Main Street, where he and his family lived for a number of years. About 1850, his residence was in Philadelphia, in which place he owned a large confectionary establishment at the corner of Ninth and Market streets. . . .

He and his wife were buried in the cemetery of the Church of the Brethren (Dunkard church), Germantown Avenue, of which they were members.

George Gearhart Hagey, . . . son of Jacob Hagey and Catherine Elizabeth Gearhart; born in Lower Salford twp., Montgomery county, Pa. Feb. 14, 1808, died at Sterling, Ill., Nov. 3, 1887; married . . . Oct. 1830, Sarah Moyer. . . .

George Hagey was probably the most celebrated clockmaker of the three generations of his family engaged in this occupation. He was also a watchmaker, and had his shop for two years near Harleysville, then seventeen years at Trappe. His residence at Trappe was opposite the Fountain Inn. In 1850 he sold property there to William R. Rittenhouse (relative of the famous . . . David Rittenhouse). He and several other parties, in 1853, sold a "Brick Messuage known by the name of The Washington Hall and the lot in The Trappe." He removed to Rockhill township, Bucks county, in 1850, where he purchased 111 acres of land. Here he continued to produce tall-case clocks of superb quality until the year 1855, when he gave up the business because of the strong competition from Connecticut shelf clocks.

The following is an excerpt from a newspaper printed in 1837, relating to George Hagey's clock shop. "On the night of 9th inst. the shop of George Hagey, watchmaker, at Trappe in Upper Providence Township, was entered by some villian or villians and property consisting of watches, jewelry, etc. stolen there from, to the value of about $1,000.00. A reward is offered for the apprehension of the thief and the recovery of the property."

He migrated to Sterling, Illinois, and there was engaged in the jewelry business until 1881, when he retired. Member of the Reformed Mennonite church, in which he was trustee and deacon.

Jonas Gearhart Hagey, . . . youngest son of Jacob Hagey and Catherine Elizabeth Gearhart; born Feb. 15, 1815, in Lower Salford twp., Montgomery county, Pa., died intestate, Dec. 27, 1895, Hellertown, Pa.; married first, ca. 1844, Anna Overbeck; . . . married second, Oct. 16, 1851, Cecilia Wolbach. . . . He and his second wife were buried at Hellertown.

He was a clockmaker, watchmaker, farmer, silversmith and auctioneer. In the field

Fig. 98. A tall clock with eight-day brass movement by Jacob Godshalk, circa 1755. This has the conventional flat top without embellishment and a sweep second hand. Courtesy of Edward Railsback and John Sweisford.

9

100

101

Fig. 99. Pennsylvania type pillar and scroll clock by John Hagey of "German Town." Courtesy of Thomas K. Leidy.

Fig. 100. Interior view of the clock in fig. 99, showing, among other features, the odd location of the bell. Courtesy of Thomas K. Leidy.

Fig. 101. Close view of the movement of the clock in fig. 99, displaying rack and snail striking. Courtesy of Thomas K. Leidy.

Fig. 102. Dial of the clock in fig. 99, showing that Hagey split the name *Germantown* into two words. Courtesy of Thomas K. Leidy.

102

First Generation	Hans Jacob Hage m. circa 1772, Elizabeth Stump
	b. 1749, Germany. Settled in Franconia Twp., Montgomery Co., circa 1767.
Second Generation	Jacob Hagey m. Catherine Elizabeth Gearhart
	b. April 24, 1775, Franconia Twp. d. September 11, 1834, Hilltown Twp., Bucks Co.
Third Generation	John Gearhart Hagey m. circa 1823, Elizabeth Nice
	b. October 7, 1799, Lower Salford Twp., Montgomery Co. d. June 30, 1855, Philadelphia.
Third Generation	George Gearhart Hagey m. October 1830, Sarah Moyer
	b. February 14, 1808, Lower Salford Twp. d. November 3, 1887, Sterling, Illinois.
Third Generation	Jonas Gearhart Hagey m. circa 1844, Anna Overbeck; m. October 16, 1851, Cecilia Wolbach
	b. February 15, 1815, Lower Salford Twp. d. December 27, 1895, Hellertown, Northampton Co.

Fig. C. The Hagey family.

of clockmaking he was probably not as well known as were his two brothers, father and grandfather. According to family tradition, only twelve tall-case clocks are attributed to him. His shop was located, first at Springtown, Bucks County, and then at Hellertown, Northampton county, where he removed soon after his marriage.

It seems likely that none of the Hageys made their own cases, as a newspaper article indicates that their clocks usually sold in the range of $40 to $100, a portion of which went to the cabinetmaker.

Montgomery County was, and still is, the home of a special religious sect; Schwenkfelder was an early group of people who came to America seeking religious freedom. In 1734 thirty-four families left Silesia, Germany, for these shores; others followed two years later, and a settlement was organized in Montgomery and Berks counties. These colonists founded an independent denomination in 1782, taking their name in honor of Kaspar Schwenkfeld (1489–1561), a German religious reformer. Their church services are simple; the group has a membership of several thousand, among which were several clockmakers.

The first was David S. Heebner (1810–1900), of Worcester Township, the son of Reverend Balthasar Heebner. His father established David in farming, but, caring little for this and possessing a naturally inventive mind, the young man drifted into clockmaking. Quite successful at this, he built a reputation until the influx of cheap Connecticut clocks halted the demand for tall clocks. Benefiting from his dual background, Heebner launched into the business of manufacturing farm machinery in 1840, in response to a call from his neighbors and friends for labor-saving agricultural machines. By 1862 the business had expanded so much that he took his sons Isaac and Jonah into partnership as Heebner and Sons Agricultural Works. A decade later this operation was dissolved; David moved into Lansdale and took sons Isaac and William into partnership as Heebner Sons and Company. In that year Lansdale was incorporated and David was elected the first burgess. He also served as postmaster.

At least three sources name Nicholas Kohl as the maker of tall case clocks in Willow Grove in about 1830. The 1850 census listed him as a watchmaker, sixty years old, and owning real estate worth $5,000.

Samuel Krauss (1807–1904), of Kraussdale, was another of the Schwenkfelders. A member of the famous family of organ builders, he was, in addition to being a clockmaker, a storekeeper, an inventor, a foundryman, a miller, and a farmer. At various times he was engaged in business in Philadelphia, Upper Milford and Upper Hanover townships, Allentown, and Coopersburg. He retired from business in 1886 and settled in Sumneytown.

There appear to have been two Kulps working in the county, Jacob in Franconia, from around 1840 to 1850, and William in Lower Salford near Sumneytown, circa 1800. Tall case clocks are attributed to William, but no record of what type (if any) that Jacob produced can be found.

At mid-century Henry Leibert, by trade a hatter and a clock- and watchmaker taught by his father, opened a store in Norristown. He later tried the jewelry manufacturing business and ultimately was killed experimenting with gun powder. In the 1850 census he was listed as a watchmaker, age forty.

David Leigh, at work in the 1840s in Pottstown, must have had a profitable trade, for he sold out to John Andre.

The Lukens family came from Holland in 1688. They were a noted clan and quite numerous; in 1776 there were eight adult males listed in the Horsham Township directory, one with as many as nine children! Peter and Seneca, grandfather and grandson, were among those named. Seneca, the son of Joseph, a farmer, learned his trade from his grandfather, who was an early, unrecorded clockmaker. Seneca Lukens became a prominent man in the township and an ingenious clockmaker by profession, who was additionally taxed in 1805 for a farm of 231 acres. He made a clock for each of his four daughters; his total production must indeed have been considerable, as his clock #41 is dated 1795. He died in 1830, having appointed his wife and son Joseph as his executors. Two sources simply list a J. Lukens in Philadelphia in the 1830s. This must have been Joseph, but his activities remain clouded.

Isaiah Lukens (1779–1846), another of Seneca's sons, was born in Horsham, where he received only a common education. By diligent, self-directed study, however, he acquired a profound knowledge of the sciences. He learned clockmaking from his father, and the reputation of excellence in his high-standing clocks spread far beyond his neighborhood and formed the basis of his future reputation. Visiting Europe, he obtained employment as a watchmaker and gained recognition for his methods of tempering steel. After three years he returned to Pennsylvania to establish himself as a builder of tower clocks, a watchmaker, and a machinist. In 1812 he made the tower clock for the Loller Academy in Hatboro.

Isaiah moved to Philadelphia in 1811, where he was listed in directories as a horologist, a town clock maker, and a mechanist. He was one of the founders of the Franklin Institute; he also built a clock for the Second United States Bank in 1820 and a tower clock for the Headhouse. His crowning achievement was the construction, at a price of $2,000, of the first four-faced steeple clock for the State House (now Independence Hall) in 1828.

Lukens enjoyed the lifelong reputation of a practical joker, and, indeed, examples which prove this are numerous. One oft-repeated tale also demonstrates his extraordinary skill. Lukens, it seems, was a frequent visitor to "Grumblethorpe," the Germantown home of Charles J. Wister, because he and Wister had kindred tastes. Wister had a workshop where he enjoyed tinkering with and creating clocks and instruments. Among his treasures was a splendid clock made by the celebrated Quaker

103

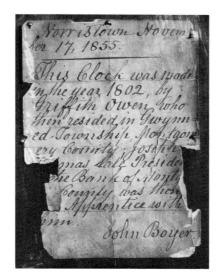

Fig. 103. Handsomely cased clock by Griffith Owen. Courtesy of Douglas H. Shaffer.

Fig. 104. Dial and hood of the clock in fig. 103. Courtesy of Douglas H. Shaffer.

Fig. 105. Paper on the inside of the clock in fig. 103. If this paper is correct, Owen is placed in Gwynned Township in 1802, but he soon moved to Towamencin Township. Courtesy of Douglas H. Shaffer.

105

104

clockmaker, Thomas Wagstaffe, of London. Apparently, it once stopped running and Wister dismantled but could not reassemble it. When Lukens next came to visit, Wister showed him the heap of wheels, pinions, and parts, and one extraneous wheel added for good measure. Of course, Lukens put the pieces all together, with one wheel remaining which he simply pocketed. When the fixed clock was back in its accustomed place, Wister asked about the wheel in his friend's pocket. Lukens calmly replied that he thought the clock would run satisfactorily without it.

Wister built, at Luken's suggestion, an astronomical observatory on his grounds, so that he could compute the correct time. Lukens made an astronomical clock and a transit instrument for the observatory.

His attachment for Germantown had a strange sequel long after his death. The tower clock he built for Independence Hall now reposes in the tower of the old municipal building in Germantown.

Only one earlier reference to Samuel Maus can be found. He was a maker of tall clocks in Pottstown around 1790 and his clock #20 is known.

A clockmaker named Moyer was most likely working in Skippackville very late in the eighteenth or very early in the nineteenth century. There is confusion over his first name; some sources name him Jacob, others Joseph. Joseph appears on the dial of a thirty-hour, one weight, chain pull-up tall clock; however, an eight-day tall clock signed "Jacob D. Moyer" is extant.

Griffith Owen, stepson and apprentice of Jacob Godschalk, is usually associated with Philadelphia. He was listed there in the 1790 census and regularly appeared in the directories until 1814. Just as Godschalk quietly slipped into Philadelphia at an unprecise date, Owen made the reverse move to Montgomery County. He even chose his stepfather's old bailiwick of Towamencin Township. Likewise, his clocks from there mimic his mentor's method of signing; "Jacob Godschalk in Towamencin" became "Griffith Owen of Towamencin."

A fleeting reference can be found to William Pennepacker, of Frederick Township, working in the 1860s. The late dating always suggests that repairing rather than making was being performed, and therefore he is included in the alphabetical listing solely as a clue to future researchers. The same is almost true of Thomas Potts of Norristown, who was said to have had some connection with David Rittenhouse in the 1760s, possibly in making instruments, except that a brass dial tall clock bearing his name and location is known. In addition, William Rapp appeared in Philadelphia directories from 1828 and onward, yet some say he was in Norristown in 1837. It seems that Rapp took over the shop vacated by Isaac Custer, but put Daniel H. Stern in charge.

Benjamin Rittenhouse, born in 1740 at Norriton, undoubtedly worked with his famous older brother David as both a clock- and an instrumentmaker. He was commissioned a captain in the local military company of Worcester and he became early in 1776 the superintendent of the Gunlock Factory. After the war he provided material aid to the organization of Montgomery County. Apparently Benjamin moved about. For example, in 1786 he advertised in Philadelphia for an apprentice for clockmaking. He was listed in directories there until 1820. In 1791 he was a judge of Common Pleas Court in Montgomery County. He died in 1825.

Daniel Scheid (also spelled Scheidt, Shaid, Shade; 1782–1878), of Sumneytown, was apprenticed at age sixteen to John Hagey. He continued his work as a journeyman for several years, before returning to Sumneytown to set up his own business. His working years continued until about the time of the Civil War; thus, his production of tall clocks was extensive. It is averred that he made all his wheels by hand, a practice followed by all too few Keystone State craftsmen.

David C. Shuler (b. 1847) was born in Trappe, where he began his trade of clockmaking and repairing in 1867. In 1901 he moved into Norristown. He made about fifteen clocks, which sold for twelve to fifteen dollars apiece. Nearly fifty years

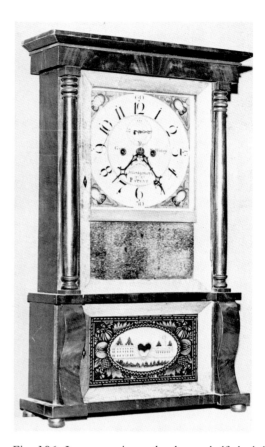

Fig. 106. Large cornice and column shelf clock by George Solliday. This was made circa 1830 in an effort to compete with the inexpensive contemporary Connecticut shelf clocks. It has a heavy eight-day cast solid plate movement with cut pinions and rack strike. The weights are compounded; the dial is painted iron; the bottom tablet is a replacement. Courtesy of Edward Railsback and John Sweisford.

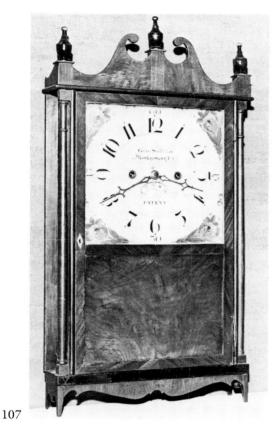

Fig. 107

Fig. 107. Pennsylvania style pillar and scroll, thirty-hour clock by George Solliday, also circa 1830. Note that the dials of both of these Solliday clocks carry the word *patent*, but what the patent covered has yet to be discerned. Courtesy of Edward Railsback and John Sweisford.

Fig. 108. Oversize Swartz clock dial with spandrels-of-the-sea. Courtesy of William A. Castle.

Fig. 109. View of Swartz movement from left. This specimen shows the time train. Courtesy of William A. Castle.

108   109

ago a writer described them as being of modern style, about three feet tall, and running eight days. Accepting the accuracy of this, we would refer to them today as grandmother's clocks, which are highly prized by collectors. Shuler and Jacob Custer (to whom a few are attributed) seem to be the only Pennsylvanians who produced these small gems. It may have been only coincidence that these contemporaries lived just a few miles apart, though Shuler admittedly only assembled parts he bought and placed them in cases made to order. Still, this does not detract from his reputation one jot.

George Solliday (1796–1871) built his clocks in Montgomeryville. He must also have done watch repairing as watchpapers of his are known. Henry Solliday (1765–1814) performed his clock making in Towamencin Township. Going by dates, one can see that Griffith Owen supplanted him and may even have succeeded to his establishment.

As already noted, the shop vacated by Isaac Custer in Norristown was taken over in 1837 or 1838 by William Rapp of Philadelphia, who placed Daniel H. Stein in charge. Eventually Stein took over the business and conducted it until his death in 1885. In the census of 1850 he was listed as a watchmaker, age twenty-eight. William Stein, twenty years old, was likewise listed.

Tall clocks bearing the name Abraham Swartz of Lower Salford have been reliably reported, but no suggestion of date or any other information has been uncovered. However, recently acquired photographs of a Swartz clock not only verify him as a maker but identify his working period. The dial bears "Abm. Swartz Lower Salford" below the date aperture. Written in pencil on the front of the seat board is " A S May 23, 1832." The dial is rather large, 13 by 18½ inches, with an arched top; this painted iron sheet is mounted directly by four posts to the front movement plate. The basket of flowers on the arched top is plain enough. The spandrels are stylized snails or whelks on a green background. The heavy brass movement is nicely finished, with rack and snail strike on the right side. A single weight on an endless chain drives both time and strike.

After many years of painstaking research in primary sources, the Historical Society of Montgomery County has identified more than twenty little-known clockmakers to add to their already prolific listing of over fifty recognized makers, a total of over seventy within the county. The compiler, the late Jane K. Burris, graciously consented to have much of her data available for this chapter.

Jacob Detweiler Custer

Jacob Detweiler Custer was born on March 5, 1805, in what was Worcester Township but is now East Norriton. His father's farm, bought in 1798, was bounded on the west by that which had been owned by David Rittenhouse. Custer, like his famous predecessor, developed his great skill entirely through self-teaching; furthermore, both Rittenhouse and Custer had Mennonite ancestors, although certainly neither of them followed this religion strictly. Finally, each had a younger brother to whom he taught clockmaking and worked with before these siblings followed their own courses.

Custer's early life was bound closely to farm work, leaving little time for anything else. It is often repeated that he had only a few months of formal education. No doubt he often arose extra early in the morning to accomplish his assigned chores so that he would have a little time to tinker with mechanical things. When he was nineteen he diagnosed, with no previous experience, why his father's watch had stopped running, and then he successfully repaired it. Next, tradition says, he did the same for a school teacher, and before long neighbors started bringing him watches and clocks to fix, particularly since the old local clock tinkerer died at about that time.

At the age of nineteen or twenty he turned his back on farming forever and set up a small shop at the corner of Ridge and Township Line, about one mile west of Jeffersonville. Here he made his first clock and so mounted it that the public could see it when passing by. Apparently, he also travelled about the area both repairing clocks and soliciting orders for his own. In about 1832 he moved to Norristown, near Main and Swede streets, to continue clock and watch repairing. He also stocked and offered to make all kinds of timepieces.

Indeed, he made tower, tall, and shelf clocks, and later he produced watches, too. Custer used steel for the arbors, but his tower clocks were generally of good cast iron, which he felt would outlast brass and cost less. He built a small factory near Main and Green streets, where his younger brother, Isaac, learned the trade. Near the factory was a school with a small bell tower, for which Custer offered to build a clock. The Town Council intervened by buying the clock for the tower in the Court House, where it remained until 1856 when a new Court House was erected. Again Custer was commissioned to supply the tower clock. His fame soon spread and he was asked to build town clocks for Philadelphia, Danville, Gettysburg, Phoenixville, Coatesville, and Falls of Schuylkill, all in Pennsylvania; Bridgeton and Glassboro in New Jersey; and Salem, Ohio, and other towns as far away as South Carolina and Alabama.

His early clocks, with wood plates and brass wheels, were typical of the variety now referred to as wag-on-the-wall of European origin. Immigrants frequently brought unsigned wag-on-the-wall clocks with them to Pennsylvania. As soon as they could afford to many of them had the clocks put into cases. All too frequently the dials then acquired names. Occasionally, these turn up at sales as genuine Pennsylvania tall clocks. Of course, Custer eventually adopted brass plates. He did a lot of experimenting with his striking mechanism; at least three completely different types were observed by that diligent researcher of Custer clocks, the late Samuel H. Barrington, who lived about two miles from the old Custer homestead. The clockmaker also used moon phase dials, which, for some reason, he would sometimes place at the bottom of the dial rather than at the time-honored top position in the lunette. At least one of his known clocks has an alarm attachment. In fact, unique features were the bench mark of his work, as evidenced by this description of one of his tall clocks examined by Barrington.

The weights are very light, the going weight five pounds, the striking weight four pounds. The strike train has but two wheels, plus an upright shaft with a revolving strike hammer in the form of a "T." One end of the "T" has a weight which hits the bell, the other end has a weight to counter-balance the striker. One arm of the "T" is straight and the other arm has a loop or half circle to contrive in it. This revolves as the clock strikes and the straight end climbs up an inclined plane and thereby hits the bell. The other end with the loop does not hit the bell, as the loop passes over the inclined plane, without elevating the weight on the end. The counting mechanism was totally different from anything I have ever seen. I shall try to describe its workings. The sum of one to twelve added, makes 78. The main wheel which carried the weight had 78 teeth. On the arbor which carries the hour hand is a wheel which is something like the well known snail, but the steps are reversed. The twelve being the high step, and the one the low, and between the steps are small notches. When the clock is ready to strike, (and there is no warning), the cam on the minute hand lifts the shifting piece out of the notch, and it slides down over the snail dropping into the nick at the far end, and an extension to the shifting piece extends out past the rim of the going wheel, and a pin in this piece drops into the space between the two teeth of the main wheel. As the clock strikes, the main wheel revolves, moving the shifting piece back up the snail till it falls in the nick it fell from. This allows a wire extending up to interfere with the revolving strike hammer; this stops the striking. At the next hour the shifting piece again slides down, this time one tooth farther, and so on. The clutch that moves when you turn the hands to set the clock is in the main wheel, which has two wheels mounted on the same arbor, and when you advance the clock to set it the weights drop as long as you keep turning the hands. The clock has the dead beat escapement, but no motion work behind the dials, as I explained the two wheels on the main arbor turn the two hands at different speeds.

It is conjectured that Custer, competing against Connecticut clock factories, made at least thirty shelf clocks, some of which were sold by his younger brother, Isaac, who had gone to live in St. Louis and work as a silversmith, and to presumably act as a selling agent for Jacob's clocks. His shelf clocks have such a unique form that they are usually described as the "Pennsylvania shelf clocks." With his ingenious mind and digital dexterity, he managed to make even shelf clocks different. Barrington owned one that had a moon in the dial and which relied on fourteen-pound lead weights to power it for eight days—an exact reversal of the four and five pounds found in the tall clock previously described. Having neither rack and snail nor count wheel, the main wheel that carried the weight had pins in it, which were spaced farther and farther apart as the number of strokes increased, the next pin raising the stop lever at the last number of the strokes. This clock also had an alarm.

According to Charles S. Crossman's *Complete History of Watch and Clock Making in America,* Jacob D. Custer was the third American maker of a serviceable watch, Luther Goddard being the first and Henry F. Pitkin the second. If Thomas Harland was also accepted as a maker, Custer would drop to fourth, but even that ranking would be noteworthy. It is believed that he made his watches between 1840 and 1845. For the time they were rather small—about two inches in overall diameter. He reputedly made all the parts of the movements except the hair spring and the fusee chain, and only the pallets were jewelled.

Custer's amazing versatility was by no means confined to horological activities. He invented the grease cup to force grease into bearings while in operation and he made many articles for the federal government during the Civil War, including Minié balls, which were mass-produced. The story persists that he made some castings for the U.S.S. *Monitor.* It has also been stated, though erroneously, that Custer invented and made specialized clockwork to revolve the beacons in lighthouses; this honor in fact goes to Simon and Benjamin (Jr.) Willard. What Custer did was apply and patent clock works with weights and maintaining power to successfully operate a fog signal bell. He supplied at least thirty-two, perhaps as many as one hundred, units to the United States Government. Custer finished out his remarkable career by devoting more time to the heavy machinery business and ultimately built a shop on Lafayette Street for erecting steam engines.

Pennsylvania Dutch Country

Fig. 110. Typical Feishtinger calendar clock. Unique location of day indicator is shown; also note small indicator for three normal and leap years. Private collection.

Berks County

Created from portions of Philadelphia, Lancaster, and Chester counties, Berks County was named for Berkshire, England, and was organized in 1752. Quakers, French Huguenots, Palatines, Germans, Amish, Mennonites, Dunkards, and Swedes settled in this rich agricultural area early in the eighteenth century. Their influence, characteristics, and customs still linger. Berks countian Thomas Rutter established the first forge in Pennsylvania in 1716. One may logically expect, therefore, to find in this land artisans of many varieties, and numerous clockmakers.

According to two sources, Henry Allebach advertised in 1829, in a German-language newspaper as a clockmaker in Reading. A fine regulator type clock by M.B. Allebach, dated 1881, is extant.

A Mr. Avise reportedly advertised as a clockmaker in Reading in 1827.

Every researcher of timepieces and their makers dreams of discovering a hitherto unlisted artist. Although very strong circumstantial evidence suggested the finding of such a person in Jacob Beilenman, working in Gabelsville around 1800 to 1810, further investigation of this man negated the evidence. The real maker in question was John Beideman, of Hamburg, circa 1800–20.

The story of Frederick Christopher Bischoff provides an interesting vignette on a trade ancillary to clockmaking. Born in Stadtilm, Germany, on February 18, 1771, he came to Reading in 1779. In January of 1803 he moved in with Benjamin Witman, a well-known maker of tall clocks, who as early as 1799 had begun the manufacture of clock dials. Witman claimed that his products were equal to the English imports. It seems that Bischoff painted the dials made by Witman. In April of 1806 Bischoff moved in with his in-laws, where he continued to paint and where he established himself as a clock dial maker. In later years he devoted himself to painting portraits and butterflies.

An earlier researcher of court house tax records states that Christian Bixler, Jr. was a clockmaker in Hamburg from 1785 to 1830. This does not agree, however, with what data is known about the prolific Bixler family whose jewelry store is still active in Easton, Pa. The first Christian Bixler (1710–62) in this country lived in Lancaster. The second Christian Bixler (1732–1811), although born in Lancaster, lived in Reading where, according to one respected author, he engaged in clockmaking between 1750 and 1790. Another respected author states that there is no record of any clockmaking, but that he engaged in various activities, including the operation of a clock store between 1760 and 1800. The third Christian Bixler (1763–1840) served an apprenticeship under John Keim in Reading, from whom he learned both clockmaking and silversmithing. It is likely that he continued as a journeyman, for account book records suggest he made about fifty tall clocks for Keim before moving to Easton in 1785 to establish his own business.

Henry Borneman apparently began making and repairing clocks in about 1840 in Boyertown; he continued this business until his death in 1890. Apparently he took his son, Joseph, on as an apprentice around 1850. It is difficult to believe that many hand-made clocks were produced at that late period.

According to one authority, Samuel Breneisen advertised as a clockmaker in the Reading *Weekly Adventurer* of May 21, 1799, before moving into Lancaster County. His brother (one authority calls George, another names William) seems to have made tall clocks in Womelsdorf around the turn of the century or a little later. It has been alleged that there was a Samuel, Jr. who was one of the last clock men in Reading, but it now appears unlikely that he ever worked anywhere but in Lancaster County.

Daniel Christ appears on the tax records from 1770 to 1820 as a clockmaker in Kutztown. Although it is difficult to refute written records, it does seem improbable that he had such a long, active career; conversely, there is little doubt that he was in business at the end of the eighteenth and the beginning of the nineteenth centuries. A clock bearing his name was sold in Berks County in 1976.

Jacob Diehl (1776–1858) was definitely a Reading clockmaker and may have been an apprentice to Daniel Rose. He operated Rose's shop from 1798 to 1804 while the owner served in the state legislature. Diehl advertised on November 27,

111

112

Fig. 111. Chippendale walnut, broken arch top with carved rosettes, unusual finials, and dentils over the arched door make this clock different from others. There are fluted quarter columns on the base and waist. The enameled dial is signed "Henry Hahn." Origin is Reading; movement #235 dates the clock circa 1803–4. Private collection.

Fig. 112. Dial and hood of a Benjamin Hill clock. Courtesy of Craig A. Newton, executive secretary and curator, Columbia County Historical Society.

1804 to indicate that he was operating independently. Examples of his work are known, and it is probable that he later moved to Bedford, Pennsylvania, because his clock #70 has that town's name painted on the dial. This move would have taken place after 1856 or 1857, when he was listed in the Reading directory as having a shop on Franklin Street between Fourth and Fifth.

John Dupuy, a clockmaker who advertised his Second Street shop in Philadelphia during the years 1769 to 1774, advertised himself in Reading in 1777. No other information can be found.

"Daniel Dyffer, Reading, Pennsylvania" appears on the dial of a clock which was probably made in about 1820. Confirming data, however, are thus far lacking.

The history of George Faber is controversial. It has been averred that he was making clocks in Sumneytown, Montgomery County before 1773, when he moved to Reading and then continued to work for several years. Though he may have been a native of Sumneytown, the reverse chronology may be closer to the truth. Daniel Rose, the eminent Reading clockmaker, was Faber's uncle, so it could be safely assumed that he learned his craft there and later returned to Sumneytown. That he conducted business there into the nineteenth century is confirmed by his clock #23, dated 1805.

Conrad Fasig (or Fesig; 1758?–1815) was at work in Reading in the late eighteenth and the early nineteenth centuries. Thus he is established as a member of the last group of notable clockmakers in the area. Clocks of his still exist.

George Fix is mentioned as a Reading clockmaker as early as 1802; it is quite likely that he worked well beyond that date and was a contemporary of Fasig's. Clocks of his also are extant. Joseph Fix, possibly a brother or son, advertised in the Reading *Adler* of March 10, 1829 that he had equipment to cut clock wheels and, indeed, at least one clock bearing his name is known. Joseph had a shop on Fourth Street between Washington and Walnut in 1856 and 1857.

Charles W. Feishtinger aided the clockmaking trade from 1894 to at least the middle of or perhaps the end of the first decade of the twentieth century. Working somewhere between Sinking Spring and Fritztown, Feishtinger made calendar mechanisms to fit up to various styles of Waterbury Victorian kitchen clocks with unmarked Waterbury eight-day time and strike movements. His patented mechanism featured individual adjustment of day, date, year, and month indexes, yet actuated as a unit in operation. The day was revealed through a slot in the base of the case, whereas all the other features were carried on the dial. Figure 110 shows a typical Feishtinger product.

Peter Gaillard advertised in the Reading *Zeitung* of April 23, 1794, that he had practiced the trade of clockmaking for many years in France. An advertisement of his from four years later is reported. He seems accepted as a clockmaker, although none of his products are known.

According to three references, Peter Gifft worked as a clockmaker in Kutztown, circa 1790–1820. A clock bearing his name was sold in Berks County in 1976.

Henry Hahn (1754–1843) advertised in the *Adler* of April 10, 1798. His era of productivity probably dated from 1790 to about 1820. He numbered his clocks, and dials of brass, pewter, iron, and white painted tin distinguished him with a bit of versatility. The Hahn clock displayed in figure 111 *is* distinctive. His shop was on Penn Street between Seventh and Eighth.

Benjamin Hill (d. 1809) operated a shop in Richmond Township. His productive period must have been roughly the last quarter of the eighteenth century, as a thirty-hour clock of his dated 1771 is known. He built the tower clock for the second courthouse in Reading; that he also produced handsome eight-day tall clocks is attested by figure 112.

The glass in the lower door of the case is a Victorian replacement, for the door was without doubt originally solid. Other timepieces of his are also reported, indicating he was a fairly active maker.

David Hollenbach worked, perhaps as an apprentice, for the well-known Daniel Oyster of Reading during the years 1822 to 1826. In August of 1826 he advertised that he had set up business for himself, an operation which continued until around 1840.

John Keim (1749–1819) was prominent in Reading city and Berks county affairs, as well as in clockmaking. His name first appeared as a clockmaker on the tax lists of 1779. The 1806 directory placed his shop on Penn Street between Sixth and Seventh. He evidently produced a goodly number of clocks. It is somewhat odd that his cases show such plain similarity while the dials are so vigorously engraved.

Some confusion surrounds John Klein. Earlier writers spelled his name Kline; they also represent him as a restless individual, ascribing him to Lancaster from 1790 to 1810, to Philadelphia from 1812 to 1820, and to Reading for the following ten years. A reputable source within the county, however, states that the name was Klein and that his place of business was in Amity Township, but declines to assess dates at work. Some of his clocks are extant.

Jacob Klingman (1758–1806) likewise poses a minor problem. His name appears on the 1784 tax list as a clockmaker, but he was certainly at work earlier, as the Women's Club of Reading owns a clock by him that is dated 1776. The oddity is

11?

Fig. 113. The exquisitely engraved silver dial of John Keim clock #137. Courtesy of Wesley G. Harding.

Fig. 114. Eight-day brass movement by Daniel Oyster, Reading, circa 1820. It has an American painted dial; the finials and feet are more modern replacements; and the door hinges are Victorian revival additions. It is certainly a desirable clock because of the beautiful case graining, the French beveled glass in the dial door, and the splendid hands. Private collection.

114

that this clock is signed by a Jacob Kling. Some earlier authorities suggest this was simply the way he signed his clocks. He moved to York and therefore will be discussed in the chapter on that county. His Reading shop was on Penn Street between Sixth and Seventh.

Practically nothing is known about Curtis Lewis (1769–1847) except that he was active in Reading and some of his clocks are in existence. His shop on Fifth Street, between Franklin and Chestnut, was possibly the former shop of Daniel Oyster.

The life of Timothy Lindsley (1791–1825) was extremely short. It seems to be agreed upon that he was at work in Reading as a clockmaker by 1815; that he advertised in the *Adler* on March 6, 1821; and that he continued to be active until his death.

Archibald Little advertised in the *Adler* issues of March 5, 1816 and April 20, 1819. He later moved to Camden, New Jersey, and finally to Philadelphia.

There is little available information about William Mears other than that he was a Reading clockmaker in 1785 and that a clock bearing his name with this date has been reported.

Jacob Mechlin, probably a French Huguenot, is said to have been a clockmaker in Alsace Township in 1759; if true, this would make him the second earliest such craftsman in the county.

Likewise, although none of his products are known, three sources maintain that the name of Abel Morris appears on the Reading tax list of 1774 as a clockmaker.

Daniel Oyster (1762–1845) is most certainly the best-known of the Reading clockmakers. The youngest child of Samuel Oyster, a blacksmith, who died when his son was only a year old, Daniel was raised by his uncle, Daniel Yoder. In 1792 he married Catharine Rose, a younger sister of clockmaker Daniel Rose. That same year he was first listed as a clockmaker. There is some reason to believe he may have plied the trade as early as 1779, which, in turn, suggests that he worked with Daniel Rose. Oyster's shop was on Fifth Street between Franklin and Chestnut. It has been determined that more of Oyster's clocks are extant today than of any other Berks County maker.

At the Sesqui-Centennial in Philadelphia in 1926, a Daniel Oyster clock, said to have been made for General Lafayette when he visited the United States in 1824 and 1825, was on display in the Pennsylvania Room. This beautiful clock has a medallion of Lafayette on the door. The timepiece in figure 114 attests to the handsome appearance of his clocks and the meticulous attention to detail—even to the use of expensive French beveled plate glass in the dial door.

Henry Roi was a clockmaker in Hamburg in the early nineteenth century. A clock signed by him was sold at an auction in Berks County in 1972. Because his last name was French for *king,* he sometimes indulged himself by signing his clocks "Henry King."

We have encountered Daniel Rose (1749–1827) twice, first in the section on Jacob Diehl and second in that on Daniel Oyster. Rose, a lieutenant in the War of Independence, was first listed as a Reading clockmaker in 1779. His best work was apparently performed during the balance of the century, for he became involved in public affairs. For example, he served for many years in the state legislature. His shop sat in a prominent location on Penn Street between Fourth and Fifth streets, now part of Penn Square. Two authors mention that Daniel Rose, Jr. was plying the trade from about 1820 to about 1837.

The clocks of Daniel Rose, Sr. are also fairly plentiful and some are quite unusual. The description of one proves this latter point: Its mahogany case is ninety-two inches tall, with rich relief carving, urn and flame finials, scrolled pediment with carved rosettes, and carved, open work ovate finial in the center with fluted freestanding columns and quarter round, column corners on the waist. The movement, as might be expected, is a brass, eight-day time and strike with moon phase, sweep second hand, and calendar which designates month, day, and date. The dial is brass and enamel, unusual in an American clock.

Charles Smith is described by three sources as a Reading clockmaker, possibly working during the 1810s and 1820s. At least one clock bearing his name is known.

Josiah Smith (1778–1860) is also accepted by authorities as a Reading clockmaker of about the same period. At least one clock of his also is known. In later years he may have moved to New York City.

Peter Snyder, Jr. was making clocks in Exeter Township in 1779 and later.

The numerous and remarkable Solliday family of clockmakers had at least one member who was a resident of and was at work in this county. John N. Solliday (1794–1881) advertised in the Reading *Postbothe* of September 7, 1816. Precisely when he started there is unknown, but in 1821 he moved to Bucks County. There does exist a shelf clock made by him that is estimated to have been produced in about 1815, quite early for Pennsylvania. The case measures 40 inches tall, 17¼ inches wide, and 7¾ inches deep. The movement is a brass, eight-day time and strike with a pendulum and crutch arrangement typical of Solliday. A finger of the crutch fits into a slit opening in the pendulum rod. The clock has the general characteristics of a pillar and scroll.[1] Attributed to Jacob Solliday, the timepiece may instead have been constructed by John N. Solliday.

Peter Spycker, Jr. merits two references as a clockmaker in Tulpehocken, circa 1784–1800.

Reading's earliest clockmaker, Valentine Urletig, arrived in Pennsylvania in 1754. His name first appeared on the tax lists in 1758; the records are murky as to whether he preceded Jacob Mechlin by a year, but that order seems to win the current consensus. He made the clock for the first courthouse in 1762. Of course his clocks have brass faces, many with moon phase and day of month features. He supposedly continued the trade until his death in 1783. Several of his clocks still exist.

Two authorities cite John Vanderslice as a Womelsdorf clockmaker in the early nineteenth century. A tall clock bearing his name appeared in the University of Pennsylvania Hospital Antique Show in April, 1975.

Henry Voight (1738–1814) presumably was a native of Reading. He was taxed as a clockmaker in 1780, but he also owned a wiremill. Soon thereafter he moved to Philadelphia and became the chief coiner of the United States Mint in about 1793; he was also associated with John Fitch in the development of the steamboat. One of his clocks sits in the Capitol at Washington, D.C. His son, Thomas, remained in Reading until about 1811, when he, too, moved to Philadelphia and made clocks. Whether he constructed any in Reading is unclear.

Thomas Wildbahn (1763–1805) was born in Winchester, Virginia and died in Philadelphia. He also lived in Reading, where he was listed as a clockmaker in 1789. He advertised in the *Adler* of May 9, 1797; his name also appeared in the 1799 directory. Many of his clocks had sweep second hands, as proven by existing examples. He was a charter member of the local Masonic lodge and served for awhile as a coroner.

Benjamin Witman (1774–1857) advertised his shop on Callowhill Street in the *Impartial Reading Herald* on July 6, 1796. One may assume that he was one of the last clockmakers in the county, but that might not have been true. An advertisement in 1799 mentioned him as a dial painter. The same year he began the manufacture of clock dials, continuing until at least 1804.

1. Lester Dworetsky and Robert Dickstein, *Horology Americana* (New York: Horology Americana, Inc., 1972), p. 108.

Anthony Zimmerman (1711–88) was taxed as a clockmaker in Reading as early as 1768. Although he lived another twenty years, nothing is known of his work.

Berks County in general, and Reading in particular, was an active clockmaking center. As indicated, handiwork of that area's craftsmen is still in existence. Occasionally, an exceptional clockmaker and cabinet- or casemaker of equal skill combined talents to produce a piece that was of museum quality. Such a timepiece is described as being Pennsylvania Dutch in character, having an unusually ornate case with a scroll top hood, the inner end of the scrolls finished with rosettes. The hood surface is covered with a leaf and flower pattern, and around the waist door is a vine design, inlaid with pigment instead of wood. The case corners are chamfered, and the quarter columns are also carved with a leaf and flower design. The wax-inlaid door (a Germanic feature) sports a floral design and the inscription, "Chr. Fahl 1801." The enamelled dial displays flowers, with an American eagle with a shield centered at the top. A calendar attachment is in a semi-circular slot. The maker of this masterpiece was Benjamin Witman.

In the mid-1750s Berkshire Furnace was put into operation about 1½ miles south of what is now Wernersville. The record books indicate that clock weights were among an extensive list of products.

Lancaster County*

Named for Lancashire, England, Lancaster County was formed from part of Chester County. Settled in 1709 by Mennonites, it was the fourth established county in the colony, thus making Lancaster the oldest inland town in America. Followed by half a dozen other European peoples, the population was a rich mixture of farmers and artisans. Elizabeth Furnace, Steigel glassware, clockmakers, Conestoga wagons, Pennsylvania (Kentucky) rifles, and, finally, watchmakers had their roots in these immigrant craftsmen.

It is fair to say that Lancaster was easily the most important watchmaking center in all of Pennsylvania. The checkered careers of the Lancaster watch enterprisers began in 1874, when John C. Adams, "The Great American Starter," appeared on the scene. Adams had previously been instrumental in starting six watchmaking firms. Early in that year, he conceived the idea of a watch factory in Lancaster; on April 23 he put out a prospectus soliciting $100,000 capital with which he would create a company capable of producing ten watches a day. Only $78,000 was subscribed, the

*In a survey of horological activities of all Pennsylvania counties, it would be a disservice to the reader to include a chapter that intended to reveal all the clockmakers of Lancaster County, as there is much more comprehensive information available. Consequently, this chapter is devoted solely to watchmaking. Those desiring the complete exposition, copiously illustrated, of clockmaking in this county are advised to read *Clockmakers of Lancaster County and Their Clocks 1750–1850* by Stacy B.C. Wood, Jr. and Stephen E. Kramer, III, with a *Study of Lancaster County Clock Cases* by John J. Snyder, Jr., published in 1977 by the Van Nostrand Reinhold Company.

largest subscribers being J.C. Adams, E.H. Perry, and E.J. Zahm. This deficit was the initial root of future difficulty.

On June 13 the company directors were elected, and they in turn appointed Zahm, a local retail jeweler, as president; John Best of Best's Engine and Boiler Company as vice president; Adams as secretary and general business manager; Perry as superintendent; and John B. Roth as treasurer. The budding enterprise was incorporated on September 26, 1874 as the Adams & Perry Watch Manufacturing Company. Best supplied one of his small buildings in which to set up machinery until the new factory was built. Many of the initial employees were stockholders, so the payroll very quickly exceeded that set forth in the prospectus, thus planting the second seed of future trouble. The company also agreed to pay Perry three dollars royalty per watch for the use of his patents. One, a design patent issued on April 11, 1871, covered the design of watch plates. The other, issued on May 30, 1871, provided an improved method of stem-setting.

C.A. Bitner, a local merchant and stockholder, donated three acres of land on the Columbia Turnpike a mile west of central Lancaster for the factory site. Work on the factory started in September. The center building was fifty feet square and three stories high; the east and west wings were each fifty by seventy-eight feet and two stories high, but these sections had basements. Again, the cost considerably exceeded the estimate. A dial house was added on the north side in 1879, and two years later another wing for offices was erected. These buildings subsequently became the nucleus of the great Hamilton Watch Company.

By the time the buildings were ready for occupancy in July of 1875, dissension had begun. Adams had planned to make ten very fine watches a day of three grades. Escapements, hair-springs, and such materials were to be imported. Perry disagreed, proposing that all parts be made at home, so to speak. The acceptance of this latter plan resulted in Adams's resignation. Perry took over as general manager and Bitner became secretary.

Foremen for the various departments were hired away from other watch factories. Additional capital was needed, so a $25,000 bond issue was floated, secured by real estate and machinery. The sale was unsuccessful, and by February of 1876, Abram Bitner acquired the bonds through a negotiated deal. Still, there was a pressing need for even more capital, but none was forthcoming.

On April 7, 1876, the first watch was reportedly finished on a rush basis. It was a 19-size, using Perry's patent stem-setting device. The variation from the standard 18-size was a deliberate attempt to compel a dealer to also buy a case with every movement, as this was the era when movements and cases were customarily sold separately. The appearance of this lone watch was insufficient to restore the company's glow. Employees were asked to forego pay days, and the situation climaxed on May 16 when the company closed its doors with liabilities amounting to $44,000.

At a stockholders' meeting, certain alleviating resolutions were passed; a new board of directors was elected, who, in turn, appointed new officers. No new money being available, an assignment was made to C.A. Bitner. Not long afterwards, a public sale was held and the assets were bought by Dr. H. Carpenter for a syndicate for $47,000, subject to two mortgages totaling $30,000 held by the two Bitners. It was reoffered for sale, but no buyer came forward. One year went by before Mr. W.N. Todd, formerly with the Elgin National Watch Company, came to examine the buildings, machinery, movements in process, and material in hand. He concluded that with $20,000 he could finish and put on the market the approximately 800 movements, some of which were financially encumbered.

Abram Bitner (b. 1836) was a dominant figure in both the first and second watchmaking firms of Lancaster County. His first job was with Bitner & Brother in the freighting business between Lancaster and Philadelphia. Following a stint in the grain business, he tried the coal trade in 1865. Next he bought 136 acres of land along the New Jersey coast, and organized and became superintendent to the Ocean Beach Association; at the same time he held an interest in the New Egypt & Farmingdale Railroad. Bitner returned to Lancaster in 1877 and was involved in the clothing business until 1879, when he became connected with the Lancaster Watch Company.

Relying on Todd's estimate, the Lancaster, Pennsylvania Watch Company was formed in August 1877, from members of the past syndicate. Work commenced on September 1, 1877, funded by $21,000 of new capital added to the $47,000 paid in a previous year. Abram Bitner was general manager and Todd served as superintendent. It was found that much of the machinery was rusty and/or out of repair, so the overhauling of the machine shop was begun by a staff of fifteen men. Production was therefore abated. Todd, unable to fulfill his contract, was succeeded in January of 1878 by C.S. Mosely, but he remained to assist in the creation of models of a new movement. The movement that this team designed was to be sold as cheaply as possible. It had a solid top three-quarter plate and a pillar plate, and was full ruby jeweled, made in both gilt and nickel, with a new stem winding device invented by Mosely and Todd. Only a few of the old Adams & Perry movements were eventually finished because the machinery was attuned to produce the new movements. Some-

115a

115b

115c

115d

115e

116a

116b

116c

116d

116e

117a

117b

117c

117d

117e

Fig. 115. a) New Era model, Lancaster, Pennsylvania, with patent pinion. Planned by the Lancaster, Pennsylvania Watch Company, Ltd. b) Comet model, Lancaster, Pennsylvania, made by the Lancaster Watch Company. c) Paoli model, Lancaster, Pennsylvania, with patent pinion, Patent Dust Proof cover, presumably mica, over exposed rim of balance wheel. Has a Keystone Watch Company dial. d) Elberon model, Lancaster, Pennsylvania, with patent pinion and Patent Dust Proof. Made by Lancaster Watch Company. e) Malvern model, Lancaster, Pennsylvania, with patent pinion, adjusted, and Patent Dust Proof (mica). The plate layout and engraving is so similar to Elberon as to make it almost certainly a product of the Lancaster Watch Company.

Fig. 116. a) The Lancaster model. This may have been planned by the Lancaster, Pennsylvania Watch Company, Ltd. b) West End model, Lancaster, Pennsylvania. The movement is so similar to the Comet's as to presume it was made by the Lancaster Watch Company. It has an unusual, cream-colored celluloid dial with the imprint of the front of a steam locomotive inside a Keystone frame. Even the hands incorporate the Keystone. c) Denver model, Lancaster, Pennsylvania, with patent pinion and Patent Dust Proof. The movement is so similar to Elberon as to make it almost certainly a product of the Lancaster Watch Company. d) Wm. Penn model, Lancaster, Pennsylvania, with patent pinion, adjusted, and Patent Dust Proof—in this instance all metal. This was introduced in 1882 by the Lancaster Watch Company. e) Record model, Lancaster, Pennsylvania. The evidence points to the Lancaster Watch Company as maker.

Fig. 117. a) Melrose model, Lancaster, Pennsylvania, with patent pinion and adjusted. Made by the Lancaster Watch Company. b) Fulton model, Lancaster, Pennsylvania, with patent safety pinion and adjusted. Made by the Lancaster Watch Company. c) Plate is simply engraved "LANCASTER WATCH, Penna." It is really Adams & Perry's #2041, a pioneer model in the saga of watches made in Lancaster. Note the peculiar regulator spring. This model came on the market in 1876. d) Also an Adams & Perry, #2077. This one does not have the same regulator. e) Franklin model, Lancaster, Pennsylvania, with patent pinion. Made by the Lancaster Watch Company. Private collection.

how, despite encumbrances, the bulk of the old movements found their way to the scrap bin.

By February there were forty-five employees, and June employment increased to sixty-three. On September 7 the capital stock was increased, but none was purchased, so the doors were closed on the last of September. The two Bitners once more offered to capitalize their $25,000 mortgage bonds, provided that outside capital of $10,000 was obtained. Despite local newspaper assistance, only $7,000 was raised. Abram Bitner contributed the remaining sum.

The company reorganized on October 31, 1878 as the Lancaster, Pennsylvania Watch Company, Ltd., with actual capitalization of only $105,000. Of course, both Bitners were directors, Abram became the general manager. To date only 100 to 150 movements of a grade called the Lancaster Watch, Pennsylvania, had been produced but a new series was planned. They were to be top quality stem wind, ¾ plate, 3 pillar, with a single roller rather than two. This stem wind was a C.S. Mosely design, with a tilting set bar with stem to pull out. The models were named "New Era," "West End," and "Lancaster, Pa." By February 1879, work on the old movements had ceased, except when called for. Before the new movements were ready for sale, however, the company again ran out of funds. In April the directors attempted to borrow $20,000, but had no success. On May 9, 1879, a new company (the fourth) was formed, called, simply, the Lancaster Watch Company.

Instead of buying, the new company leased for not less than three and not more than five years, agreeing to: pay six percent interest on $80,000 capital, interest on $50,000 real estate, and taxes and insurance; keep machinery in good repair; and purchase new machinery as needed, reducing payments accordingly. Again both Bitners were stockholders and Abram was manager. The new movement was pushed to production for shipment by August. It was still a 19-size, but a change in both marketing philosophy and supply policy dictated a reduction to 18-size to fit the Howard cases. It was decided to furnish this movement in four grades, known as the "Keystone," the "Fulton," the "Franklin," and the "Melrose." Other grades were added later, and the watches were finished daily by 125 employees. Any present-day factory manager would instantly recognize the unprofitable ratio, and sure enough, the funds ran out again. At another of the recurrent emergency meetings it was reported that a total of 334 movements had been finished, 220 of which were the Keystone grade.

As a palliative, new partners with additional cash were admitted. A second series was started, consisting of three movements in which the yolk was fastened to a plate with screws. A smooth year passed and by October 1880, 1,250 movements had been completed and the monthly payroll had reached $6,700. In fact, in January, 1881, the capital was doubled. Simultaneously, the Lancaster Watch Company paid off the $25,000 mortgage of the Lancaster, Pennsylvania Watch Company (the second company) and bonded the property for $50,000. In June Mosely resigned as superintendent and was succeeded by Russell Lyle.

During 1880, an average of forty movements per day were turned out by 175 employees. The next year the same number of employees pushed the output up to sixty movements daily. That autumn a new series was planned. These had the yolk fastened in the regular way (in the center with a screw), had intermediate winding and set wheels, and were lever set. This third series was ready to market by May, 1882. Production rose to seventy-five per day that year; moreover, a new grade called "Lancaster, Pa." was marketed. It was high grade with cap-jeweled escapement having end stones, gold settings, expansion balance, and Breguet hairspring. It was offered in both nickel and gilt finish, and about two hundred were made. Truly, 1882 was a vintage year, for the "Delaware" was added to the line. It also was offered in both gilt and nickel, and boasted a patented dust-proof cover over the escapement. The "William Penn" was the final model started that year.

This burst of activity was compensated for in 1883, when five grades of ladies' 8-size movements were started, but only between fifty and seventy-five were finished. Including these ladies' movements, some thirty varieties of watches were offered, which, again, a modern manager would recognize as too many for a relatively small factory. As of April 1, 1883, the Lancaster Watch Company surrendered its leases from the Lancaster, Pennsylvania Watch Company, Ltd., and the two consolidated, making, technically, the fifth in the series. This time a capitalization of $248,000 was shown; the same officers remained and both Bitners stayed on the Board of Directors. The factory had been closed for two weeks during the consolidation, but it reopened on April 16; on May 15 it closed due to some difficulty with several foremen over pay during these two weeks. The matter was settled and work started again on May 21. Abram Bitner took a leave of absence. On July 31 the factory again closed, leaving several thousand movements in various stages of completion. The foremen and others came forward with the proposition of investing a portion of their wages to keep operators going. Accordingly, the factory opened again in mid-August, but after one month the proposition disintegrated, forcing the directors to borrow $25,000 on a bank note. By year's end 8,900 movements had been completed.

In February 1884, Abram Bitner forced the appointment of a committee to investigate the company's affairs because its debt had climbed to around $100,000. Bitner offered to take over all the stock in exchange for assuming the indebtedness. The larger stockholders agreed, and he secured additional stock by paying ten cents on the dollar. Soon he owned 5,625 of the 8,000 outstanding shares. New directors and officers were elected, and Abram Bitner was made secretary-treasurer. Fortunately, during this fitful, torturous period, the watches that did reach the consumer were recognized as being of superior quality.

In 1886 an entirely new company of well-to-do Lancaster men organized the Keystone Watch Company. This sixth company had a fully paid capital of a half-million dollars, so it bought outright all of the existing plant and its real estate. Foolishly, they lowered the quality of the watches and, according to John J. Bowman, adopted various unorthodox marketing practices that placed Lancaster watches in poor repute with the regular watch trade. In his *Complete History of Watch Making in America,* Charles S. Crossman stated that Bitner, still superintendent, contracted with Oppenheimer Brothers & Veith of New York to take all the watches produced. Apparently the arrangement survived the change to Keystone, and the "new" company continued to move a considerable part of their production through the New York firm. Any surplus was sold directly to the consumer by various methods. Henry G. Abbott claimed in *The Watch Factories of America,* however, that the entire output was sold to Atkinson Brothers of Philadelphia, who, in turn, sold chiefly to the jobbing trade. In any event, many models were produced. The trade hostility put Keystone into bankruptcy by 1890, and the assets were sold at a sheriff's sale in 1892 to a group of Lancasterites who, in that same year, bought the Aurora Watch Company of Aurora, Illinois. This firm had also floundered into bankruptcy. The stage was now set for the creation of lucky number seven in this corporate parade that spanned only eighteen years.

The Hamilton Watch Company began operations on June 15, 1892, and continued running for over three quarters of a century. Named for the famous Philadelphia lawyer, Andrew Hamilton, who was responsible for the formal founding of Lancaster in 1730, the company employed the best of the Keystone and Aurora equipment. A combination of circumstances predestined success: capable people were in charge; the capitalization was adequate; and, though standard time had been established almost a decade before, serious railroad accidents had occurred which were traced directly to inaccurate timepieces. Adverse publicity forced the railroads to adopt official inspection services, which required all employees in charge of train operations to

118a

118b

119

carry watches of approved quality and which demanded periodic watch inspection and certifications.

Consequently, Hamilton's first watch, designed by Henry J. Cain, was an improved 936 grade, 18-size timepiece, which could meet the new railroad specifications. This watch, with a 17 jeweled, open face, full-plate, nickel finish movement, adjusted to temperature and positions and had a patent regulator, a Breguet hairspring, and a double-sunk dial. Grade 937 was identical, except it was in a hunting case. This watch soon became a favorite, and increasing demand quickly established a sound basis for a profitable business.

At the turn of the century, Hamilton produced the favorite watch for the ever-increasing number of railroad employees. From letters of praise, the company coined two pre-eminent advertising slogans: "Hamilton, the Railroad Timekeeper of America" and "Hamilton, the Watch of Railroad Accuracy." The advertisements appeared in prestigious magazines, such as the National Geographic. Number 936 was modified in 1898 and 1899 to become the famous #940. This phenomenally successful "Railroad Timekeeper of America" was still being advertised as late as 1912 in terms as superlative as any that Madison Avenue has coined in latter years.

From 1893 to 1928, fourteen grades of 18-size, open face and twelve grades in hunting cases, ranging from fifteen to twenty-three jewels, were offered. All were lever-set, fitted with three footed dials, and almost all were sold uncased, so the buyer could select any standard case.

In the infancy of the twentieth century, the line of railroad watches was supplemented by a line of fine, smaller dress watches for men. The buying power of women was recognized in 1908 by the introduction of 0-size pendant and wrist watches. The management laid great stress on its fine automatic machinery, superlatively trained artisans, and rigid inspection. Reportedly, a Hamilton pocket watch was used continuously for twenty-five years without a cleaning or oiling, after which it was returned to the factory and found to have sustained only normal wear and to be still keeping time within acceptable limits.

Eventually the 18-size railroad was succeeded by an even finer, smaller 16-size model. By 1912 men's dress pocket watches were reduced to a thin 12-size, soon followed by a small 6/0-size wrist watch for women. After World War I, this movement was cased in wrist watches for men; the returning veterans created a demand that overcame the general prejudice against these "sissy" timepieces.

From 1928 to 1940, public tastes dictated the marketing of smaller watches, still with the same rugged dependability and accuracy. The sizes of ladies' watches were

Fig. 118. a) This photograph illustrates the vicissitudes of the horological researcher. The watch dial is marked "New Era" and the plate is engraved "New Era, U.S.A.," though it is in a Keystone Watch case. New Era was a model name used by two of the Lancaster firms, so it is a Lancaster watch, not a product of the New York Standard Watch Company, which also used the name. b) The dial of the movement is marked "K.W. Co." and its plate engraved "Lancaster, PA.," so this was made by the Keystone Watch Company between 1886 and 1892.

Fig. 119. This is clearly a product of the Keystone Watch Company, probably from about 1890. Like the West End (figure 116b), it has the unusual cream-colored celluloid dial with the imprint of the front of a steam locomotive inside a keystone frame. These two watches may represent the earliest application of this material to watch dials.

also reduced, to 18/0, 21/0, and 22/0. Male customers also demanded thinner and smaller dress pocket and service wrist watches, so the 10 and 14/0 sizes were marketed. Hamilton joined forces in 1928 with Sangamo Electric Company of Springfield, Illinois, to form the Hamilton-Sangamo Corporation for the manufacture and sale of fine electric clocks. This operation was sold in 1931 to General Time Instruments, Inc.

From 1910 through 1942, Hamilton made approximately 57,000 watches of grade #999 for Webb C. Ball of Cleveland, Ohio, all 21 jewel or 23 jewel. In 1939, 1940, and 1941, Hamilton made nearly 3,700 watches of grade #998 for Ball. All these can be identified by a "B" preceding the serial number.

During the same time span, several technical developments put Hamilton in a position to meet the demands of the war that was nearing. A time microscope was invented, which reduced the final timing adjustment period from weeks to minutes. Elinvar hairsprings, which significantly reduced errors resulting from temperature variations, magnetism, and rust, were introduced into the railroad watches. By the time World War II exploded Hamilton had prepared for all watches, except for the very smallest, an improved hairspring alloy called Elinvar-Extra. These hairsprings were fabricated entirely within the Hamilton factory—from raw material to ingot, to rod, to wire, to hairspring.

During America's participation in the Great War, Hamilton standard watches were used by the A.E.F., and special navigational watches were produced for the U.S. Navy. Hamiltons were the official watches for many businesses and activities, such as the first domestic airmail service inaugurated on May 15, 1918, between New York and Washington; they were also used by such airlines as Transcontinental & Western, United, Eastern, and Northwest. Unofficially, Hamiltons were used for a myriad of important events, such as polar expeditions, transoceanic flights, stratosphere balloon flights, ocean voyages, and African explorations; it is documented that they performed unfailingly. Countless hundreds of watches were presented to heroes, outstanding public officials, and champion athletes. Important personages, such as King Albert of Belgium, eagerly bought them.

In 1923 Hamilton bought the Illinois Watch Company of Springfield, Illinois, which it operated until 1937. In 1931 the firm obtained the rights to the name "Howard," formerly the trademark of the famous E. Howard Watch Company. The watch movement and case industries had been plagued occasionally over a period of many decades by attempts to upset orderly marketing practices. From its outset, Hamilton had been most ethical in this respect. The Great Depression, however, fos-

120a

120b

120c

120d

121a

121b

121c

121d

Fig. 120. a) Hamilton, Ezra F. Bowman model. b) Hamilton, The Union model. c) Hamilton, Electric Railway Special. d) Hamilton, 940 model.

Fig. 121. a) Hamilton, 974 model, adjusted, 17 j., circa 1917. b) Hamilton, Ezra F. Bowman with full plate and safety pinion, circa 1894. c) Hamilton, 940 model, adjusted, safety pinion, 21 j., circa 1898—the first famous railroad watch. d) Hamilton, The Union, full plate, safety pinion, unusual regulator control, circa 1896.

tered a host of new evils. Characteristically, Hamilton met these new cutthroat pricing practices with a new, even more ethical distribution plan. Its list of distributors was reduced to thirty-nine financially stable firms, and the country was divided into twenty-one sales zones, thus reducing competition. The plan was highly successful; the trade greeted it as a great contribution to orderly merchandising. Thus, marketing quality went apace with product quality. Many factory improvements and additions were made.

War brought a drastic change to the venerable old Columbia Pike institution. Modern warfare demands all sorts of devices from the watch and clock trades, and in mind boggling quantities. The U.S. Navy had depended upon European sources for fine handmade chronometers for navigation. Very quickly their supplies were depleted, and, subsequently, the enemy denied us some sources. Hamilton was asked to perform the impossible—to design a chronometer that could be mass-produced, and then to prove it in the doing. The first mass-produced chronometers in the world were therefore produced in Lancaster. Toward the end of the war, more were finished per month than were produced in any prewar year, in the world. These instruments were so accurate that the testing procedures at the Naval Observatory were inadequate, so Hamilton had to invent and build the equipment to measure deviation down to $\frac{1}{100}$th of a second per day.

Other war products included fine navigational timepieces, time fuzees, many types of service watches, navigational instruments, and a miscellany of highly specialized timing instruments.

Reconversion to peacetime production was accomplished in 1947, with nine laboratories set for applied research and problem solving. Improved spring-driven men's wrist watches were marketed before the end of the decade.

Hamilton was indeed the only American watch factory that manufactured high-grade products exclusively since its inception.

Ezra F. Bowman (1847–1901) exhibited from boyhood a decided inclination toward mechanics. His father recognized the wastefulness of the apprentice system, whereby the apprentice received about two years of instruction and gave to the preceptor two or more years of routine labor. He calculated that the student who paid for his instruction would become a wage-earning journeyman sufficiently sooner. Therefore, after Ezra received his primary education from a local school, his father employed a European master watchmaker to teach his son. This had a profound effect on Ezra's future vocation.

Upon completion of this training, Ezra worked for H.Z. Rhodes & Brothers in

Lancaster, where he acquired a reputation for his mechanical skill. When the Adams & Perry Watch Manufacturing Company began operations, Bowman transferred in, and being assigned to the model department, he worked on the first model made by them. When financial difficulties loomed, Bowman was one of those employees who agreed to forego his pay in the belief that he was helping a new local enterprise stay alive.

In 1877 Ezra opened a jewelry store at 106 East King Street, which specialized in the sale and repair of watches and clocks. The prosperous shop moved such large quantities of merchandise that Bowman was accorded a jobber's discount. Smaller retail shops soon fell into the habit of picking up their needs from him, rather than ordering farther afield and waiting for delivery. Thus, Bowman "backed" into the wholesale business; he moved into larger quarters in May, 1882, and adopted a new set of marketing rules: "Positively no goods sold at retail; no goods sold to peddlers; price lists sent to regular jewelers only." The shop's growth continued and, as usual, additional capital was needed, so Bowman took Willis B. Musser, his brother-in-law, as his partner. On January 1, 1883, the firm of Bowman & Musser came into being; it continued until 1894, when Musser took a position with the Trenton Watch Company. The Non-Retailing Company was created to absorb the watch and chain departments. Ezra retained the tool, material, and trade repairing departments under the name of Ezra F. Bowman & Company.

Fig. 122. Ezra F. Bowman pocket watch in a gold hunting case.

Bowman had always dreamed of producing a high-grade domestic pocket watch to equal any offered in Europe. In the fall of 1879, he ordered a small group of watchmaking equipment from Hart & Sloan of Newark, New Jersey. Most of it came from the defunct United States Watch Company. He set up this equipment on the floor above his jewelry business, proposing to create watches in modest quantities. In January of 1880, he hired W.H. Todd, the former superintendent of the Lancaster Watch Company. Todd immediately proceeded with the production of a prototype watch and of small tools that had not been purchased. Only five artisans were employed, but by early 1882 they had ready thirty-odd watches and others were in process—altogether, about fifty watches were planned. At least forty-nine reached the market.

Except for the balance and the dial, the whole movement was made on the premises. They were all 16-size, nickel finish, stem wind, fully jeweled, and ¾ plate—well finished and handsome.

Small scale, almost custom, manufacturing, resulted in a high cost with little margin for Bowman. His dream was easily realized, but not on a competitive economic basis. Americans were not yet ready to pay $125 for a domestic watch. The pragmatic Bowman therefore decided that the watch business should be stopped so his entire time and talent could be directed to his wholesale business, which was expanding rapidly.

In the summer a sale was made to J.P. Stevens of Atlanta, Georgia. For some time, Stevens had been buying movements, primarily Hampdens, then finishing and fitting them with a special regulator of his own design. He now organized a new firm called J.P. Stevens Watch Company and chose Todd as his superintendent. Todd again designed the prototype, which closely resembled the Bowman watch with the Stevens regulator. This firm folded in 1887, and the machinery was dispersed for the third time.

Todd was a great specialist on hairsprings, especially in the hardening and tempering of them. Certainly this talent contributed to the excellent time-keeping abilities of the Bowman and Stevens watches, thereby fostering the tradition of technical progress at the other series of firms which, years later, induced Hamilton to adopt Elinvar.

In 1887, at the suggestion of friends in the trade and because of his own youthful training, Bowman opened the Ezra F. Bowman Technical School to teach watchmaking, jewelry manufacturing, repairing, and engraving. An immediate success, it soon became one of the outstanding schools of its kind in the country.

With the departure of Musser, the burden of the thriving business and the school operation was too much for Bowman, so in 1896 he put the business in the hands of a liquidator to insure full justice to his creditors while he concentrated on the school. Affairs were settled by 1899, and he began in the retail jewelry business. Unfortunately, this operation was not firmly established by the time of his early death in 1901.

Bowman's two sons had been thoroughly trained to continue the business, John conducting the school and Charles operating the store. Their management was indeed successful. During the period of the two World Wars, enrollment at the school grew to about 125 students. Although John died in 1959 and Charles in 1964, the entire operation continues to be a viable and venerable institution at Duke and Chestnut streets, under the ownership of E.H. Parkhurst.

The last of the Lancaster watchmaking firms was pioneered by another rugged individual, William W. Dudley. Born in 1851 in St. John, New Brunswick, he began his career at the early age of thirteen as an apprentice to a Canadian marine chronometer-maker. Eventually he migrated to Waltham, Massachusetts, to become a

Fig. 123. Movement of Ezra F. Bowman pocket watch #41.

model-maker at the Waltham Watch factory. As it was with many of his colleagues, Dudley made frequent moves, working variously for the Illinois, the South Bend, and the Trenton watch companies; finally, he served as designer and superintendent for Hamilton from 1906 to 1920. Dudley retired at age 69 to found his own watch company.

He had always had an enormous interest in Free Masonry, and despite his peregrinations, he belonged to many of the various organizations within that over-all body. Combining his two loves, he apparently tinkered with designs of watches having or composed of Masonic symbols. In 1918 he started serious work on a prototype with bridge plates in the form of Masonic symbols. By June of 1923 he had received a design patent for his creation, which called for the center wheel bridge to be a crescent with star and scimitar, although production models used the square and compass framing the letter *G*.

Considering how many tens of thousands of Masons there are in the world, sales prospects for a Masonic watch seemed grand. It is not surprising, then, that two local jewelers, George Adams and John Wood, joined forces with Dudley in June, 1920, to incorporate the Dudley Watch Company, with Wood as president, Adams as secretary and treasurer, and Dudley as vice president and superintendent. Property was bought at South West End and Maple Avenues and a 10,000-square-foot building of 2½ stories was erected.

The company's power train and escapement was purchased from Waltham. Cases were bought from Wadsworth, Keystone, and Star; they were gold or gold-filled, faced with either a solid or glass back. Dials and hands matching Dudley's specifications came from Switzerland. At first the jewels were burnished into their settings by hand, but later they were made by Vallorbs, a local jewel manufacturer; by 1925 even this was subcontracted to a Swiss firm for cost savings. In general, the winding and setting power control mechanism and the Masonic symbol plates were made in the factory. At full production, eighteen to twenty men were employed, and most were ex-Hamilton men who were also Masons.

In 1922 the first 14-size, 19 jewel watches were ready to market, at prices ranging from $125 to $250. A salesman named Bostwick was sent out to market them. His first trip seemed to betoken success, as he sold directly to retailers, most of whom put a few in stock. Unfortunately, on his second trip Bostwick found most of these still in the stocks because men were starting to favor wrist watches. In 1923 Dudley attempted to counter this by designing and then offering a smaller 12-size, 19 jewel model, chiefly using Swiss parts. These were somewhat more successful, but, still,

Fig. 124. Dial of open face Dudley Masonic watch.

Fig. 126. The beauty of this Sheraton style mahogany and cherry clock by Cooper reflects the judicious use of decoration which results in an attractive and finely balanced piece of furniture. The clean moon phase dial features beautiful floral spandrels. The center arbor carries hour, minute, sweep second, and date hands. The finials are nicely balanced; below the center finial are acanthus leaf carvings, used in ancient times atop columns by the Greek and Romans. The carved rosettes on the arch scrolls are cleverly balanced by the turned feet. Courtesy of the Fred F. Groff Funeral Home.

Fig. 127. Note the change in the center finial and the subsidiary dials for seconds and date. Courtesy of Douglas Doughty.

Fig. 128. Note the four finials, the extra carving, different spandrels, and a grain-painted case. Courtesy of Douglas Doughty.

127

128

No less than three historians have outlined briefly the career of peripatetic John Esterlie (b. 1778), who was born near Shamokin. He first practiced his trade in Lebanon, but moved to New Holland in Lancaster County in about 1812. Although he moved back to Lebanon, he eventually stayed in New Holland, where he remained in business until his retirement in about 1830.

Jacob Goodhart (also Guthard, Gudhart) came from Reading, Berks County, and succeeded Jacob Graff as clockmaker. When Lebanon was organized as a county, Goodhart was appointed a justice of the peace and was one of three assemblymen elected. He served three terms in the state legislature, until 1818. When Lebanon was incorporated as a borough in 1821, he was chosen to serve as chief burgess at the princely salary of $5 per year. From 1826 to 1829 he was county treasurer, and in 1840 and again in 1846 he was recommissioned as a justice of the peace. Despite all these civic duties, he found time to make clocks, for there are still many of his clocks in the vicinity.

Possibly the earliest clockmaker in Lebanon was Jacob Graf, as there is extant a clock marked "1735—Jacob Graf." That he was listed as a clockmaker on the list of 1750 taxables is significant because such artisans at that time were usually called "watch makers"—erroneously, of course, by our standards. He might eventually have moved to Lancaster, as one reliable source places a Jacob Graff there as a clockmaker in about 1775.

Philip Maus is recorded as a maker of tall clocks, several of which are known. It is believed that his #44 was made in about 1800.

Emanuel Meily (Meyli, Milay) is dated by different sources at different times—he appears to have worked in the early decades of the 1800s. While his name is seen upon many clocks originating in Lebanon, very little is known about him, other than that he was evidently a dealer who traded many items besides clocks. Clocks are also extant whose dials appear to be signed "Emanuel Weily." It is likely that the lettering on all these clocks is in German-style script, rendering it very difficult to discern "M" from "W." There is also a suggestion of a Samuel Meyli (also Meily, Milay) working around 1800 to 1810, although he is listed on the tax records as early as 1769 as a clockmaker. There is a strong suspicion that these two men were one and the same.

Clockmaking continued in this county into the twentieth century in the person of Reverend Harry E. Miller (1873–1947). Born in Schuylkill County, as a boy he worked in the coal fields. At fourteen he came to Lebanon to apprentice at the Lebanon Manufacturing Company. After graduation from college and seminary, he became pastor of the Salem United Brethren Church in Lebanon. Apparently, at an early age he was interested in tall case clocks, and he did a lot of repairing. When he wanted one for himself and could not acquire it, he built one. Therefore, clockmaking was started as an avocation. His clocks were well made, so his reputation spread and he always had plenty of orders. Supposedly, up until 1942 he built 394 tall clocks; these found their way all over the United States.

Indeed, he was unique in both clerical and horological annals.

Gustavus Stoy (1777?–1816), probably born in Lebanon, made clocks there from 1795 to 1805, when he moved to Lancaster. He became an innkeeper in that town, but continued his clockmaking and, apparently, watch repairing, as the inventory of his estate included "1 set of watchmakers tools," valued at $150. He served briefly in the War of 1812.

That Stoy was a craftsman who did not construct exclusively tall clocks was proven by the appearance at the National Association of Watch and Clock Collectors Convention in June, 1973, of a square bracket clock, with balance wheel escapement and rack lever striking mechanism, which was signed "Gustavus Stoy Lebanon."

From April 1969 to August 1970, a series of articles ran in the Lebanon *Daily News* entitled "Lebanon County Antiques." In this history of the county as seen through its artifacts, ten men were mentioned as clockmakers. Seven of these men have already been mentioned. Interestingly, the articles placed Emanuel Meily in Meyerstown rather than in Lebanon. Three new names appeared: Andrew Robb, a jeweler, circa 1820; Joseph Drayer, circa 1820; and Peter Spyker (Spycker), of Williamsburg (now Jonestown), working before 1771. As of April 1974 at least one clock bearing the name of each of these men exists in the Lebanon area. These clocks do not necessarily prove that each man was a maker; indeed, nothing seems to be known about Drayer, and Robb may have handled clocks made by others but bearing his name. The case for Spyker is strengthened by two other sources listing him as a clockmaker in Tulpehocken around 1784 to 1800.

Lehigh County

Named for the Lehigh River, Lehigh County was formed from part of Northampton County. Swiss and German settlers came in as early as 1715, and the county was organized in 1812. Horological research is rendered difficult in this area for two reasons. First, the chief city was originally called Northampton, but later changed to Allentown to honor Chief Justice William Allen of Pennsylvania. Sometimes, then, when an artisan's place is given simply as Northampton, it is hard to decide if the community or the neighboring county is meant. Second, the boundary between Lehigh and Northampton counties passes through Bethlehem, making it almost impossible to say in which county a clockmaker working after 1812 actually was.

Jacob Bishop's name appears on the 1789 tax list for Salisbury Township. In about 1810 he evidently moved into Allentown, for a J. Bishop is recorded there as the builder of tall clocks. Indeed, a splendid tall clock exists; it is both signed and dated, and the face bears a unique two line inscription: J. Bishop/Allentown, Northampton. On the back of the dial is the date 1794. This is a singular example of a clock signed with both names of his communities.

Another documented maker is Jacob Blumer (1774–1830), born in Whitehall Township. Although his name is on the Salisbury Township tax records of 1798 to 1807, he, too, gravitated to Allentown. His clock producing years are generally agreed to be about 1798 to 1820, with time out to serve as lieutenant of the "Northampton Blues" in the War of 1812. He apparently took a partner, Joseph Graff, for part or all of 1799. It may be assumed that he was a complete craftsman, capable of producing a whole clock, for it is recorded that he "worked all week and finished completely 30-hour clock which was $16 clear to me."

Blumer was well educated; however, because he was more mechanically inclined, he embraced clockmaking. His products are highly prized. He served as town clerk from 1812 to 1829, and died at a relatively early age.

Although there is one reference to John Ealer in the town of Northampton in the early 1800s, there is nothing to substantiate this. Another authority indicates that the name should be Baler.

While Jacob Geiger was listed on the tax records of Salisbury Township from 1770 to 1789, it is generally agreed that he was also in Northampton from 1787 to 1790, making tall clocks before moving to Maryland after 1793. That Geiger made superb clocks is attested by a piece that sold at an auction in May, 1977. This walnut Chippendale tall clock with a brass movement is housed in a case featuring ogee feet, fluted corners to the hood, an arched panel door with brass escutcheon, and a scroll top hood with rosettes and finials. The signed arched brass dial has a second hand and calendar, and four brass dolphin and cupid spandrels. A circular brass medallion in the arch is etched with a profile of Major General Richard Montgomery in full uniform with gun and sword. This is a "bespoken" clock, and it would be interesting to know by whom, for the general was killed during the assault on Quebec in the Revolutionary War.

Several authorities place Joseph Graff in the town of Northampton around the 1790s to the early 1800s. He did, however, appear on the Bethlehem tax record for 1799, which is somewhat puzzling because in that year he was Jacob Blumer's partner in what is now Allentown.

Sources have regularly omitted Jacob Hartz of Northampton on the tax records as a clockmaker from 1790 to 1828, perhaps because that is the only evidence of him. Likewise, there is scant evidence for Peter Hendrick, listed in 1848 in Upper Macungie Township, and Nathan Kimble and Jacob Kitchline, both in Upper Milford Township, in 1856 and 1801 respectively.

John J. Krauss (Krausse, Krouse) is noted by one source as being at work in Northampton in about 1830.

Samuel Krauss (1807–1904), of Kraussdale, Montgomery County, was a member of the famous Schwenkfeld Krauss family of organ builders. In addition to laboring as a clockmaker, he was a storekeeper, an inventor, a foundryman, a miller, and a farmer. At various times, he was engaged in business in Philadelphia, Upper Milford

Fig. 129. J. Bishop clock. Courtesy of Harold A. Verwohlt.

Township, Upper Hanover Township, Allentown, and Coopersburg. In 1886 he re-tired from business and settled in Sumneytown. According to his ledger, he built sixty-three tall clocks in Lehigh County, where he signed his pieces "Saml. Krauss Lehigh County," using the German "s."

The names of Charles Massey and Nathan Metzger are found nowhere else but on the 1847 tax records for Allentown. This, however, could be the same Massey who was listed in Philadelphia directories from 1837 to 1839 and who issued watch papers.

Peter Miller (1772–1855) was carried on the Lynn Township tax records for the long period of 1800 to 1840. One writer states that Miller was working in Ephrata around 1800 and that his total working years were from about 1793 to 1837. Apparently quite a craftsman, he made both wood and brass movement clocks, twenty-four-hour and eight-day. It is generally agreed that he probably produced more tall clocks than any other maker in Lehigh County, and was therefore the best-known maker. The authors of the *History of Lehigh County, Pennsylvania* state: "He made the historic 'Peter Miller' grandfather clocks which became noted all over eastern Pennsylvania and was an exceptional mechanic in wood and brass materials."[1]

Although not a clockmaker according to the general usage of the word, Solomon Moyer of Allentown deserves some mention. In 1887 he obtained patent #369,462 for a universal clock. The invention, or at least its dial, must have been complicated. It is illustrated in Nutting's *Furniture Treasury* and described as an astronomical clock which shows the time for the entire globe and the position of the stars at all times. The Universum Clock Company of Boston used New Haven Clock Company movements to which its appurtenances were added and then cased.

John Murphy, originally from Ireland, was included on the Salisbury Township tax records from 1770 to 1789. He was probably the earliest clockmaker in the county, having established himself there as early as 1775, according to one source, while the tax records date him at even five years earlier. Because he stayed in the county until about 1790, a great number of his clocks have "Northampton" as the place name. He may have moved to Chester County, as there was a clockmaker named John Murphy in Pikeland Township around 1790. Thomas Murphy, who may have been a relative, was at work in the town of Northampton around 1830.

It is commonly believed that Henry Rentsheimer (also Rentzheimer) was a clock-

1. Charles Rhoads Roberts et al., *History of Lehigh County, Pennsylvania* (Allentown, Pa.: Lehigh Valley Publishing Co., 1914), p. 32.

maker in Salisbury Township, but there are differing opinions as to exactly when he labored. Two sources agree on 1785 to 1788, whereas the tax records extend his working period to 1807.

Jacob Solliday was discussed in the Bucks County chapter, but a brief summary will be given here. The son of the original Frederick Solliday, Jacob was a well-known clockmaker in Bedminster at the close of the Revolution. Along with his son Peter, he pursued the trade as late as 1807. The exact date of his move to Lehigh County is unknown. His clocks are marked "Jacobe Salede—Bucks County" and "Jacob Solliday—North Hampton."

Jacob Stein (1771–1842) made many tall clocks in Allentown and was at work probably from about 1820 to 1840. He and his son George must have worked together during that period, as clocks exist which are signed "Jacob Stein & Son."

Joseph Weiss (1802–63) remained on the Allentown tax records for the long span of 1820–60. That he reputedly made a large number of clocks is odd because his working period saw the end of the demand for fine tall clocks and the tremendous marketing thrust of the inexpensive Connecticut shelf clocks. There is extant, however, a unique grandmother-sized clock, 53 inches tall, housed in a case of the pillar and scroll variety. The wood is curly maple, and the scrolls are carved with molded borders. The dial is signed "Joshua Weiss Allentown"; Weiss's Christian name was sometimes given as Joshua. One author has reasoned that this clock was made before 1811;[2] if true, it may have predated the Connecticut pillar and scroll, based on the knowledge that Northampton was renamed Allentown in 1800 and remained so until 1811. Conversely, if 1802 can be accepted as the birth year of Joseph (or Joshua) Weiss, it must follow that the clock was made after 1838, which would be consistent with the period that other Pennsylvanians, such as Jacob Custer and John Scharf, were making pillar and scroll clocks. Of course, the possibility that Joseph Weiss and Joshua Weiss were two different artisans must also be considered. Joseph Weiss most probably was the last clockmaker of any note in the county.

Two references to Martin Weisser as a clockmaker in Allentown were found, one indicating that he worked sometime after 1825, the other that he dated about 1830. He is listed on the tax records from 1847 to 1849.

Martin Weiser (also Weizer), a veteran of the War of 1812, was a lineal descendant of the great diplomat to the Indians, Conrad Weiser. Martin was one of the

2. Mark E. Shanaberger, "Pillar and Scroll Clock Cases Tell Their Own Story," *Timepieces Quarterly* 1, no. 1 (November 1948): 11.

best-known makers in the county, having been one of the first to construct what are now known as grandfather clocks. Many specimens of his skill in this line are still to be found in the rural districts of the county. Known as a wit and a master of sarcasm, Weiser made periodical trips through the county to sell, clean, and repair clocks, and it was his custom to remain overnight and to have meals with his customers. Because of his flashes of wit which spiced his conversation, the old clockmaker was usually a welcome guest, but sometimes he joked unwisely. An oft-repeated story tells that he was a dinner guest at a home where the china was beautiful, but the coffee was weak. Upon tasting it, Weiser blurted out: "Ei, Mommy, was here ier shea g'schar. Mer kou die blummer derfoon ein keipichy saena dorrich der koffer" [Why, Mother, what beautiful dishes you have. You can see the flowers on the cup through the coffee].[3]

Several authorities agree that Solomon Yeakel (1773–1814) was a clockmaker in Upper Milford Township. That he does indeed appear on the tax records from 1800 to 1841 makes the paucity of information about him, his products, and his production all the more puzzling.

Yet, this is no more baffling than the existence of a walnut, thirty-hour tall clock with a painted dial signed "Solomon Yeakel, Barks County." There is no such county in Pennsylvania.

3. Roberts, *History of Lehigh County, Pennsylvania*, p. 1378.

Northampton County

Formed from part of Bucks County and named for the Earl of Pomfred of Northamptonshire, England, Northampton County was organized as early as 1752. The early settlers were a mixture of nationalities: English, Scotch-Irish, Germans, French, and Dutch. Thomas Penn personally named the town of Easton, and the first courts were held there in the same year. This was also the scene of many conferences between the whites and the Indians. General John Sullivan launched from Easton his campaign against the Indians to avenge the Wyoming massacre. The Moravians laid out Bethlehem in 1741, and the first stars and stripes of the United Colonies were flown at Easton on July 8, 1776. Such an early, rich, and varied background would lead one to expect a host of craftsmen; in the field of horology, there is no disappointment.

Abraham Andreas (1725–1802) was born in Fredericktown, Montgomery County. Initially a millwright, he learned clockmaking (where or from whom is unknown), moved to Bethlehem in 1736, and eventually married the stepdaughter of another clockmaker, Abraham Boemper. (The tax records of Bethlehem Township during the period of 1770 to 1793 list Boemper as a clockmaker.) When Boemper died in 1793, Andreas succeeded to his business and continued with it until his own death. Actually, silversmithing may have been his primary occupation.

Henry Andreas (1762–1802), the second son of Abraham, learned watchmaking in Philadelphia; the identity of his teacher is unknown. He returned to Bethlehem in 1800 to carry on his trade.

130   131

Charles F. Beckel (1802–80), of Bethlehem, was an apprentice watchmaker and silversmith under both John S. Krause and Jedediah Weiss beginning in 1815. He started his own shop in 1826 and later took Henry D. Bishop as his apprentice. Around 1825 Beckel decided to go into the iron foundry business, so Bishop took over the clock business.

Two earlier compilers dismissed Josiah O. Beitel as a maker of tall clocks in Nazareth with no ascribable date. Now, thanks to good fortune, a great deal of his fascinating story can be recounted. Beitel (1811–98), of Nazareth, is generally believed to have been the first Moravian clockmaker in Pennsylvania. The chapter entitled "Jewelers and Opticians" in *Two Centuries of Nazareth* briefly describes him: "Beginning with Josiah O. Beitel, who manufactured clocks and dealt in jewelry at 135 S.

Fig. 130. Attractive tall clock by Josiah O. Beitel. Notice unusual hood treatment and fan ornamentation above the waist door. Courtesy of Robert J. Beitel, M.D.

Fig. 131. Close-up of dial (see fig. 130) displays the unusual combination of geometric line and mollusk spandrels. Courtesy of Dr. Robert J. Beitel.

Fig. 132. Josiah Oliver Beitel clock in the president's home, known as Frueauff House, at Moravian College. Notice the marvelous wood graining of the case, the magnificent fan ornamentation atop the door, and the applied rosettes on the horns of the broken arch top. Courtesy of Moravian College.

Fig. 133. The marvelous dial of the clock in fig. 132. Courtesy of Moravian College.

Fig. 134. Time train side of the clock's movement. Courtesy of Moravian College.

Fig. 135. Strike train side of the clock's movement. Courtesy of Moravian College.

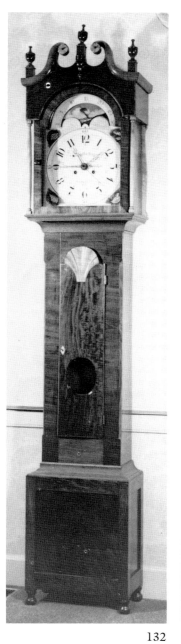

132

133

134

135

Main Street from 1832 to 1877, Nazareth has had eight jewelers in its business history. In 1868 Beitel took in partnership his son, Richard, who took over the business in 1877." This reference undoubtedly gave rise to the myth that Brother Beitel had a small factory producing both wood and brass movement clocks.

This idea is disproved by Josiah's great grandson, Robert J. Beitel, Jr., M.D., who states that various family estimates rank J.O. Beitel's output at approximately twenty to twenty-five clocks. Dr. Beitel and his brother know of the existence of only eight, possibly nine clocks. The doctor is the proud possessor of a beautiful cherry-cased piece, made by Josiah for Solomon Kahler. Figures 130 and 131 show that heirloom. Notice the mollusk motif spandrel paintings, which suggest an English dial and fan ornamentation on the door. The mollusk spandrels and the door fan decorations contribute to the generally similar appearances of the two clocks displayed. The pendulum rod is interesting, as it appears to be an attempt at some variation of gridiron. The really startling features of this clock are the date and number. Beitel supposedly made clock #18 in conjunction with his old preceptor, Jedediah Weiss, and the dial indeed confirms this; however, a clockmaker at age nine is not likely. Furthermore, his diary confirms there is no error in his birth year. Upon realizing that the date does not square with the data recorded in the Nazareth history, one suspects the dial may have been repainted at some time and the wrong date applied. There still is no explanation as to why, after making seventeen clocks, he chose to accept Weiss's help on this one; nor does this piece figure into the balance of clocks he is estimated to have made.

Not all of Beitel's clocks stayed close to Nazareth. In the Harris Ferry Tavern room of the Penn Harris Hotel in Harrisburg, Pennsylvania, stands another magnificent Beitel piece with the typical mollusk spandrels and fan top door.

Those clocks thus far described have brass movements. Some of his descendants maintain his first clock, containing a wood movement, found its way to the Moravian settlement at Gnadenhutten, Ohio, but, unfortunately, searchers there have been unable to find it.

Beitel learned his trade from Jedediah Weiss of Bethlehem. He married Maria Kern in that town in 1833. A good musician, he was a member of the church choir and a trombonist. He was also a member of the school board, and he served as chief burgess during the Civil War. Four of his sons entered the jewelry and so-called watchmaking businesses. Another great-grandson, Dr. J.J. Longacre of Cincinnati, Ohio, states that Beitel not only cured the cherry wood for his clock cases, but he set up a special cabinet shop where all the work was done to make and decorate the cases. Chances are the existence of this shop gave rise to the "factory" myth. Dr. Longacre also reports that his illustrious ancestor made four-faced clocks for church steeples and town halls.

The year 1825 found the fourteen-year-old Beitel in the Nazareth Boarding School, unhappy and wanting to leave school to learn a trade. Desiring to become a silversmith, he begged his parents to apply to Mr. Weiss to take him on as an apprentice. They finally consented, and he went with Weiss on April 18, 1825. His day book (now in the possession of Dr. Longacre) is written in the nature of a personal diary, or recitation, of his comings, goings, and doings; nothing is actually reported about the teaching and learning process of his apprenticeship, which apparently was not as strict as earlier apprenticeships, as he seemed free to come and go pretty much as he chose.

> July 20, 1825 Mr. Weiss and I went to Nazareth to clean the tower clock. Mr. Weiss rode up with Mr. Haus. I walked. The next day Mr. Weiss, my father and myself went early in the morning on the job we alluded; it being cleaned around dinner time, the rest we finished in the afternoon. Mr. Weiss going home the same day permitted me to stay.

> November 12, 1825 Mr. Beck coming to Easton brought along Thomas Albright, he being now by the trade Robert's watchmaker, gave me order to paint a dozen watch papers to sell by the pair. I will not mention how many papers I have sold until this time. [There follows a list of names totaling sales of 177 pairs of papers. It is curious that these were always prepared and sold in pairs.]

> April 11 [1826] Francis Linnerd [another of Weiss's apprentices] got zubbelt by the ear of his Master on account of not doing that immediately which he was ordered to do.

> August 8 I finished a 30 hour clock which was the first one that I have yet had made. It was for my Uncle Mr. Romig in Gnadenhutten, Ohio.

> Sept. 16 I went on a visit to Nazareth. The next morning after breakfast I tuned our pihano [sic] and playing on a good while, I went into our garden where I eat peaches in abundance. In the afternoon my father required to repair three watches among which of them was one that was laying five years in the wasser [sic]; on opening it we found that all the iron work was rusted in pieces and unfit for use. [This and other entries indicated that Josiah's father apparently had the ability to repair clocks and watches.]

October 26 I made a second clock, likewise a 30 hr. one for Jacob Bauer near Nazareth.

November 1 I went out cleaning clocks for the first time which gave me very much pleasure. As Mr.————living about five miles from here, asked Mr. Weiss whether one of us could not come out and clean his clock. He answered yes and then went out on the first of November. Having finished his clock I stepped over to Mr. Carr where I cleaned his 8 day clock and remaining there until the next morning. I then went to Mr. Kock about 8 miles from here. After having cleaned his clock I went to Menckes and cleaning Mr. Shaefer's wooden clock. I proceeded to Caspar Meyer's where I cleaned his two clocks, likewise to Mrs. Brown's 8 day clock. Coming thence I proceeded to Mr. Schneitzer. After having cleaned his I returned home, being out two days $6.00.

December 1 Went to clean Mr. Swartz's 8 day clock; and after I had it finished I returned to old Mr.————so I cleaned his 30 hr. clock, remaining there overnight; the next morning I went to Mr. Young and cleaned his dead beat clock and after him I cleaned Mr. Smidt's 30 hr. clock and then returned home. $3.00.

On the second Christmas Day it snowed all the day so persons could go slaying [*sic*] but I, not minding the weather, sat down pretty near the whole day, cleaned and repaired watches. [This and other entries tell that the Moravians apparently celebrated Christmas for two days.]

January 26 [1827] I made my third 24 hr. clock for Daniel Ritter, and went with him that day to his house to set it up.

May 1 Mr. Brader brought in his 8 day clock to get it cleaned. After I had it cleaned he took me with him to his house to set it up. I took a grand dinner with him. After having a good deal of fun, one of his boys took me again.

October 19 I finished my first 8 day clock.

The day book ends with an entry which explains that he has been there for three years and is still joyful and rejoiced, even more than before, in fact, because Francis Linnerd is gone.

In addition to Henry Bishop (already mentioned under Beckel), there was a Moritz Bishop in business as a clockmaker in Easton in about 1786 and for quite awhile thereafter. No relationship between the two has been established.

The multiple generations of the Bixler family must be put into their proper ordering, even though their roots began outside of this county.

Christian Bixler I (1710–62) was the son of Johann J. Bixler, a Swiss, who came to Lancaster County in about 1702. No proof positive has been found to prove he was a clockmaker, but it is suspected that he had some knowledge of the art and that he instilled this into his son.

Although Christian Bixler II (1732–1811) was born in Lancaster County, he moved to Reading (the date is uncertain), where he worked as a clockmaker from 1760 to about 1790.

Christian Bixler III (1763–1840) was born in Robeson Township, Berks County. He served an apprenticeship under John Keim in his father's shop in Reading, learning both clockmaking and silversmithing. It is strange that he was not his father's pupil; perhaps it was because of a desire to learn two trades, or Keim may have been developing an enviable reputation as a teacher. Bixler continued working in Reading as a journeyman, then he moved to Easton in 1784. The following year he established a shop there which remains in business to this day.

It is averred that he made about 465 clocks between 1784 and 1812. The casting and most of the forging he performed himself, or it was done under his direct supervision. His clock #446 was illustrated in the March, 1975 issue of ANTIQUES magazine.

The Bixler store is under the management of Mr. K.H. Mitman, the husband to the last of the Bixler line. In his possession are what amount to the day books of Christian III, which show the numbers of the clocks and the names of the original owners. Drawings of all the types of clocks are there showing all the details—the layout, the number of teeth in wheels and pinions, dimensions, and dates of manufacture, with serial numbers which reached up to nearly 200 before the end of the eighteenth century. It is interesting to know that the original clock, watch, and silver store and the Bixler home were at Bank and Northampton Streets, and were bought from John Penn, descendant of William, for thirty-eight pounds, six shillings, and sixpence.

The business interests of Christian Bixler III were varied, for in addition to the retail shop, he owned a sawmill, farm land, and a shop for making barrels and other containers. Later he used the same facilities for making his clock cases of mahogany, pine, maple, and fruitwoods. He also produced very fine silverware.

A civic-minded man, he was one of the founders and directors of the Easton National Bank; he was a founder and incorporator of the Easton Water Company, and also of the first Delaware River bridge in 1804 and of the Wilkes Barre Turnpike. In his spare time he served terms as burgess and county treasurer.

According to the records, Bixler made different types of clocks but, in harmony with the times, he concentrated heavily on the tall case variety. He was very particular about the pivot holes, which he drilled and polished to such smoothness that they approached jewels in reducing friction. Wheel and pinion teeth were also finely finished. His dial decorations were artistic, often featuring garlands of flowers, fruit, or cherubs. His cases were examples of the finest joiner's skills, yet even his superb clocks eventually succumbed to the influx of inexpensive Yankee shelf clocks.

Bixler produced beautiful shelf clocks. For example, in his day book is recorded a clock with the serial number in sequence with other numbers and carrying this entry, "Made for Myself, One Shelf Clock." The drawing of the movement matches the movement in the clock. It is brass, eight-day, rack and snail strike with repeater cord. He was indeed a top-notch craftsman. He even manufactured bracket clocks at a time when some of the few other native manufacturers relied on English imports, in whole or in part.

Around 1825 Daniel Lewis Bixler began an apprenticeship under his father; he carried on the business after his father's death in 1840. This halted any clockmaking in the family, but David did perform some clock and watch repairing as an adjunct operation to the store. He was eventually succeeded by his son, Christian Willis Bixler, and, in time, Christian was succeeded by Arthur B. Bixler, who worked until his death in 1945. Philip Bixler Mitman is being groomed to one day take over the business from his parents, Kathryn Bixler Mitman and K.H. Mitman; thus he will assume a firm which is already "America's Oldest Jewelers."

John (or Johann) Boehner was born and trained as a clockmaker in Gruenberg, Bohemia. He arrived in Georgia in 1736 with the early group of Moravians. Like others of his sect, he drifted up to Bethlehem after its founding, arriving there in 1748, and plied his trade for an undetermined amount of time.

Abraham Boemper (1705–93), born in Herborn, Nassau, Germany, learned the clockmaking profession in Marburg. After living in Holland for a brief period, he went to Surinam as a missionary and then to New York, where he served as an agent for missions of the Moravian Church. After his wife died, he moved to Bethlehem and remarried in 1748. This was undoubtedly when he started his clockmaking and silversmithing. His firm in Bethlehem was passed on to Abraham Andreas in 1793 upon Boemper's death.

Little is known about George Bush's early life until he served as an apprentice under Christian Bixler from 1806 to 1812. He then entered the clockmaking business for himself in Lower Smithfield Township. Either he had an odd numbering system

Fig. 136. A superlative bracket clock by Christian Bixler III of Easton. This is his number 327. Private collection.

Fig. 137. Tall case clock, #64, by Isaac Grotz, of the one-day, pull-up variety. Notice the fine dial. Private collection.

13

137

or he was a prodigious producer during his relatively short career, as his tall clock #213, with calendar and moon phase, is extant. Besides tall clocks, he made what was then called the "hanging half case clocks." He also dealt in materials for tall clocks. His business operations ceased in 1837, and he died in 1843.

Michael Bush (any relationship to George is unknown) has been mentioned as an Easton maker of tall clocks. A respected collector living in Bucks County attests to having seen a tall case clock with the marking "Michael Bush, #96" on the dial.

Tax records place George Detrech as a clockmaker in Lower Smithfield Township from 1807 to 1828; Frederick Folger was a clockmaker in Easton in 1807; and Martin Ginkinger was a fellow tradesman in Lehigh Township in 1795 and 1796. None of these three, however, are listed in any of the early clockmakers reference books.

Isaac Grotz (1784–1835), of Easton, first learned the blacksmith's trade, but turned to clockmaking when he was still a young man. This combination of trades was quite common in Europe and England in the earliest days of making tower and turret clocks, probably before 1635. He may have learned clockmaking from Christian Bixler. With the tools and knowledge of both trades, he could do most of his own rough casting. Apparently, a good number of Grotz's handsome products were of the one-day, pull-up variety.

Grotz stayed in the trade until his death in March 1835, which resulted from what was probably pneumonia, contracted while he was out setting up some of his clocks a few weeks earlier. It had been his custom to travel by ox sled in the winter to deliver clocks that had been ordered.

A letter from an owner of a Grotz clock tells more of the story.

> My husband's family possess a beautiful clock made by an ancestor, Isaac Grotz from Easton. Jacob Grotz and Jacob Grotz, Jr. were also clockmakers in the late 18th century. I have seen three of these clocks. All of these Grotzes were from Easton and, according to a map of Easton in 1776, they lived two blocks from the known clockmaker, Moritz Bischoff. He died at the age of thirty-three after which his widow sold the shop to Christian Winters who was also a clockmaker. Another clockmaker living at about the same time and same general location was John Murphy.[1]

The Jacob Grotzs, senior and junior, are nowhere else listed, so two hitherto unrecognized clockmakers may be discovered. Moritz Bischoff is quite likely the

1. Letter received from Mrs. A. Newton Bugbee, Jr., March 16, 1973.

Moritz Bishop described earlier. John Murphy was described in the Lehigh County chapter.

Nathan Gulick (1777–1826) began building fine tall clocks in the 1790s and continued until 1818, when he moved to Maysville, Kentucky. Unfortunately, he survived his father, Samuel, a clockmaker in Northampton, by only one year.

Jonas Gearhart Hagey (1815–95) was a clockmaker, a watchmaker, a farmer, a silversmith, and an auctioneer. He was probably not as well known in the field of clockmaking as were his two brothers, father, and grandfather. According to family tradition, only twelve tall case clocks are attributed to him. His shop was located first at Springtown, Bucks County, and then at Hellertown, Northampton County, where he moved to soon after his marriage.

That Elisha Kennedy was an Easton clockmaker in 1786 and 1787 is confirmed by tax records. There is not, however, any further record of him there; furthermore, an Elisha Kennedy advertised in Middletown, Connecticut, in 1788. Because these are the only two men of that name in the horological reference books, the chances are great that these refer to the same maker.

John M. Miksch established his own watchmaking and silversmithing business in 1822; he was ultimately succeeded by Edward F. Erwin, and he died in 1882. Erwin continued the business for about one decade, yet whether he ever made any kind of a clock is unknown. Thus, except for the Bixler family, these two men and J.K. Rauch were probably the last of the clockmaking breed in the county.

Abraham (or Abram) Miller was a successful clockmaker for about twenty-five years in the early nineteenth century. Clockmaker George Peter also labored during that period in Lower Smithfield Township—from 1803 to 1804, according to tax records—although he is not mentioned in any of the clock reference books.

James K. Rauch was an apprentice to Jedediah Weiss, whose business he took over in 1865 and apparently continued until around 1892.

Jacob Roberts, a contemporary of Abraham Miller's, served as apprentice to Christian Bixler; however, he never met with any great success.

Thomas Roberts was listed on tax records for 1815 through 1835 as an Easton clockmaker.

John Shuman of that same town has thrice been mentioned as a clockmaker who worked around 1780 to 1790. No other particulars have been given about him.

John George Weiss (1758–1811), born in Bethlehem, took up clockmaking in 1795 as an upgrading of occupation from nail, lock, and gunsmithing. His aptitude for this trade must have been great, for, with only two year's experience, he was able to attract an apprentice, J.S. Krause.

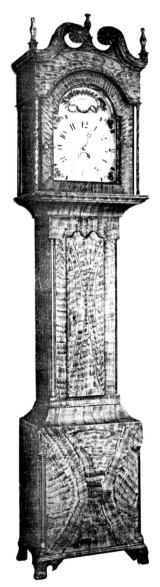

Fig. 138. Tall case clock, made in Lehigh Valley, Pennsylvania, circa 1820. Courtesy of *Spinning Wheel* magazine, June 1974.

John's son, Jedediah Weiss (1795–1873), was still a minor when his teacher, J.S. Krause, died in 1815. He took over Krause's clockmaking and silversmithing business and operated it quite successfully until his retirement in 1865, when it was passed on to J.K. Rauch. In addition to Rauch, Weiss had other apprentices, such as Beckel and Beitel, who made reputations for themselves, and Francis Linnerd, whose name never appeared in connection with his trade after he left Weiss.

This magazine excerpt attests to the skill of Weiss and the ingenuity of his inventions:

> Improved clock. Mr. J. Weiss of Bethlehem, Pennsylvania has invented a clock which for simplicity and beauty of construction is pronounced to be a most exquisite piece of mechanism. It is calculated to run for eight days; but its construction is so simplified that only three wheels are used for the running and striking parts, whereas in ordinary clocks, eight wheels, besides the fly-wheel, are employed. The escapement, too, is an entirely new and very ingenious contrivance; the pendulum is suspended horizontally and is supplied with a mode of compensation, believed to be perfect, that regulates the movements of the clock in the most accurate manner.[2]

Christian Winter was on the tax records from 1793 to 1799. He died in 1800 and his will confirmed his occupation as a builder of tall clocks in Easton.

Not all the clockmakers in the twin counties of Lehigh and Northampton signed their works, eye-arresting though they might be, as proven by the masterpiece in figure 138. This tall case clock, with grained decoration freely applied in lampblack on a faded mustard yellow ground over a tulip wood carcass, features an astonishing combination of naive and sophisticated elements. The crimped rosettes, the dumbbell finials, the massive moldings, and the overall abstraction of the feather-graining are provincial in feeling. However, the use of fluted quarter-columns, the carved bracket in the door of the case, and the nicely shaped ogee feet suggests that the anonymous craftsman was familiar with the work of late eighteenth-century Philadelphia cabinetmakers. Neither the maker of the thirty-hour clock movement nor the cabinetmaker has been identified, but the history of ownership, the proportions of the case, and the works indicate that the clock was made in Lehigh Valley, Pennsylvania, in about 1820.

Not all the creators of clock movements made their own cases, and, again, the joiners go unheralded because they did not sign their cases. Figure 139 shows a case made in Bethlehem to house works brought from Germany perhaps 150 years ago.

Fig. 139. Unsigned clock case made in Bethlehem to house a German movement. Courtesy of Miss A.K. Krause and N.F. Beacham.

2. *Scientific American,* December 11, 1847.

York County

York County, formerly a part of Lancaster County, was organized in 1749. When the Continental Congress fled from Philadelphia, it met in York from September, 1777 to June, 1778. Here Congress received the news of Burgoyne's surrender, approved the Articles of Confederation, was notified that France would come to the aid of the colonies, welcomed Baron von Steuben and Marquis de Lafayette and commissioned them major generals in the Continental Army, and issued the first Thanksgiving proclamation. The first iron furnace west of the Susquehanna was erected here in 1762, and three years later Codorus Forge was built on this land. York County produced cannons and cannonballs under the supervision of James Smith, a signer of the Declaration of Independence. A water-powered stone grist mill has been in continuous operation here since 1740.

German, Scotch-Irish, and Quaker settlers assured the county of its fair share of artisans and, indeed, a satisfying number of clockmakers can be described.

John Elias Abel (alternately Appel), thrice listed as a clockmaker in Dover, probably worked during the 1770s. His will, however, dated August 5, 1778, names "clogmaker" as his vocation. To this date, no clock by him has been reported.

Jacob Beck (or Becker), of Hanover, is listed by several authorities as a clockmaker in the 1820s, but no other information can be found.

Caleb Bently was briefly described in the Chester County chapter. A traveler, he plied his trade of clockmaking and silversmithing in York around 1780 before moving on to Leesburg, Virginia, and ultimately to Maryland.

George Carson is cited by at least two authorities as a clockmaker in York from approximately 1810 to 1820. He advertised on August 10, 1819 as a clock- and watchmaker stationed on Main Street next to the post office.

Veazey Chandlee (1804–81) was one of the prolific Chandlees described in the Chester County chapter. One of the fourth generation, he was the son of Ellis. Benjamin Chandlee of Baltimore, the son of Goldsmith, taught him the clockmaking trade. After the death of Ellis Chandlee in 1816, the clan gradually discontinued clockmaking and began to scatter. Veazey and his brother, Lilburn, moved to York County, where Lilburn ran a farm and did shoemaking. Veazey also farmed and did clock and watch repairing, and he possibly made a few clocks to order.

Richard Chester (b. 1770) is said by several sources to have been a clock- and watchmaker, although it can be questioned whether he actually made watches. Born in East Berlin, he was the son of an English schoolmaster who later became a tavern keeper. From whom or how he learned his trade has not been discovered, but it is fairly certain he made clocks in East Berlin prior to his move to Hanover.

On March 25, 1799, Chester bought six acres of land in Hanover priced at 153 pounds of Pennsylvania lawful money. The payment plan called for the clockmaker to deliver three watches to the value of 18 pounds and 15 shillings, and four eight-day clocks valued at 76 pounds. Also, a debt against a third party amounted to 20 shillings. He was also to deliver one faceless clock priced at 7 pounds, 7 shillings and 6 pence. The cost of the entire delivery of clocks would amount to 153 pounds.

A number of clocks marked "Richard Chester" are in existence, of both the thirty-hour and the eight-day types. Most were done in the Chippendale design, with finials and broken arch, and with or without rosettes.

Amos Clark, working in the 1790s through the 1810s in the borough of Lewisburg, manufactured large eight-day clocks. The artistic decoration on many of them was done by Miss Pamela Lewis, an amateur artist and a teacher.

No reference books include George Clark, but in the Hammond-Harwood House, a historic landmark in Annapolis, Maryland, sits a tall case clock, dated 1791, whose movement is attributed to George Clark of Hanover, Pennsylvania. The clock's case was made in Baltimore.

Authorities seem to agree that Frederick B. Cook (1808?–1842) worked in Columbia from 1828 to 1832 and then in York from 1832 to 1842. He was both a silversmith and a clockmaker. One of his eight-day clocks, with broken scroll and painted dial, is known.

Phineas Davis (1795–1835) was one of that relatively small group of clock- and watchmakers who achieved great fame in an entirely different field. Born in New

Fig. 140. A handsome clock by F.B. Cook of York. Note that the finials are of mixed design, two urns and one acorn. From the collections of the Historical Society of York County, Pennsylvania.

Hampshire, he wandered down through the northeastern states in search of employment, and finally settled in York in about 1810. Jonathan Jessup took him into his home as an apprentice, and Davis stayed on for six years to thoroughly learn both clock- and watchmaking. The tale persists that he constructed a gold watch the approximate diameter of a dime. Jessup, recognizing potential, encouraged him to study from his collection of books and especially to explore scientific subjects.

In 1821 Davis formed a partnership with Israel Gardiner in an iron foundry and steam engine machine shop. After building stationary engines of Davis's design, the partners in 1825 built a sixty feet long, ironclad steamboat, the *Codorus,* for use on the Susquehanna River. This was the first iron boat in America, but often the Susquehanna was too shallow to permit its travel. The boat's engine worked at a high pressure (100 psi). In 1831 Davis completed for and delivered to the Baltimore & Ohio Railroad a locomotive, the *York,* which met the company's specifications (that the locomotive burn either coal or coke, consume its own smoke, and pull fifteen tons at fifteen miles per hour). The following year he and Gardiner placed in service the *Atlantic,* the first of the "grasshopper" engines. During a trial run, however, a misplaced rail threw the *Atlantic* off the track and Davis was killed.

Thomas Edmundson (b. 1773) is recorded as a clockmaker in York around 1790 to 1800. On August 9, 1788, he was released from Warrington Meeting to York Meeting because he was apprenticing with Elisha Kirk. The *York Recorder* of January 28, 1800 carried an advertisement of the sale of the property of "Thomas Edmundson of Warrington Township, clockmaker." So far none of his clocks have been reported.

John Filber is twice listed as a clockmaker in York from about 1790 to 1810, and again after 1820. At least one mahogany-cased tall clock with an enameled dial exists.

Much and little can be told about John Fisher (1736–1808) born in Pfeffingon, Swabia, Germany. Brought to America in 1749 and almost immediately orphaned, young John worked on a farm until 1756, when he turned up in the town of York as a wood carver and the pioneer clockmaker of that area. His education for these crafts remains a mystery; nevertheless, he was an exceedingly brilliant artisan.

Fisher was not only the pioneer clockmaker in the county, but he was also one of the most prolific and may well have been the most talented. The *Maryland Gazette* for September 10, 1790 carried an article which described his most noteworthy achievement.

> A description of a curious Time-piece completed by Mr. John Fisher, York-Town, Pennsylvania, May 23, 1790; the astronomical part of which does the greatest honour

141

142

143

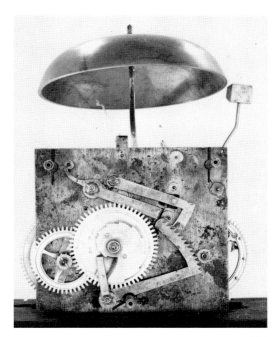

144

Fig. 141. The York County gem by John Fisher. Courtesy of Miss Patricia E. Kane, assistant curator, Mabel Brady Garvan Collection, Yale University Art Gallery.

Fig. 142. Very plain tall clock by John Fisher. Courtesy of Lee Davis.

Fig. 143. Refinished dial of the clock in fig. 142. Note that Fisher signed it "York Town." The straight lines through portions of the spandrels are an enigma. Courtesy of Lee Davis.

Fig. 144. Movement of the clock in fig. 142, clearly showing the rack and snail striking control. Courtesy of Lee Davis.

to the inventor. This Timepiece performs the office of a common eight day clock, but runs thirty-five days; it exhibits the time of the Sun's rising and setting, its destination, the longest and shortest days in the most distant parts of the world, all of which is clearly elucidated by a globe, affixed about three inches from the centre; it has the moon circulating round the verge of the globe, which makes all the different vicissitudes that the real moon seems to make to us in the Heavens. The dial plate is circular and of fourteen inches diameter; in the centre are disposed the date, minute, and second hands, and in the north of them the hour hand operates. This plate is elegantly engraven, and is by no means void of taste; round the verge it is ornamented with the twelve signs of the Zodiac, the seven planets, and twelve months, with the exact number of days in each month in a year. The operation of winding this machine is performed on an entire new plan, and constructed in such a manner as not to affect it going. The whole is executed with fourteen wheels and a suitable number of pinions, and contained between two brass plates, six inches long and three wide; it is kept in motion by two common clock weights, and that motion kept regular by a seconds pendulum.

145   146

This remarkable tour de force is now the property of the Yale University Art Gallery as part of the Mabel Brady Garvan Collection.

Although there is available a translation of a paper written in German by John Fisher, clockmaker and engraver of York, detailing family history from 1688 up to his time, no further light is shed on his clockmaking activities. That he also made fine "ordinary" tall case clocks is attested by figures 142, 143, and 144.

Peter Ford (also Foard) was listed as a clockmaker in York County's first census in 1783. Two authorities say he continued with that trade until 1819 or 1820; that, however, is the total of our knowledge of him.

Fig. 145. David Gobrecht clock with inlaid case and six finials. Courtesy of Edward J. Gobrecht.

Fig. 146. Dial and hood of the clock in fig. 145; picture shows inlaid rosette in the arch. Courtesy of Edward J. Gobrecht.

Fig. 147. Splendid Daniel Grumbine clock. Notice the strong finials, the elaborate dial decoration, and the matching door hinges. From the collections of the Historical Society of York County, Pennsylvania.

Christian Forrer (1737–83), of Nidau, Switzerland, apparently earned his clock-maker's certificate at age sixteen. He and his brother, Daniel, came to America in 1754 to settle in Lancaster County. In March 1774, Christian bought some land in Newberry Township, York County. There he made clocks, ran a ferry across the Susquehanna, and farmed until his death. His estate inventory included clock makers' tools valued at forty pounds and one unfinished clock. Though this particular clock had a wooden movement, he also produced ones made of brass. Several of his clocks are known.

According to the administration bond of his estate in 1800, Jacob Gartner was a clockmaker in York County. There is some suggestion that he may have been such for a decade or more, but nothing definite has been discovered.

The Deeds Book of York Township reports that John Gemmill, clock- and watch-maker, bought lot #124 in December, 1756. One reference places him in York from 1756 to 1760; another quotes the same years, but puts him in Lancaster, Carlisle, and York. While this latter theory is perfectly possible, it seems improbable that he would carry on his trade in three different communities at one time. In any event, he did make tall clocks, one of which is cased in walnut, with a broken arch top, a hood with rosettes, bracket feet, a brass movement, and a dial with spandrels.

David Gobrecht (b. 1775) was born in Lancaster, but when he was four his family moved to Hanover, where his father, Johann, served as the second pastor of Emanuel Reformed Church. David somehow learned silversmithing and clockmaking. A number of his eight-day tall clocks are known, many with flat top cases. One clock, made sometime around 1800, has a well-proportioned case surmounted with a broken arch, complete with rosettes and tall single finial.[1] This David Gobrecht clock (figure 145), belonging to a fifth generation descendant, has quite a unique top.

Interestingly, the Philadelphia paper *Poulson's Adventure* of December 30, 1829, stated that David Gobrecht was the first native American to engrave in steel. He engraved a medal for the Franklin Institute of Philadelphia and also one for Charles Carroll, of Carrolton, Maryland. A fair number of his silver spoons also remain.

Not much is known about Eli Gobrecht, other than that his name appears on several clocks of the nineteenth-century vintage. One is a thirty-hour clock. His ancestor, Edward J. Gobrecht, knew only that Eli lived several miles from his grandfather's farm.

Nothing is known of Jacob Gobrecht, the grandfather of Edward Gobrecht, ex-

147

1. Dworetsky and Dickstein, *Horology Americana*, p. 19.

cept that his name appears on a clock and that he was a farmer in Union Township of what is now Adams County.

Christian Grove was a clockmaker in both Heidelberg Township and Hanover during the early 1800s. So far, only several of his products have been catalogued.

Two authorities cite William Grove (1807–1874) as another Hanover clock-maker working during the long period of the 1830s to the 1870s. At least one of his tall clocks has been identified as having been made in either 1834 or 1837.

Various sources mention differing working dates for Daniel Grumbine (1801–82); all agree that he toiled in both Hanover and East Berlin. Grumbine built tall clocks, starting supposedly in about 1820 as an apprentice to a Mr. Hansel. Circumstances suggest, however, that his mentor was actually George House of Hanover. His reported products are all eight-day; one is marked "Daniel Grumbine, East Berlin, Pa." and the rest read "Daniel Grumbine, Hanover, Pa."

Benjamin Harlacher (1777–1829) is listed in two reference books as a clockmaker in York County from 1799 to 1829. Actually he was a native and resident of Washington Township.

The story of Jacob Hostetter (1754–1831) can be more fully recounted, as he was the best-known of all the Hanover clockmakers. Though also described as a watch-maker and a silversmith, he learned clockmaking, his chief trade, from Richard Chester. He made beautiful timepieces, mostly eight day with painted dials. There are probably a hundred or more of them in existence, cased in styles varying from simple walnut flat tops to the most ornate Hepplewhite. He may have had a small brass foundry, which would have enabled him to make the complete clock movements.

In 1825 he moved to Lisbon, Ohio, where his son, Jacob, Jr., had gone three years earlier. There the father and son team continued the clockmaking trade until the el-der died. He was the first Pennsylvanian horologist included in the *Biographical Di-rectory of the American Congress, 1774–1927.* The entry reads:

> Jacob Hostetter, a Representative from Pennsylvania, was born near York, Pa. May 9, 1754; attended the common schools; pioneer in the manufacture of the tall eight day clock; member of the General Assembly of Penna. 1797–1802; elected as a Democrat to the Fifteenth Congress to fill the vacancy caused by the resignation of Jacob Span-gler; re-elected to the Sixteenth Congress and served from November 16, 1818, until March 3, 1821; moved to Ohio and settled in Columbia (County) where he died June 29, 1831.

One Hostetter descendant suggested that Jacob set up a watchmaking establish-

Fig. 148. The Kirk-Jessup clock. From the collections of the Historical Society of York County, Pennsylvania.

ment in Ohio and that he was also instrumental in applying clockwork to revolving lighthouse beacons. The former theory has never been confirmed; the latter is disproved by official government sources. He did, however, turn to the design and manufacture of tower clocks.

The son Jacob evidently worked with his father in Hanover for a number of years before moving to Ohio in 1822, where he continued the trade.

Watchpapers bearing the name of Samuel Hostetter of Hanover as a clock- and watchmaker exist. There are two passing references to him that suggest he labored in the 1820s.

Hanover was certainly blessed with a surplus of skilled craftsmen; another silversmith and clockmaker, George House, was at work there from the 1790s until around 1830.

Jonathan Jessup (also Jessop; 1771–1857) was born in Guilford County, North Carolina. His mother took Jonathan to York when he was thirteen years old to apprentice him to her cousin, Elisha Kirk, to learn clock- and watchmaking. A tall clock, signed "Elisha Kirk, No. 67 and Jonathan Jessop, No. 1, 1784," is extant. This piece is displayed in figure 148.

The clock's date may mark the formal beginning of Jessup's apprenticeship, and the piece, perhaps worked on jointly as the training progressed, might have been given as a gift to Jessup when he became a journeyman. When Kirk died, he willed his tools to his son, Aquila, but Jessup inherited his business. The *York General Advertiser* carried the following advertisement on October 19, 1791:

> Jonathan Jessup, Begs leave to inform the public in general, and his friends in particular, that he continues to carry on business at that noted stand formerly occupied by Elisha Kirk, deceased, where he makes all kinds of Clocks, and will constantly be supplied with an assortment of new Watches, of the first quality which he means to sell on the lowest terms, for cash, short credit, or county produce.
>
> N.B. As he has been absent for some time, he fears the workmen left in the shop has [*sic*] not given general satisfaction in watch repairing; therefore engages to rectify such deficiencies, gratis. Those who favor him with their custom, may depend on being served with punctuality and dispatch; and hopes his exertions to please may merit a continuance of their favors.

Fig. 149. A more typical Jessup clock. Private collection.

This advertisement offers some insight into Jessup's character; it also raises some interesting questions as to where he had been and for how long, how many work-men were employed and what size the establishment was, and why no mention is made of his silversmithing.

Jessup was a man of exceptional mechanical skill, so his clocks, all eight-day, were known to be fine pieces. Also a reputable engineer, he supervised the building of the Washington branch of the Baltimore & Ohio Railroad. He was interested in a mill for making cotton cloth, and he developed and perfected the York Imperial apple. He was both a founding director of the York National Bank and one of the early heads of the Vigilant Fire Company. Still, clockmaking was his first love right up to the time of his death.

Joseph U. Jessup (1796–1859), Jonathan's son, undoubtedly learned his trade from his father. He advertised as a clock- and watchmaker on May 6, 1823, apparently for the first time, at his father's location. It is likely that as his father became more engaged in outside activities, Joseph increasingly "tended store." At least two of his clocks are reported, both eight-day.

One reference can be found to a John Keplinger working in Hanover in the early 1800s. There were Keplingers established in Baltimore, Lancaster, and Gettysburg; perhaps some future researcher will establish a connection.

Aquilla Kirk, the son of the famous Elisha Kirk who inherited his father's clock-making tools, has no known products. There may have been some, however, because he flourished in York during the 1790s and then moved to Baltimore.

Elisha Kirk (1757–90), a pewterer and one of the best-known clockmakers in the county, was born in Chester County on Christmas day. His Quaker parents transferred from Bradford Meeting to Warrington Meeting, York County, in 1770, but Elisha went back to Chester County in August of 1774. He lived there with Isaac Jackson for six years while he was an apprentice. In 1780 Elisha returned to the town of York and bought land. He was the first president of the Vigilant Fire Company, a position later assumed by his pupil, Jonathan Jessup. Although he lived only thirty-three years, he produced at least ninety-five clocks.

Three sources refer to Timothy Kirk (no relation to Elisha) as a clockmaker in York Township in the 1780s. He was, however, listed in the 1783 census as a joiner. He may have made some clock cases—perhaps he occasionally bought a movement, cased it, and sold it as his product.

Daniel Klingman is also accepted by three authorities as a York Township clock-maker, but no life span dates are known and even his working dates are loosely ex-pressed as being from the early 1800s to possibly 1830. Thus far, only one of his products has been officially reported: it is a mahogany, eight-day clock with beauti-

Fig. 150. Tall clock by Joseph U. Jessup. From the collections of the Historical Society of York County, Pennsylvania.

Fig. 151. Somewhat plain, severely cased clock by Elisha Kirk. From the collections of the Historical Society of York County, Pennsylvania.

Fig. 152. "Daniel Klingman, York Town" clock in mahogany case with urn and spear finials. In addition to moon phase, dial has small, circular calendar ring. From the collections of the Historical Society of York County, Pennsylvania.

Fig. 153. A slightly more elaborate Daniel Klingman clock, with fancier finial curves of the broken arch. Dial has sweep hand calendar and somewhat unusual painted birds. From the collections of the Historical Society of York County, Pennsylvania.

Fig. 154. Jacob Klingman clock with sweep second hand and painted bird on the dial. From the collections of the Historical Society of York County, Pennsylvania.

150

151

152

153

154

ful inlay and a broken arch bonnet with three urn finials. The timepiece shown in figure 152 may be that Daniel Klingman clock, except that it also has a calendar ring.

In this instance the spirit of the chase was amply rewarded when another Daniel Klingman clock was found (fig. 153).

Jacob Klingman (1758–1806) may have been born in Reading, for he worked there before coming to York. The Woman's Club of Reading owns one of his clocks, dated 1776. One author has stated that his clocks were signed "Jacob Kling," though certainly not all were, for figure 154 shows one that is definitely signed "Jacob Klingman."

Jacob Koch of York Springs was a maker of clock cases, primarily for John Albert. The report that some dials bear his name is completely misleading in this instance.

Conversely, Richard Koch (1774–1836) was both a silversmith and a clockmaker in York Township. Some authorities maintain that he did not enter into these trades until 1805 and then he pursued them until his death. His will stipulated that any of his sons who learned his father's trade could have all his tools and materials. Only one of his clocks is known; it is signed "Richard Koch, York"—that is the only available detail. A Richard Koch clock was sold at an auction near Reading in October, 1973.

John Latshar, born in Latshaw, was listed as a clockmaker in York Township on the 1779 and 1780 tax lists; after that he moved to what is now Adams County. He may also have been a silversmith.

Godfrey Lenhart (1754–1819) was also a clockmaker and a silversmith in York Township. His shop was a one-story log building, located at Continental Square and N. George Street. Several of his clocks are extant. His #30, a thirty-hour clock, supposedly sat in the York County courthouse and was used to time the sessions of the Continental Congress when that body met there from September 30, 1777 to June 28, 1778. Other clocks of his, with broken arches and scroll tops, are recorded. A most unusual example of his work is shown in figure 156. The spartan appearance of its case reminds one of the similar Shaker clocks.

George Long of Hanover was evidently a clockmaker of considerable repute. Some believe he worked in the period of 1790 and 1810; however, he was definitely entered as a clockmaker on the tax lists for 1779, 1800, and 1801. At least three of his clocks have been reported: all are of walnut and have painted dials; one has a thirty-hour and two have eight-day movements. One of his clocks is on display in the Hammond-Harwood house in Annapolis, Maryland. Authorities there think that the Hepplewhite case may have been made in Baltimore. Another of his clocks, marked "1780," is described as having inlaid eagles and stars, and a fine dial with a music box attachment capable of playing eight tunes.

Fig. 155. "Richard Koch, York" clock with sweep seconds and calendar hands. From the collections of the Historical Society of York County, Pennsylvania.

3

Fig. 156. Perhaps the plainest, most unattractive of the Pennsylvania tall clocks. It has a sweep second hand. From the collections of the Historical Society of York County, Pennsylvania.

John Long, also of Hanover, seems to have been at work sometime during the first two decades of the nineteenth century. At least two of his clocks are known.

John Michael labored in Hanover one, perhaps two decades earlier than John Long. He was not officially listed for his trade until 1965, when one of his clocks showed up at a local farm sale. It had an eight-day movement with moon phase, and it was housed in a Chippendale case, with broken arch and all finials intact.

There is one reference to Lewis Michael as a clockmaker who worked in York from 1788 through the 1790s. One thirty-hour tall clock signed by Lewis Michael exists, but that does not establish him as a maker. The earlier compiler probably based his dating on Michael's advertisement of April, 1788, announcing that he had set up shop in York Township to repair various instruments, clocks, etc.

An 1811 deed conveyed property to John Norton of York Borough; by an 1812 deed this same property was conveyed away by John Norton of Manchester Township. Although he was described as a silversmith, at least three clocks bearing his name are known.

F.B. Cook, a clockmaker in Columbia, Lancaster County from 1828 to 1832, began work in York in 1832 and continued there until his death in 1842. Around 1846 his widow married Francis C. Polack, who succeeded to Cook's clockmaking and silversmithing trade.

Joseph Rothrock (b. 1755) was a native of York Township. His father, Philip Jacob, arrived there from Germany in 1733. Joseph served as a private in the American Revolution. The York Township tax list of 1783 lists him as a silversmith; that he was also a clockmaker is certain because several of his clocks still exist. One carries the number 101, which suggests diligent production efforts. All of his clocks are eight-day, with painted dials and walnut cases.

No evidence has been confirmed about Richard Sauter of Hanover, who reputedly made two tall case clocks for John P. Senft in or around 1776 for the tremendous price of $125 each. The clocks are described as being in solid walnut cases about six feet tall, which, if true, is quite short.

None of the standard horological reference books mention Peter Schutz (d. 1790?), another silversmith and clockmaker from York Township. A deed from March 1758, indicating that he purchased land, describes him simply as a silversmith. He left at least four known clocks, although there may be many more. One of the four has an unusual pewter face, signed "Peter Schutz/Uhrmacher at York," the whole surmounted by crossed arrows. Only one other Pennsylvania clockmaker designating himself "uhrmacher" (German for watch- *or* clockmaker) has been noticed.

The Pennsylvania archives record that George Schwartz, a clockmaker of York

Township, enlisted on January 16, 1776, at age twenty-two, in Captain Grier's Company of the Sixth Pennsylvania Battalion. He then dropped out of sight. His clockmaking activities, if any, must have been short-lived before his enlistment.

Peter Schwartz, a party to many land transfers from 1772 to 1799 in York Township and Freytown, was described as a clockmaker and a silversmith. The 1783 census placed him in York as a clockmaker. Thus far, only a thirty-hour clock, made in 1771, with a brass face and a broken arch top, has been reported.

Mathias Smyser poses the premier clockmaking mystery of York County. A perusal of the half-dozen or so horological reference books, plus a check of the historical society notes failed to find any mention of him, yet figures 157 and 158 display two clocks that bear his name. Both appear to be solid, nicely cased clocks. Though less ornate than the other, the clock in figure 158 has a standard second hand and a circular calendar ring. Notice the eye-arresting candle-like finials.

Colorful Jacob Spangler (1767–1843), of York Township, the eldest son of Rudolph Spangler, is the only other Pennsylvanian clockmaker listed in the *Biographical Directory of the American Congress, 1774–1927:*

> Jacob Spangler, a Representative from Pennsylvania, . . . attended the York County Academy; engaged in surveying; served as a trumpeter in Captain McClellan's light horse company of York in 1799; county commissioner in 1800; postmaster of York 1795–1812; deputy surveyor of York County 1796–1815; again county commissioner in 1814; elected as a Federalist to the Fifteenth Congress, and served from March 4, 1817; until his resignation on April 20, 1818; surveyor general of Pennsylvania 1818–1821; commander of the State Militia, with title of general; chief escort of General Lafayette from York to Harrisburg on his visit to the United States in 1825; clerk of York County Court until 1820; again surveyor general of Pennsylvania from 1830 to 1836.

Somehow he found time to build tall clocks; six of them, all with painted dials and eight-day movements in walnut cases, are in existence. Each is signed "Jacob Spangler, York-Town." An "S" has been cut into the second hand of each clock.

From the pen of a great grandson of Rudolph Spangler (1738–1811), we have learned something about this important cabinet- and clockmaker. Rudolph was the son of Balthasar, who emigrated from Baden, Germany, to the Codorus section of York County in 1732. When Balthasar died in 1770, he left to Rudolph a small tract of land near his farm. Apparently, Rudolph neither lived on it nor farmed it, for by 1760 he was a practicing clockmaker and silversmith in the near town of York. Dur-

Fig. 157. "Mathias Smyser, York Town, Pa." clock made in 1827. In addition to the hour and minute hands, the center arbor carries a sweep seconds hand and a calendar date indicator. From the collections of the Historical Society of York County, Pennsylvania.

Fig. 158. A somewhat plainer, but still attractive clock by Mathias Smyser. From the collections of the Historical Society of York County, Pennsylvania.

160

157   158   159

Fig. 159. Magnificent clock by Rudolph Spangler. From the collections of the Historical Society of York County, Pennsylvania.

Fig. 160. Dial and richly carved bonnet of the clock in fig. 159. The scroll top and finial are unique among Pennsylvania tall clocks. From the collections of the Historical Society of York County, Pennsylvania.

ing the American Revolution, he joined the Sixth Company of the York County mi-litia, became its captain, and marched his men to eastern New Jersey in 1776 to form the "Flying Camp." In 1801 he was elected treasurer of York County; in 1803 he was appointed burgess of York; and in 1810, the year before his death, he was sent to the State General Assembly.

At least five of his clocks survive, some signed "Rudy Spangler, York Town." One, seen in figure 159, was signed "Rudolph Spangler." It is one of three brass-dialed, pre-Revolution varieties, made of cherry wood and being a full nine feet tall. The un-usual top has twin scrolls, so high as to be almost called Swans-necks, and a unique center finial that is a magnificently carved fleur-de-lys. It has an eight-day brass movement and a neatly engraved brass dial. Numerals are on the moon phase disc it-self rather than on the surrounding portion of the dial. It also has a date slot.

Joseph Taylor presents another puzzle: one compiler simply lists his name and "York P. and ca. 1785"; another compiler places him in York in the 1780s through the 1800s but states he was a dealer who cased movements made by others and ped-dled them in what was then western Pennsylvania. A third source maintains that he was making clocks in York Township in 1783 and that his clocks #97, #103, and #108 (one of which is a ninety-six hour clock) are known.

The Taylor mystery does not end here. One (and only one) previous chronicler re-ports that a John Taylor was at work before the Revolution in New Jersey, that he served in the war, and that afterwards he settled in York. While there, he joined Cap-tain Spangler's Volunteers, who marched to the defense of Baltimore in August, 1814.

Richard Taylor is omitted by one compiler; he is simply listed as working in York, circa 1785, by a second; and a third states only that his clock #99 is known.

In Bottstown, an early settlement formed to rival York, Henry Weigel was making clocks in about 1827. Five of his tall, eight-day clocks, with broken arch tops and painted dials, are known.

According to his own advertisement, Benjamin Willard was absent from Grafton, Massachusetts from about 1775 to around 1783 or 1784. His whereabouts have not been satisfactorily detailed, yet there was some speculation that he spent part of that time in York County. He did marry a York woman, Margaret Moore, but it now seems certain that the next time he was in York was in 1802 to sell some of the Moore property.

Fig. 161. Regardless of who made it, this clock is signed by Joseph Taylor. From the collections of the Historical Society of York County, Pennsylvania.

Center of the Commonwealth

Adams County

Adams County was formed from York County in January of 1800. Although clock-makers were among the artisans of the county, this group was not as prolific as that of the parent county, which was settled earlier and had a much larger population.

John Albert was primarily regarded as a silversmith in Huntington Township, circa 1814, but he was also a maker of clock movements. Cabinetmaker Jacob Koch, of Menallen Township, usually built the cases for Albert, although three clocks made entirely by Albert have been located. Figure 162 illustrates one of his clocks.

Unfortunately, it is not known where Albert and Koch learned their trades, for both of them produced some interesting features and unique—considering the environment and the early date for the area.

William W. Bell (1777–1842) was included on the Gettysburg tax lists for some twenty years; usually marked as a silversmith, in 1809 he was classified as a clock-maker and in 1821, as a clock- and watchmaker.

Samuel Fehlinger, who labored in the early nineteenth century, left only one tall clock, signed "Samuel Fehlinger, Gburg." No other information has been discovered.

Alexander Frazer was included in the 1860 census as a clock- and watchmaker in Menallen Township. However, tall case clockmaking in Pennsylvania had ceased by that date because of the challenge of the inexpensive Connecticut shelf clocks; therefore, it is safe to conclude that the census incorrectly applied the term "maker" to a man who was actually a repairer.

162

163

164

Daniel Grumbine was listed by an earlier compiler as a clockmaker in East Berlin from 1824 to 1860, but no corroborating evidence has been located. Likewise, Jacob Housel, of Hamilton Township, was identified as a clockmaker in 1821, but no substantiating proof has yet been found.

Samuel Keplinger (1770–1849) is mentioned by several compilers as a clockmaker in Gettysburg. Indeed, he advertised in 1807 as both a clock- and a watchmaker. One source states that two of his clocks are known, while another infers that more are extant, describing them as being rather tall and quite handsome. Keplinger

Fig. 162. John Albert clock, housed in elegant though simple case by Jacob Koch. Courtesy of H.H. Heilman, Jr.

Fig. 163. This close-up reveals not only the moon phase but also the beautifully wrought hour and minute hands, calendar hand, and sweep second hand. Courtesy of H.H. Heilman, Jr.

Fig. 164. The bell horn for better sound emission is unusual yet not uncommon in Adams, Franklin, and Cumberland counties. Courtesy of H.H. Heilman, Jr.

165

must have been a good mechanic, for he was granted a patent on May 4, 1820, for a machine that made watch chains.

John Latshar of Reading Township is described in *The Book of American Clocks* as a clockmaker who worked between 1780 and 1784. However, no other data has been found.

David Little has been mentioned as a clock- and watchmaker in Gettysburg in 1821. George Long, of the same town, appeared on the assessment list of 1807 as a single man and a clockmaker. Joseph Mathias has also been suggested as a Gettysburg clockmaker, though in the 1830s and the 1840s, but no supporting evidence is offered. Finally, the 1821 list of occupations of Gettysburg taxables refers to George Welsh as a justice of the peace and a clock- and watchmaker.

One tantalizing mystery remains buried in the clockmaking history of Adams County. The 1810 census for the district embracing Huntingdon, Latimore, Tyrone, and Reading Townships listed one "clock makery" but offered no further identification. This could have been a sole proprietor who was already known, a sole proprietor not yet known, or, perhaps, several workmen attempting simultaneous production of several clocks.

Fig. 165. The novel side movement window. Courtesy of H.H. Heilman, Jr.

Bedford County

Bedford County, formed from a part of Cumberland County, was first settled in 1751 and was laid out in 1771 at the request of John Penn. The county was named in honor of the Duke of Bedford. The county seat, Bedford, is historically important, being both the crossroads of well-used trails east-west and north-south and a vital staging area for mounting attacks on the French and repelling Indians and for pioneers venturing beyond the Alleghenies. Despite its early settlement and strategic location, however, this county produced no clockmakers of distinction during the colonial or Yankee periods.

A researcher for the Bedford Heritage Commission wrote to tell us: "In Waterman's *History of Bedford, Somerset, and Fulton Counties,* published in 1884, on page 249, I found a William Vickroy, clockmaker, was listed as a tax paying inhabitant in Bedford Borough in 1795. On page 250, I found a Jacob Diehl, clockmaker, was listed in the 1810 tax records. Three Diehl clocks exist, two locally and one in a museum in New England."[1] Unfortunately, a survey of several reference books failed to locate any data on Vickroy. Better luck was had tracing the other name. Jacob Diehl (1776–1858) worked in Reading, Pennsylvania, operating the clock shop of Daniel Rose while Rose served in the state legislature. He later took over the shop and operated it until 1804, when he dropped out of sight, so far as earlier compilers could as-

1. Letter received from V.E. Whiskers, May 7, 1974.

certain. A vague reference to his clock #70 being marked "Bedford, PA." tentatively marks Diehl's later working place.

An ingenious clockmaker from the twilight of the nineteenth century is described in this letter to the *Bedford Gazette*:

> Electric clocks were very much more of a novelty back in 1894. The account of a Bedford jeweler who secured a patent on this type of clock is reprinted from the Gazette files.
> "J.W. Ridenour, the enterprising jeweler of this place, has secured control of the patent of an electric clock of Mr. Wubbeler's invention. This is perhaps the most unique clock ever invented in that it is the only reliable electric clock running independently.
> "At a glance it resembles any ordinary eight-day clock, but upon closer inspection it is found that it has only three wheels—one for the second, one for the minute, and one for the hour hands. These wheels with a magnet, a small weak battery and a pendulum, constitute the entire machinery of the timepiece. It does not require any winding and needs no attention whatever, except that once in a year, the batteries ought to be renewed, which costs ten cents. But its greatest merit is its time-keeping qualities."[2]

No additional information has been found concerning Ridenour. How he and the inventor came together is still a question, nor is it known if he arranged for the manufacture and sale of this unique electric clock. The April 12, 1893 issue of a horological review contained this information about the inventor and his invention:

> 494,832. ELECTRIC CLOCK. Herman Wubbeler,
> Beaver Falls, PA., filed May 21, 1892,
> Serial No. 433,905. (No model.)
>
> In an electric clock, the pendulum provided with a lateral operating arm, the electromagnet, the armature-lever, the impulse spring carried by the armature lever and adapted to engage said operating arm, the seconds ratchet engaged by a pawl upon the pendulum, the circuit closer adapted to be engaged by the pendulum and the circuit breaker operated by the armature lever.

At a much later date, approximately 1950, there was still laboring a local practitioner of an art that was then over a century outdated. An agent for the Department of Public Welfare interviewed an old man in Bedford County who had made a con-

2. Letter received from V.E. Whiskers, January 25, 1974.

traption which ground teeth into discs of wood from one inch to six inches in diameter. The motive power was an old sewing machine operated by a foot treadle. The control that determined the diameter and number of teeth was a wooden disc with a thin sheet of metal on one side, in which were punched a number of small holes. By fastening a small arm into one of these holes and then working the treadle, the operator could cut the teeth accurately. Iron wood and dogwood were used for these wheels, as they were the least likely to shrink or split.

The old man claimed he was making the cog wheels for clockmakers who used wooden cog wheels instead of metal.[3] It would be interesting to know who those customers were at so late a date.

Cumberland County

Named for a shire in England, Cumberland County was set apart from Lancaster County in the 1730s. Aggressive Scotch-Irish pioneers were its first settlers; then, just before the Revolutionary War, many Pennsylvania Germans began to move in. The county was organized in 1750.

Cumberland County's military history began with the French and Indian War. Fort Franklin was built at Shippensburg in 1740; in 1753 Fort Lowther was erected at Carlisle and was followed by Fort Morris in 1755. Provincial soldiers were present there as early as 1750 and Indian councils were held in the area. Colonel Henry Bouquet joined General John Forbes here in their expedition to capture Fort Duquesne in 1758. Hessian soldiers captured at Trenton built the guardhouse at Carlisle Barracks in 1777. The military post, the second oldest in the nation, is still used by the U.S. Army. Carlisle, an armament center during the Revolution, was occupied by confederate troops during the Civil War.

Thousands of pioneers passed through the county on their trek westward. The Carlisle Indian School was in session from 1879 to 1918. The Naval Supply Depot at Mechanicsburg is one of the largest in the United States.

Daniel Drawbaugh, of Eberly's Mills, is indeed the most famous clockmaker and inventor from Cumberland County. Much has been written about Drawbaugh, variously referred to as the "Edison of the Cumberland Valley" and the "Wizard of Eberly's Mills."

Had Chief Justice Waite of the United States Supreme Court died five days earlier than March 23, 1888, the name Drawbaugh might today be synonymous with the telephone instead of Bell, and the horological world might have been without an electrical timing device created as an example of perpetual motion. Daniel Drawbaugh of Eberly's Mills . . . apparently produced the first instruments embodying the principles of the modern telephone. Had he had the foresight to see in that "talking machine" not a mere toy but a discovery of revolutionary commercial significance, his name might stand today among the immortals. But Drawbaugh was not a business man; he lived and died poor, his name remembered only around a small segment of Pennsylvania. . . .

The "electric clock" was not a simple device operated by alternating current, as those in common use today, but a ponderous contrivance standing six feet high—its pendulum alone weighing approximately twenty-four pounds. The pendulum was propelled by an ingenious arrangement of permanent magnets and electromagnets, which were wired to draw latent electrical energy from the ground through a well six feet deep, lined with fine plates and filled with carbon. The clock was acclaimed at the time as "the nearest thing yet to perpetual motion.". . .

People today remember Daniel Drawbaugh for his magnetic clock. Despite the fact he devoted most of his time for a decade to developing his talking machine and spoke of little else, a witness, Jacob Shettel, in the telephone suit testified, "I did not think there was half the value in that (the talking machine) that there was in the clock—I never considered the talking machine, as my mind was taken up with the clock." As a consequence, Shettel chose to exploit the clock rather than the telephone.

Unfortunately for posterity, the clock ultimately proved a failure. It was capricious in electric storms as Drawbaugh originally rigged it up and likely to be affected by extraneous metallic substances in the earth. But it created a lot of talk.

Originally the earth battery gave the pendulum propulsion in but one direction, the pendulum's weight swinging it back. When it was changed, first to dry cell and then to house current power, it was fixed so that the pendulum received propulsion in both directions, thus improving its timing.

Only a few of the clocks were ever made, Drawbaugh himself having made only three. One of the earliest clocks was exhibited by one Leonard Johnson at "10¢ a look" at Harrisburg in 1874. Johnson's advertisement read "Greatest piece of mechanism of the age. All should see it. Magnetic clock. Seven feet by two feet three inches. Pendulum weighs 25 pounds. Motive power is derived from the earth by means of two small metal plates buried in the ground to which two insulated wires are attached and ingeniously connected with the works of the clock."

Another of the clocks was acquired by St. John's Lutheran Church, Camp Hill, in 1871. Laid outside in the church attic, it was purchased for $10.00, by Sam N. Miller, a member of the church council, in about 1910. Miller rigged it to operate from a dry cell battery. His daughter, Mrs. Kenneth Ivory, Mechanicsburg, had it for a time but, since it had to be bolted to the wall, she found it cumbersome in various moves and gave it to her sister, Mrs. H.C. Maeyer, Washington, D.C.

A third clock was the property of the late Rev. L.C. Smiley, a Lemoyne, Pennsylvania jeweler. The clock was bought by the elder Smiley when Drawbaugh's property was sold and is now owned by the Pennsylvania Historic & Museum Commission. The beautifully carved and ornamented solid walnut case is nearly seven feet tall and three feet wide at the base. It has an open dial, decorated in gold leaf with black numerals. The massive brass pendulum with two pairs of compensating rods weighs roughly twenty-four pounds. The clock is not one operated by alternating current as those in common use today. It has no motor, but is driven by the pendulum. Motive power to run the clock was originally derived from the earth by means of two small metal plates buried in the earth, to which two insulated wires were attached and connected with the works of the clock. The clock thus utilized the earth's rotation in its own magnetic field. Originally the earth battery gave the pendulum propulsion in one direction, the weight of the pendulum swinging it back. Mr. Smiley adjusted the clock to propel in both directions, thus improving its timing; and operated the clock on a dry cell battery, then on house current. To avoid the use of a battery to drive the clock, a rectifier to provide direct current from a house current source was provided, so that Drawbaugh's original mechanism has not been affected in any way. It is believed that this clock is the one that was exhibited at the Centennial in 1876 and at expositions in Paris, London and Berlin.

An alternate description is that the clock is over six feet high, and, unlike other clocks, the pendulum is its motor. It is suspended on an edged pivot of hardened steel to reduce friction to a minimum. This pendulum weighs about twenty-four pounds. Its central rod terminates midway between the ball and point of suspension, and at this place there is an ordinary permanent magnet. Fastened to the back of the clock case and at right angles to the permanent magnet, is an electro magnet, the wires of which run into the earth. The earth becomes the battery feeding this magnet. When the pendulum is swung from the perpendicular, the opposite poles of the two magnets first attract and then repel, thus keeping up the oscillation. There are but four bearings that are subjected to friction, and this the least possible amount. Latent currents from the earth are secured by digging a hole six feet deep and three in diameter, and placing fine plates at the bottom, to which the wires are attached. Coke or charcoal is then dumped about the plates to retain moisture and the hole is filled with earth. The affair is a marvel of simplicity and ingenuity and can be run so that it will not gain or lose more than two seconds in a year. Contemporary observers reported the clock had two drawbacks, namely: it needed its inventor to regulate it and in electrical storms it ran wild. They were quick to praise it, however, as the only piece of machinery in the world operated entirely by electrical forces drawn from the earth and as the nearest thing yet to perpetual motion.

The company formed by Shettel made two clocks. Another version of the clock, but without original works, is supposedly owned by a Drawbaugh relative in the Harrisburg area.[1]

Sometime in 1868 Drawbaugh started experimenting with the electromagnetic clock. A complete clock was set running in 1869 or 1870. It is now asserted that he personally made four clocks—the last in about 1878.[2] The concept of such a clock was not original with Drawbaugh, for Alexander Bain of England had anticipated him as early as 1847. As one earlier writer commented, there was great similarity between the clocks of these two men, although there is no hint that Drawbaugh knew of Bain's prior production.[3]

The legal battles, which, oversimplified, were Bell versus Drawbaugh, dragged out over eight years, finally culminating in a United States Supreme Court 4 to 3 decision for Bell. According to George Swetnam, it is the longest opinion given up to that time by that high tribunal.[4] Swetnam's article contains an amusing story about how a smart young man made money by divining the final decision (while poor Drawbaugh received nothing).

John Eberly, for whom Eberly's Mills may have been named, is sometimes mentioned as a clockmaker. No corroboration of this has been found, although the written history of Cumberland County notes marriage ties between the Eberly and Erb families.

Earlier clock historians associated the name Erb only with Lancaster County, but two family members have been discovered who belonged to Cumberland, heart and soul. The first Erb family left the Palatine region of Europe in September 1736, and settled in Lancaster County, but Christian Erb of the third generation moved to Cumberland in 1810 and located near Wormleysburg. His oldest son, Abraham, built the first clock placed in the courthouse in Carlisle in 1846. Abraham Erb was considered one of the most skilled mechanics of his day. Besides manufacturing

1. James W. Gibbs, "Daniel Drawbaugh—Tragic Genius," *Bulletin of the National Association of Watch and Clock Collectors, Inc.* 7, no. 3 (April 1956):158–63.

2. Ibid.

3. George Swetnam, "Clockmakers and Watchmakers of Western Pennsylvania," *Bulletin of the National Association of Watch and Clock Collectors, Inc.* 9, no. 8 (February 1961): 547.

4. Ibid.

166

167

Fig. 166. Jacob Handel clock in magnificent case. Courtesy of an anonymous owner.

Fig. 167. Fine dial of the clock in fig. 166, with special features and magnificent sweep second hand. Courtesy of an anonymous owner.

clocks, he traveled over the country once a year, carrying his book of 4,000 names with him, to keep his clocks in good running order. His son, also named Abraham, followed the trade and was still repairing clocks at age eighty.[5]

Jacob Engle is recorded as a maker of tall case clocks in Carlisle, circa the 1780s through the 1800s. He must not be confused with another Jacob Engle, who made clocks and watches at a much later date in Millersburg, Ohio.

One source lists John Gemmill as a maker of tall clocks, variously in Lancaster, Carlisle, and York, during the approximate period of 1756 to 1760. That he worked in three towns in so short a period, while not impossible, seems improbable. Another source described him as a bona fide clockmaker, who had worked elsewhere but appears to have settled finally in Carlisle during its frontier days as an important military and trading post. An excellent tall case clock bearing both his name and "Carlisle" was once owned by Edward Martin, senator from Pennsylvania.

Two references mention John Green as a clockmaker, also in Carlisle, during the early nineteenth century.

Likewise, two sources regard John Greer as a clockmaker and possibly a watch repairer in Carlisle during the 1770s.

> JOHN GREER. All persons indebted to the estate of John Greer, late of Carlisle, Clock and Watch-Maker, deceased, are requested to make speedy payment. William Oliphant, Administrator. (*Pennsylvania Packet,* February 28, 1774)

Bernard Handel has been identified as a clockmaker in Carlisle, perhaps from 1780 to 1810. Another compiler refers to him as the Bernard Hendel who conducted a jewelry store and advertised himself as a clock- and watchmaker during the first quarter of the nineteenth century. The assertion has also been made that Hendel bought movements, put his name on them, and put them in his own cases. The discrepancy in name was resolved, however, when a clock was located in 1972 that definitely bears the name of Bernard Handel. The discrepancy in time is not so great a matter as it might appear. Whether he did or did not produce clock movements is not now likely to be determined.

The story of Bernard's older brother, Jacob Handel, listed in Carlisle during the 1760s through the 1780s, is very similar. Figures 166 and 167 show one of his

5. Levi E. Martin, *Biographical Memorial of John Eberly and Genealogical Family Register of the Eberly Family* (New Kingston, Pa.: United Evangelical Publishing House, 1896), pp. 31, 70.

clocks. Truly a gem, it is an eight-day brass movement with sweep second hand; full calendar of day, date, and month; moon phase; position of sun; and painted iron dial. Further, the case is signed by its maker, Jacob Wain, Harrisburg—this is a rare practice. It, too, is a gem, constructed of solid, light mahogany or walnut with a broken arch; a finial; French feet; and string, bellflower, and fan inlays, all finely executed and shaded. To top it off, there is even an eagle on the waist above the door. This tour de force is presently owned by a recognized connoisseur of fine clocks. The signed case proves that. Jacob did not have to depend on Bernard for cases. Perhaps Bernard is erroneously ascribed as a casemaker. It is therefore safe to assume that Jacob did make his own movements.

Clockmaker Solomon Gorgas, of Ephrata, moved to farm in Lower Allen Township, Cumberland County, in about 1800. There in May 1806, a son, William Rittenhouse Gorgas, was born. Although his father apparently relinquished clockmaking to pursue farming, he most likely taught the art to his son. At least one tall clock signed "William Gorgas" on the back of the dial is in existence, having been recently verified. William was a director of two banks and of the Harrisburg City Passenger Railway Company, as well as serving both as a legislator and as a senator.

Dauphin County

John Harris came to the lower mideastern area of Pennsylvania as an Indian trader before 1715, and established a ferry and trading post there in 1720. His son continued and founded Harrisburg. Dauphin County was organized in 1785 and was named in honor of the heir to the French throne. In 1812 it became the state capital, and developed into an important canal and rail center, and a military and manufacturing core.

It is not surprising, therefore, that Dauphin County can lay claim to a dozen clockmakers, but it is amazing how little is known about them. Only on Frederick Heisely has any appreciable data been accumulated.

George Beatty (1781–1862) came over from Ireland to settle in Harrisburg; the date and circumstances of his settling have not been found. He became the brother-in-law of an already established clockmaker, Samuel Hill, and under Hill's tutelage he learned the trade. It is believed that he established his own business in about 1808, though he possibly simply continued Hill's business following his death in 1809. Either way, Beatty conducted his trade over an unusually long span, right up to his death. Judging from an example of his product, he was an ingenious mechanic.

There is some confusion over Thomas Dickey (b. 1793?). That he was indeed a clockmaker is certain; the location where he plied his trade is a question. One source lists him as being in Marietta, Lancaster County, from 1810 to 1820; in Middletown at the decade's start; and, finally, in Harrisburg after 1820. Another source indicates that he was in Marietta and later in Harrisburg, and mentions that he was listed among the taxables of 1812 through 1814, but fails to say where. A third source places him in Harrisburg as early as 1814 by citing Dickey's advertisement that he "begs leave to inform the Publick that he has commenced the business of a clock-maker and watchmaker next door above the Tavern."

Joseph Doll (b. 1768) is believed by some authorities to have been a clockmaker, first in Lancaster city and then in Harrisburg. Though the facts are still meager, records clearly show that he was born in Lancaster and that his mother died on February 9, 1810, in his home in Harrisburg. According to a newspaper advertisement from September 20, 1797, Joseph Doll was both a clockmaker and a silversmith in Harrisburg; in an advertisement from June 1, 1811, he termed himself "Watch and Clockmaker," and also noted that he carried a stock of "Gold and Silver Ware." It is not known from whom he learned his trade, nor for whom he may have worked as a journeyman. By contemporary custom, he probably would have been ready to set up his own business in about 1791. Thus, his location for six years is unaccounted for.

There is one bit of evidence that informs that he worked only in Harrisburg. One of his clocks, which is now in the Ford Museum, has an eagle inlaid into the case. Authorities know of only about a dozen clock cases with eagle inlays, and these originated in Manheim and Harrisburg. While Doll did not put the name of the town in which he worked on his dials, the conclusion is clear.

Frederick Heisely (1759–1839), born in Lancaster, was in service with the Second Pennsylvania Regiment during the New Jersey campaign of 1778. Presumably, he then became apprenticed to the well-known Lancaster clockmaker, George Hoff, whose daughter, Catharine, he married in November 1783. The young couple decided (for reasons unknown) to move to Frederick, Maryland, and while there he constructed a tower clock that is now in the Smithsonian Institute.

After a decade, they returned to Lancaster so that Heisely could go into partnership with his father-in-law. They advertised to announce the news.

> GEORGE HOFF & FREDERICK HEISELY Inform their friends and the public in general that the Clock & Watchmaker's Shop, between the Courthouse and the jail, formerly kept by George Hoff only, is now carried on by Hoff & Heisely, jointly, who now make in addition to what was usually made in said shop, all kinds of Surveyors' Instruments, such as Land Compasses of different kinds and sizes, Chains, Scales of any dimension; Protractors, of different sizes and forms; best steel-pointed Dividers; stiff and jointly Draw-Pens, &c. &c.
>
> Said Heisely has carried on the Instrument making business, in

Fredericktown, in Maryland, upwards of ten years with great success. His Instruments are scattered from one extremity of the state of Maryland to the other, as well as through Virginia and Kentucky, and are universally approved of. He flatters himself to meet with equal success in that line.

Hoff and Heisely hope, by their strict attention to both branches of business, as heretofore, to merit the patronage of a generous public. (*Lancaster Journal,* January 22, 1796)

It has been suggested that the partnership lasted about eight years; evidently this was not true, for it seems to have lasted even less than one.

The Partnership of Hoff & Heisely being dissolved, the subscriber begs leave to inform his friends, and the public in general, that he has removed to the house formerly occupied by the Editor of the Lancaster Journal, and opposite to the Post and Printing Office of Mr. Hamilton, where he intends carrying on the Clockmaking business in all branches, and repairing watches in the neatest and best manner, and on the most reasonable terms. He also makes, as heretofore, all kinds of Surveyors' Instruments. He hopes, by his strict attention to business, and constant indeavours [*sic*] to please, to merit the future custom of his old friends, and the public in general. He expects a few elegant Silver Watches, which he intends to sell at the most reduced prices.

Frederick Heisely
Lancaster, Nov. 18, 1796
(*Lancaster Journal,* November 25, 1796)

The period of 1797 to 1811 is a blank; it must be assumed that Heisely quietly pursued his trades. Around 1811, he and his family moved to Harrisburg, where he was in business with his older son, George Jacob, until his retirement. Heisely was also the Dauphin County treasurer from 1827 to 1829. Contrary to earlier opinion (some believe he moved to Pittsburgh), he lived until his death in Harrisburg.

Frederick Heisely's clock production is usually thought to have been in tall clocks, though more recent information indicates he also made short clocks. A quarter of a century ago, a Heisely mantel clock was identified which dates in the early 1800s. It has an eight-day, brass movement, and a time and strike, without a silencer. The dial, tympanum, and spandrels have prettily enameled decorations.[1] Exhibited at the annual convention of the National Association of Watch and Clock Collectors, Inc. in

---

1. *Timepieces Quarterly* 1, no.2 (February 1949).

Pittsburgh in June 1973, was a conventionally shaped bracket clock by Frederick Heisely, Harrisburg, made probably during the first part of the nineteenth century. The movement, however, was not of traditional design, as it had a pin-wheel escapement.

It actually might be wise to allow D.H. Shaffer, an eminent clock authority, to describe the bracket clock for us:

> There were a few spring-driven clocks in America before 1840. Foremost among these were the American bracket clocks. These finely made clocks were usually faithful to the design of the English bracket clocks. Sometimes a native craftsman departed from the customary plans to produce an item of special interest to us today. The springs for these clocks, as well as many other basic components of the movements, were imported from Europe. American makers often simply finished and assembled these clocks. The limited availability of spring-driven clocks shows that it was not impossible to produce such items, merely difficult. Steel of the quality required to form coil springs was not then available on this side of the Atlantic, making it necessary to import the springs that were to be used. This additional cost made coil springs unsuitable for modest priced clocks.[2]

At the Watch and Clock Collectors convention, a tall shelf clock by Jerome & Darrow and one very similar to it by Heisely were shown. The resemblance between the two pieces was so apparent as to cause speculation over whether Heisely used Jerome & Darrow movements in this particular style of clock. One noted authority on Pennsylvania clocks offered this hypothesis:

> George Hoff favored the use of lantern pinions and increased and simplified their preparation by making only a few sizes and tooth counts. During his association with Hoff, Frederick Heisely observed this and used lantern pinions in his brass eight day repeating movements with the strike train between the plates. This plus somewhat less fine finish and other innovations made it possible for him to make good shelf clock movements competitive with similar contemporary Connecticut movements. It is possible he traded movements to Jerome & Darrow for finished cases. He may well have been the only Pennsylvania maker of tall clocks who successfully switched to shelf clocks in a commercial sense.[3]

2. D.H. Shaffer, "A Survey History of the American Spring-driven Clock, 1840–1860," *Bulletin of the National Association of Watch and Clock Collectors, Inc.* supplement 9 (Winter 1973).

3. E.F. LaFond, Jr., "Frederick Heisely Strikes Again—or, After You, Mr. Heisely," *Bulletin of the National Association of Watch and Clock Collectors, Inc.* 13, no. 3 (April 1968): 227–49.

It is now generally accepted that Frederick Heisely *did* make the A-plate movements sometimes found in Jerome & Darrow cases.

George Jacob Heisely (1789–1880) was born in Frederick, Maryland. It is likely that he worked as an apprentice to his father, Frederick Heisely, when he was in business over the years of 1797 to 1811. The father and son were in business together when they moved to Harrisburg.

George served in the military briefly during two wars. From August to December 1814, he was with the Harrisburg volunteers of the Pennsylvania Militia, in and around Baltimore. Almost a half-century later, he was a member of the Home Guards when Lee invaded Pennsylvania in 1863. George was also a flute player, and the legend persists that he chose the tune which was mated to Francis Scott Key's verses and which eventually became our national anthem, "The Star Spangled Banner."

Like his father, he made at least one tower clock and, again like Frederick, he was buried in Harrisburg.

Frederick Augustus Heisely (1792–1875) was, like his brother, born in Frederick, Maryland, and he also served in the War of 1812 with the Maryland Militia—he may even have been wounded. Presumably he also learned his trade from his father, as both he and George continued making surveyor's compasses. Frederick Augustus is the Heisely who moved to Pittsburgh in 1836. He was already listed in the 1837 directory; his advertisement showed a surveyor's compass and stated that he made clocks and watches. The 1839 directory listed him as a watch- and an instrumentmaker. From 1849 his name appeared intermittently in directories until 1873.

It is generally agreed that Peter Hineberger (1784–1869) was in Harrisburg from 1790 to 1830 and that he built tall clocks and made flat silver. He eventually moved to Harrisonburg, Virginia, possibly because large numbers of persons of the same general European origin as our Pennsylvania Germans settled in that area.

Samuel Hill (1765–1809) was born in England and learned his trade there. He came to Harrisburg in 1785 and must have immediately set up shop, for he was on the 1786 assessment list. Thus, he was the first clockmaker in Harrisburg and likely the first in Dauphin County. He married Nancy Beatty, an Irish girl, and taught her brother, George, the art of clockmaking. Hill is described in Egle's *History of Dauphin and Lebanon Counties* as "ingenious and skillful." His first shop was located on the south side of Second Street, and his second, near Bombaugh's tavern, was where he worked until his early death.

Hill's clocks were not all alike in either mechanism or casing. Escapements in some works were placed at dead center, while others were a recoil placed immediately in

Fig. 168. Traditional bracket clock from the early nineteenth century. Courtesy of *Timepieces Quarterly*.

front of the back plate—an unusual placement. It is believed that the cases used by both Hill and Beatty were made by Samuel Berryhill, the only Harrisburg cabinet-maker assessed at that time. One known Hill clock has a cherry case, inlaid with walnut veneer paneling; a bird's eye maple door; and a turreted hood with six finials. This unusual design may have been a model for a later clockmaker named Grosch who worked in Marietta because at least one pillar and scroll with multiple finials is known. Another Hill clock is of the traditional tall case design with the broken arch, or scroll top, design. Considering Hill's English origin, it is not surprising that the name Osborne is found on the dial plates that support the moon phase and calendar mechanism. Osborne was a contemporary manufacturer of dials and false plates in Birmingham, England.

Thomas Leschey is confirmed by three sources as a clockmaker in Middletown during the very early portion of the nineteenth century, yet no additional information can be supplied.

Similarly, little is known about Anne Scott, who was listed as a Harrisburg clockmaker at the middle of the nineteenth century. This dearth of knowledge is a pity, for women horologists in America were precious few. The somewhat late date mentioned raises the suspicion that she might really have been a repairer or a clock dealer.

An identical conclusion could be drawn for H. Steckman, despite his listing by two sources as a maker of tall clocks in Middletown around 1850 to 1858, and for Charles D. Walters, who is simply mentioned as being in Harrisburg in the 1850s and the 1860s.

The Historical Society of Dauphin County owns a tall case clock signed by Jacob Winterode, the upper portion of which is shown in figure 169. Nothing is presently known about this man except that two sources include him as a maker of tall clocks in Dauphin County. Still, both were unable to ascribe either a location or a date.

Mention must be made of the Apostolic clock in the Hershey Museum, undeniably the most famous timepiece in the county and possibly in the whole southeastern portion of the state. Its maker, John Fiester, was born in 1846 in Lancaster County.

The clock consists of three sections. The lower section houses a music box, which plays upon the appearance of the trumpeters at the time of the apostles' procession in the upper section.

The middle section contains the representative forms of the elements of time. The face depicts the seconds, minutes, and hours, the day of the week and of the month, the month of the year, the signs of the zodiac, and the phases of the moon. Centered above the face, a form depicting childhood appears on the approach of the first quarter of the hour. Father Time then strikes one with his scythe. On the approach of the

Fig. 169. Jacob Winterode clock with minute, hour, sweep second, and calendar hands operating off one arbor. The hour hand appears to be a replacement. Courtesy of the Historical Society of Dauphin County and the late Mrs. John Tilman, curator.

Fig. 170. The world famous Apostolic clock. Courtesy of Mr. John Strawbridge III.

APOSTOLIC CLOCK

second quarter, another form, Youth, appears and Father Time strikes two. On the approach of the third quarter, Middle Age appears and Father Time strikes three, whereupon the apostles' procession before Christ begins and the music box plays a selection. At the approach of the fourth quarter, Old Age appears and Father Time strikes four. The skeleton, representing death, strikes the hour.

The upper section of the clock is where the procession of the disciples takes place at the approach of Middle Age, depicting the betrayal of Christ that occurred in his middle age. As the procession begins, the Apostles parade out and face Christ, who raises his arms as if to bless them. The three Virgins appear in the top center and observe the procession. Upon the appearance of Peter, Justice raises her scales and Satan appears behind her, watching for the appearance of Judas.

As Peter approaches Christ, the cock crows and Peter turns his back to Christ, depicting the denial. Upon the appearance of Judas, Satan withdraws from his window; he reappears, following Judas to see that he ignores Christ. Satan then withdraws and reappears behind the clock, observing Judas as he fulfills his promise. Satan withdraws from view, as do the three Virgins, and Justice lowers her scales, depicting the end of the procession.

Eleven years were required to construct this masterpiece, which stands six feet tall and is three feet wide. Tradition has it that the clock was initially exhibited from a wagon traveling from town to town. While in Manheim, maker Fiester was in some way befriended by a Mr. Danner, and the clock later served as repayment to Danner for his kindness.

Franklin County

Named, of course, for Benjamin Franklin, Franklin County was formerly a part of Cumberland County and was organized in 1784. It was a frontier against the Indians and it even figured into the Civil War. Mercersburg and Waynesboro were named for Hugh Mercer and Anthony Wayne, both generals in the Revolutionary War. Although never particularly noted for early craftsmen or industry, Franklin County can claim some fine clockmakers.

Alexander Scott carried on a clockmaking and silversmithing business in Chambersburg from about 1800 until his death in 1821. He manufactured a large number of eight-day tall clocks, which were celebrated for their correctness as timekeepers. It is interesting that he was an uncle of Thomas A. Scott, the first president of the Pennsylvania Railroad; furthermore, it is possible that he had James Thomson as an apprentice.

James Thomson (1790–1876) was born near Chambersburg, but moved to Pittsburgh in 1812. From then until 1825 he carried on a clock- and watchmaking business there. Scott being in Chambersburg, he probably learned the art while still in that area. Later he was engaged in building steam engines and freight cars; he served as mayor of Pittsburgh, and, finally, he was an engineer for the Pittsburgh Gas Company.

At least three tall clocks, beautiful in structure and excellent at keeping perfect time, are known to have been made by James Wilkins (1794–1858). Born near Mercersburg, he married Catherine Spangler, who *may* have been related to the

Fig. 171. James Wilkins tall clock.

clockmaking Spanglers of Hagerstown, Maryland and York, Pennsylvania. The best known Wilkins clock is now at the Mercersburg Academy. On the back of the gong, James Wilkins wrote his name and "1820," the year he made the clock. His son, George, eventually serviced the clock and put his name on the gong. Still later, his grandson, Wesley Fallon, a jeweler, repaired the clock and added his name. This particular clock is doubly valuable as James' brother, Marshall, a cabinetmaker, made the case. Another clock, ninety-nine inches tall, has a seatboard signed "Made July 1834/by James Wilkins/at Mercersburg/Franklin Co./Penna." The case of this one was possibly also made by Marshall. Elsewhere in the clock is another inscription, "Rep.d 1852/by Wm. H. Wilkins."

Jacob Wolf has been identified as a clockmaker in Waynesburg, Greene County. In truth, Wolf really belonged in Waynesburg, Franklin County, where he was identified as a silversmith and a clockmaker in the 1790 census. The community was Wallacetown until 1797, when it became Waynesburg, which it remained until 1831 when it was renamed Waynesboro to avoid confusion with other communities named after Anthony Wayne. Jacob Wolf bought land and built the establishment where he apparently lived and conducted his clockmaking business until his death.

Several Wolf clocks are extant. One is simply signed "Jacob Wolf"—no place given—so it was presumably made before 1797. Its cherry wood case is of a plain, simple style, with chamfered corners on the waist, free-standing round columns on the hood, and a molded scroll top with urn finials. The dial has Roman numerals; a sweep second and a day-of-month hand both work off the center post; the spandrels have a gesso dotted outline; and a moon phase dial is present.

A second Jacob Wolf clock has a signature and a location, so it was made after 1797. Its case has crotch veneer panels, cross banding, tapered turned pillars on the hood, a molded scroll top, and urn finials. This dial has Arabic numerals, pineapple spandrels, a slot calendar, a separate ring seconds hand, and a moon phase.

Several others of his pieces are in tiger-maple cases, some have seashell pattern spandrels, and one has hands that appear to be made of cast gold and silver.

Charles Young appears to have been the first clockmaker in Chambersburg and perhaps in the county—one source dates him circa 1750 to 1780, another circa 1760 to 1770, and another simply before the Revolutionary War. Figure 174 shows a clock attributed to him. Springs were necessary, as the motive power for a clock of this sort would be almost nonexistent in the colonies at that time by native manufacturers. Assuming the dating is correct, there is the possibility that the movement is English. Contrariwise, one very respected museum curator speculates that the dating might be closer to 1780 and that the movement is American.

Fig. 172. Jacob Wolf clock.

While a discussion of electric clocks may not be compatible with the title of this book, they played an interesting role in the horological history of this county. *The Keystone* for July 1899 contained this account of the "Electrical Programme Clock."

Our illustration [absent from here] shows an ingenious electrical programme clock made by jeweler Frederick Frick, of Waynesboro, Pa. Mr. Frick explained his invention at a recent meeting of the Philadelphia Horological Society with the result that the society passed unanimously the following commendatory resolution:

The Horological Society of Philadelphia has examined the Frick Electric Programme Clock, and finds it to be a most ingenious, useful and practical invention for the purpose of distributing time signals in schools, colleges and manufacturing establishments, or other places where accurate time signals are required.

As explained by Mr. Frick, the programme mechanism proper consists of a programme dial which is driven by a suitable mechanical motor and an automatic switch and connections, all of which are mounted on a suitable base. The programme motor is started once each five minutes, when it revolves the programme dial one space, or five-minute period, and is reset for the next movement.

In the programme dial are as many circles of holes as it is desired to give different programmes or schedules. Tapered pins are inserted in these holes by the figures on the dial to the times it is desired to have the signals given.

The programme mechanism in the case with the time movement is designed for giving different programmes on different days and nights of the week. In this clock there are six commutators, which are carried by the insulating posts at the motor end and by suitable commutator adjustors at the dial end. The commutator adjustors have vertical elongated holes in them, and when the commutators are in their normal positions they rest at the lower ends of these elongated holes and below the path of the pins in the programme dial; consequently, when in this position no signals can be given. The automatic switch drum is made of an insulator, and has as many circular rows of holes as there are commutators, each row having fourteen equally spaced holes, seven holes being for the seven days and seven for the seven nights of the week. In these holes are inserted pins which automatically ring into and out of service the respective commutators on the proper days and nights of the week. Each morning and evening of the week the automatic switch drum is revolved one space by means of the cam and bell-crank lever at back of programme dial, and each such movement throws into or out of use one of the commutators. It will be apparent that by using different circles of holes in the programme dial for the programmes for the different days of the week these different programmes can be brought into and out of service on any days desired by simply placing the pins in the proper holes in the switch drum, setting the pins by the index on the ratchet wheel at upper end of switch drum.

In its entirety, the clock is very complete and effective for the purpose intended.

173

174

Mr. Frick held two patents for the programme clock. He also received two electric clock patents in 1902.

According to Ralph M. Verdier, member of the National Association of Watch and Clock Collectors, Inc., the program clock systems were first started in or around the year 1888 by the McCaskey Clock Company. That company was purchased by Frederick Frick in or around 1899 and later was sold to Landis Engineering & Manufacturing Company.

The *Jewelers Circular-Weekly* for August 19, 1908, contained this notice of a patent issued to Frank F. Landis.

895,772 SECONDARY ELECTRIC CLOCK
Frank F. Landis, Waynesboro, PA.
Filed September 11, 1906. Serial No 334,174
In a secondary electric clock, the combination of the frame, the dial train, comprising a ratchet wheel, electro-magnets, a lever provided with an armature adjacent to said magnets, another lever pivoted on the opposite side of the frame, the inner ends of said two levers being pivotally connected by a link, the pivots in the two ends of leading to said receptacle, a reciprocating slide an opposed yieldingly mounted bar, and means for operating the slide to cause it to engage and hold a coin between it and the yielding bar and in engagement with the reciprocal chute.

Landis manufactured the Frick clocks until approximately 1923, when the company designed the Landis line. In 1930 the company was sold to J.G. Mumma, of Waynesboro, who renamed it the "Landis Program Clock Company." He sold it in 1937 to the Cincinnati Time Recorder Company.

A catalog of the Landis line, seen by this author, displayed at least eighteen different clock and time interval program machines.

Fig. 173. Another Jacob Wolf clock.

Fig. 174. A unique Chippendale walnut shelf clock from Pennsylvania, circa 1760–70. The floral-engraved brass dial bears the marking, "Charles Young, Chambersburg." Courtesy of John S. Walton, Inc.

Juniata County

175

Formed from part of Mifflin County and named for the river that ran through its land, Juniata County was organized in 1831, a rather late date. German and Scotch-Irish settlers drifted in about 1754 but endured Indian attacks. Mifflintown was laid out in 1791 and, with the advent of the canal, the area became a lively trade center. This seemingly would be a good home for various craftsmen, and perhaps it was, but not for clockmakers.

No previous studies of clock- and/or watchmakers have identified even one in this county. John Shallenberger has been mentioned, but there is difficulty in placing him. His name was on the dial of a tall clock that featured a brass movement, a sweep second hand, and a bell stamped "John Willbank, Phila. 1839–1841." As it turns out, this bell had to have been a replacement and, therefore, was no useful clue as to the approximate working date of Shallenberger.

An inquiry to the Juniata County Historical Society brought a prompt reply from its president, David A. Shellenberger. He turned out to be the great-great-great grandson of Johannes Shellenberger, who was, indeed, a clockmaker in this county and a man who was proud of his craft, wishing to be identified as "clockmaker." This is illustrated by both his will—in which the words, "John Shellenberger, Senr. clockmaker," appear twice—and by his wife's.

A booklet was published in connection with the Fayette Township sesquicentennial (1810–1960) which mentioned John Shellenberger, a clockmaker from Ge-

Fig. 175. Moon phase and calendar ring.

Fig. 176. Moon phase and calendar hand.

Fig. 177. Moon phase and sweep second hand.

Snyder County

Snyder County was formed from a piece of Union County and was named for Simon Snyder, a governor of Pennsylvania. An Indian massacre occurred shortly after the area was opened for trading, in about 1754. The county was organized rather late—in 1855.

If it has no other claim to horological fame, Snyder County is known to collectors as the home of the maker of perhaps the most graceful Pennsylvania pillar and scroll style of shelf, or mantel, clock. His story has been described thus:

> Johann or John Scharf was born in Switzerland on 12 December 1778. He was married and had at least two children when he came to America. His wife died during the voyage and was buried at sea. The year of his arrival is not known, but was probably about 1815. He first located in Philadelphia, but later sojourned in Lancaster County in or near Ephrata and married a second wife, by the name Anna Katharina Wonfiedler. To them was born a son, his only child by this second marriage, Joseph Scharf, on 14 May 1821. Of this there is definite written record. When the Scharfs arrived in Selinsgrove is not known. One of his clocks has been found with the usual "John Scharf, Selinsgrove" (sometimes just "J. Scharf") on the face of it that had a *repair date* of 1829 pasted inside the case. Hence he was in Selinsgrove as early as 1829 and probably before that. The old clock maker died in the home of his son, 19 January 1859—age 80.[1]

1. Letter received from Brian W. Kauffman, May 28, 1974.

In his *Pennsylvania Clocks and Clockmakers,* George Eckhardt suggests that Scharf was already a trained clockmaker when he emigrated. While he made other varieties of shelf clocks, he is best known for his fine eight-day, time and strike, brass movement clocks, in pleasing pillar and scroll cases. His are generally less heavy than other Pennsylvania pillar and scroll clocks.

Another clockmaker—heretofore unlisted except in one apparently incorrect reference—also lived and worked in Snyder County. An interesting tale has been provided:

> Undoubtedly the outstanding clock-maker of Snyder County was Michael Wittenmyer of Middleburg, the father of 10 children. The story is that shortly after his marriage he bought a lot on a side street in Middleburg and began excavating the cellar for a house and store. While thus engaged, Albright Swineford, the founder of the town (1800) remarked, "Your store should be located on the corner lot on Main Street." To which Wittenmyer replied that he could not afford such a prominent place for his business. Swineford told him that if he would make him an eight day clock, and another 24 hour clock and give him his present lot, in exchange he would give him the lot on Main Street. There opposite the present Reformed Church, he built his home, store and tavern.[2]

Another letter adds to what we know about Wittenmyer:

> Michael Wittenmyer, born in 1772, married Mary Magdalena Wittenmyer, daughter of Andreas and Susannah Wittenmyer, in 1795. They lived in Middleburg and had 10 children. Michael was a noted clock maker, a merchant, a student, and a music master, and possessed a fine bass voice.
>
> In the cellar of the original log house Michael had his work shop and forge. He is supposed to have made forty clocks before he died, one for each of his children and thirty others.
>
> Michael was a modest man and did not sign his works, as is usually done, on the dial. A few he signed inside the case. Therefore, the location of only about six or eight is known. In his cellar work shop, Michael did all the work on his clocks, smelting the brass shavings and fashioning the works in his forge. The brass he got in Reading, riding there on horseback and bringing the metal back in saddle bags. He bought the dials; cabinet makers built the cases. Besides making clocks—which he did in his

2. Letter received from Charles F. Snyder, February 22, 1973.

183

Fig. 183. Gracefully proportioned Pennsylvania pillar and scroll clock by John Scharf, Selinsgrove. Courtesy of Thomas K. Leidy.

Fig. 184. The clock in fig. 183 with door open to show extremely legible dial and curiously formed weights, which appear to be original. Courtesy of Thomas K. Leidy.

Fig. 185. The clock in fig. 183 with dial removed to reveal the unusually small, compact movement for a clock of this size and design. Courtesy of Thomas K. Leidy.

184

185

spare time—Michael was the auditor of Penn Township in 1803; the paymaster of the 77th Regiment in the War of 1812; and the first postmaster of Middleburg, appointed 13 December 1814 to 1829. He was appointed justice of the peace in 1829 and served many years. He died in 1850.[3]

3. Letter received from Brian W. Kauffman, May 28, 1974.

The Scenic Northeast

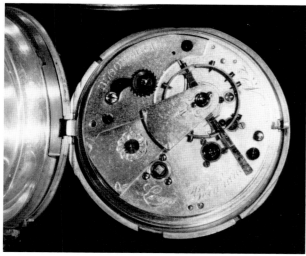

Fig. 186. Dial of chronometer by Louis Bernhard, Bloomsburg, Pa. Courtesy of the Pennsylvania Historical and Museum Commission.

Fig. 187. Back plate showing detent escapement of chronometer No. 2 by Louis Bernhard, Bloomsburg, Pa. Courtesy of the Pennsylvania Historical and Museum Commission.

Columbia County

Columbia County, another former section of Northumberland County, was the center of much Indian activity, especially during the Revolutionary War. Organized in 1813, it was named to commemorate the writing of the patriotic song, *Hail Columbia*.

Columbia County claims only one maker, but he was a true horologist, capable of producing a chronometer watch and an astronomical clock. In addition, Louis Bernhard (1839–1921) possessed considerable skills in other arts, as detailed by J.H. Battle:

Louis Bernhard, watchmaker and jeweler, Bloomsburg, was born in Bavaria, Germany, 1839. When he was a year old, his parents immigrated to America, settling in New York City, and a few years later in Wilkesbarre [sic], Pennsylvania. Here our subject passed his youth and early manhood, meanwhile obtaining a good education in the Wilkesbarre schools. When seventeen years of age, he began an apprenticeship at the watchmaking trade with John F. Jordan of that place, under whose instruction he remained several years, and in 1858 located at Bloomsburg, where he established the watchmaker's and jeweler's business, which he still continues. He exhibited at the county fair in 1859 a chronometer watch, all the parts of which were made by himself. This, without doubt, was the first watch ever made in Columbia County, and since then he has made many. During his residence in Bloomsburg he has had eleven apprentices, all of whom served their time and subsequently made a success of their vocation. Mr. Bernhard is also an architect, and has furnished plans for many buildings, among them the Lowenberg & Cadman block, the Episcopal parsonage and his residence on Fifth Street. Even the iron fence surrounding his well-kept and ornamental grounds was cast from designs drawn and furnished by him. In his house many evidences of his mechanical skill and artistic talent meet the eye, as he is also an artist in oil painting and a carver in marble and wood. Among the articles of the latter class may be mentioned a most elaborately finished case of black walnut, an astronomical clock of most intricate and perfect workmanship, which runs for two months after one winding, and valued at upward of $500; an elegant inlaid box for his drawing instruments; a large black walnut looking-glass frame, elaborately carved, reaching from floor to ceiling; a center table; and many other handsome articles. His walls are hung with several oil paintings executed by himself, several landscapes representing some of the choicest scenery in the vicinity of Bloomsburg, also several copies of famous paintings, among them *Shakespeare and his Friends*. All of these paintings are well executed and denote a high order of artistic skill.[1]

The astronomical clock that Battle describes as able to run for two months on a single winding is now in the Museum of the National Association of Watch and Clock Collectors, Inc. The description of its "most intricate and perfect workmanship" is quite accurate; however, it would be more properly referred to as a thirty-day regulator timepiece.

The William Penn Memorial Museum in Harrisburg has a splendid wheel cutting engine that is signed "Louis Bernhard, Maker."

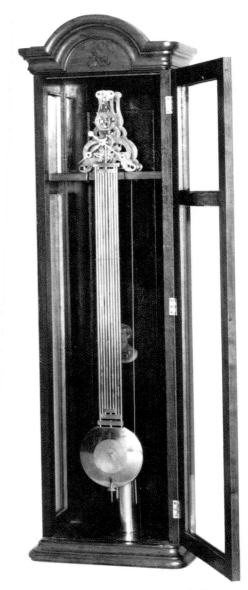

Fig. 188. Louis Bernhard regulator clock. Courtesy of the N.A.W.C.C. Museum.

1. J.H. Battle, *History of Columbia and Montour Counties, Pennsylvania* (Chicago, 1887), p. 323.

Luzerne County

In 1753 the first settlers arrived in the Luzerne County area from Connecticut. The land claims they made conflicted with those from William Penn. The ensuing difficulties, together with Indian uprisings, had a negative effect on any possible widespread, diverse settlement. Even so, Luzerne County was organized as early as 1786 from part of Northumberland County and was named for Chevalier de la Luzerne, French minister to the United States. The region's emphasis on coal mining was apparently not inviting to an influx of craftsmen and artisans.

Stephen D. Engle (1837–1921) was born on a farm in Sugarloaf Township, Luzerne County. His ancestors had come from Holland by way of Germantown. Engle's father and two brothers were watch tinkers by trade. Even as a lad, Stephen had an abundant desire and aptitude for tools and had more exposure to practical mechanical learning than formal education. At sixteen he left home to learn the watch tinkerer's art from one of his brothers. An attempt was made to indenture him, but he refused. Engle claimed that he invested all his free time for six months into building a complete watch, which passed his father's scrutiny and thus ended talk of the indenture.

He later lived in White Haven for two years, where he began to experiment on clocks. From there he moved to Hazleton, where he resided until his death. To earn his living, he practiced dentistry and made watch cases, gold chains, and jewelry, but he continued to experiment with mechanical organs and mechanical movements for clocks until he felt he could design and build his dream—an apostolic clock. He calculated wheel trains and made figures and drawings of the astronomical arrangements at such a protracted feverish pace that he nearly ruined his eyesight and his health.

Told to rest, he claimed he could not until his clock works were "broken," "knocked loose," and "bent and out of adjustment." So he continued, and at long last his dream creation was completed. Although photographs are not available to illustrate it, a word picture of it, written by Captain J. Reid, can be included here.

> The lower section, or base, of this clock is four feet nine inches high, eight feet wide, and three feet deep. The centre of this section contains the weights and a revolving horizon, twenty-six inches in diameter, giving the apparent motions of the constellations in the Zodiac from East to West. In the centre of this dial is a six-inch terrestrial globe, which revolves on its axis once in twenty-four hours; representing the Moon, it revolves in twenty-nine and one-half days, showing its position each day with reference to the Sun, Stars, and Earth.* At the lower part of the dial the Stars pass behind a fixed Sun and twilight, showing what constellations are not visible at certain periods. All the machinery is visible in the centre of the dial, and the movements can be seen. This section is very elaborately ornamented with flat-fluted columns, gilding, and grotesque lion heads.
>
> Above this lower base, in the centre, arises the clock and apostolic tower, the lower section containing the hour-strike, time, quarter, apostolic train, and chimes. In front of this section, at the base, on either side, are dials. The left one represents the tides and the right one represents the seasons and inclinations of the earth's axis. In the centre between these dials is a revolving cylinder representing the day of the month. Above this is the large dial representing minutes, hours, and the phases of the moon, with revolving cylinder at the right showing the day of the week and another at the left showing the month. Above this is an oval niche, where Youth, Prime of Life, and Old Age appear during the hour. In the right of this is an alcove which contains "Father Time," with his scythe, hour-glass, and bell on which to strike the quarter-hour with the scythe. On the left is another alcove, containing the figure of Death, holding a thigh-bone in his right hand and a skull to strike the hour on. Extending up the corners of this section, half way, are four Corinthian fluted columns, with gilt fluting and gilt capitals. Above these are four Egyptian gilt columns with lion-head capitals. The top section, near the base, has an open court, and on either side, and beyond in the

---

*Although this is an exact copy of the original description, it is easier to understand if it is revamped to read: In the center of the dial is a 6″ terrestrial globe representing the moon. It revolves on its axis once in 24 hours and also revolves in 29½ days, the complete moon cycle.

centre, are doors where Christ and his apostles appear, and Satan also. On either corner are two gilt columns, and on the right, at the top of the column stands the Cock that crows. On the left is the figure of Justice with scales, which she raises during the appearance of the apostles. Above the figure of the Saviour and apostles is a balcony, with folding doors leading into it, where the three Marys appear. On either side of this are two windows with shutters, where Satan appears alternately with his three-pronged harpoon. Above this is a battlement roof containing a Roman soldier, who paces his beat continually, and right-about-faces at the end of his beat.

When the hour hand approaches the first quarter, Father Time reverses his hour-glass and strikes one on the bell with his scythe, a bell inside the clock responding, and Youth appears. Three minutes previous to the half-hour, a bell strikes, followed by the music of the organ. At the half-hour Time again reverses his glass and strikes two on the bell, a bell inside responding, when Youth passes and Manhood appears. One minute after this a chime of bells is heard, when a folding door opens in the lower porch and one at the right of the court, and the Saviour comes walking out. Then the apostles appear in procession, Peter in the centre and Judas in the rear. As the first one approaches the Saviour a folding door above in the balcony opens, and the three Marys come out, walking in single file, and stand facing the audience. Mary, the sister of the Virgin, stands on the left, the Virgin Mary in the centre, and Mary Magdalene on the right, viewing their friends. As the apostles come opposite the Saviour, they turn towards him; the Saviour in return bows to them, except Peter, who turns in the opposite direction; then the Cock on the right flaps his wings and crows, and Satan also appears above at the left window; then the figure of Justice raises her scales. Judas, as he advances, does not look upon the Saviour, because the Devil follows immediately after him on foot, and goes back the same way he came; the Devil stays long enough to see that Judas is all right, but returns again for fear, and disappears to appear again above at the right window. Satan appears six times at different places. At the third quarter, Father Time strikes three with his scythe, and turns his hour-glass, when the bells respond.

Then Manhood passes and Old Age comes into view. Three minutes previous to the hour the organ peals again, and, as it arrives, the skeleton figure of Death strikes the number with a human thigh-bone on the skull. One minute after the procession of the apostles again takes place, and, besides these two voluntary movements, they can be produced twice on the first quarter, and twice again on the third, making, in all, six apostolic processions each hour.

At the right of the clock stands a second tower, four feet five inches high, built in two sections, the lower one containing an organ that plays during the Apostolic March, beautifully ornamented in front with gilded pipes. From the upper section appear two figures, Orpheus and Linnus, representing Music, who appear with harp and pipes when music is heard and disappear as it ceases.

At the left stands a third tower of corresponding height, ornamented in front with gilded flutings and embellishments, containing a mechanical fife. From the upper section appear twenty life-like figures, typical of the "Spirit of '76." The background presents a woodland scene, and while the fife plays a soul-inspiring melody, the brave Continentals march boldly on to the Battle of Monmouth, and Mollie Pitcher, the heroine of the American Revolution, appears bearing her memorable water-keg, turning to cheer the soldiers as she follows her husband to the field of conflict.

The clock produces forty-eight moving figures, or TWENTY-SIX MORE THAN ANY OTHER CLOCK IN THE WORLD! It also operates more dials, has more wonderful mechanisms and more delicate movements, besides being more beautifully designed and finished, than any mechanical invention or work of art beneath the sun.

Two other horologists are reported in Luzerne County. James H. McGlynn and William P. Howells, both of Wilkes-Barre, patented what they called a "clock-alarm."

Pike County

Pike County, originally a part of Wayne County, derived its name from Colonel Zebulon Pike and was organized in 1814. Dutch settlers came to the area as early as 1682. The principal commercial development was lumbering, which was not conducive to an influx of artisans.

Considering the size of Pennsylvania and the number of substantial communities, it is strange that watch case establishments appeared in only Philadelphia and one other community—Milford. This town boasted two such firms, both staffed primarily with foreign workers. One, known either as Berthoud & Courvoisier or as the Gold Watch Case Factory, was founded by two Swiss, Ferdinand Berthoud and J.W. Courvoisier, in 1877; at its zenith the operation employed about thirty workers, many Swiss. Their products were high quality gold cases in two grades. Courvoisier left in 1883, and operations continued for eleven years.

The other firm, the Silver Watch Case Factory, was founded in 1863 by a Frenchman, Desire Bornique. It carried between sixty or seventy employees, many French; produced, obviously, only silver cases; and lasted until 1885.

In a history of northeastern Pennsylvania written by Beers in 1900, there is a reference to clockmaker Peter Henzel, who worked in Lehman Township until 1842, when he moved to Wayne County to begin farming. The *Book of American Clocks* mentions a Hetzell in Milford around 1834—this is obviously the same man.

Schuylkill County

Formed from sections of Berks and Northampton counties in 1811, Schuylkill County was organized that same year. Its name is Dutch for *hidden stream*. Although settled as early as 1747, the county became known principally for its anthracite coal production and so did not prove attractive to craftsmen.

The county's historical society and other sources could not suggest a single name; however, the region was not devoid of possible makers.

Brady & Elliott, of Pottsville, issued watch papers in 1853 proclaiming themselves watchmakers and jewelers who carefully repaired and warranted clocks and watches, and sold jewelry, silverware, and like products.[1]

George Michael Deuble (b. 1798) was a native of Baden, Germany, and learned the weaving and watch- and clockmaking trades there. In 1825 he immigrated to America, coming first to Philadelphia and then to Mahonoy City, where he began making clocks.[2] In 1831 he settled in Ohio. He always pursued his clockmaking trades, never taking up the weaving.

George Grim is listed in Drepperd's *American Clocks and Clockmakers* as a tradesman at work in Orwigsburg from the 1810s to the 1830s.

1. Dorothea Spear, *American Watch Papers* (Worcester, Mass.: American Antiquarian Society).
2. James W. Gibbs, *Buckeye Horology: A Review of Ohio Clock and Watch Makers* (Columbia, Pa.: Art Crafters, 1971), pp. 40–41.

190

Some years ago, one of Philadelphia's well-known antique dealers, Frank S. Schwarz & Son, offered for sale a tall clock signed "C. Cret—Orwigsburg." Figure 189 displays that timepiece.

This particular clock and its maker have become rather well known in collectors' circles. Chris Bailey of the American Clock and Watch Museum has seen one clock similar to this with the complications and another with a conventional dial. Several serious investigations have been performed in Schuylkill County for information on C. Cret, but they resulted in no information. Apparently, such a name does not appear in any annals. Perhaps, though, the imagination can help find an answer: when the maker's alleged name is pronounced quickly, it sounds like *secret,* which could be a very clever pseudonym to conceal forever the maker's real identity. He may even be hinting about the trick by printing the name and writing the town in script.

Fig. 189. The plain but somewhat stylish case of the "C. Cret" timepiece. Courtesy of Frank S. Schwarz & Son, Philadelphia.

Fig. 190. The splendid dial of the clock in fig. 189 with unique painted spandrels. Courtesy of Frank S. Schwarz & Son, Philadelphia.

The Western Frontier

Allegheny County

The name for Allegheny County was derived from the Allegewi Indian tribe. The county was formed from sectors of Westmoreland and Washington counties and was organized in 1788. Possession of the fort at the river junction that controlled the Ohio Valley was for long a focal point of campaigns and battles. At the threshold of thousands of miles of inland waterway lay Pittsburgh, early on named "the Gateway to the West." Its fortuitous location gave rise to the multitude of industries that has long characterized Pittsburgh, but this field of giants had a minimal effect in attracting individual craftsmen.

Although there are over two dozen names previously recorded as clockmakers, later information substantiated considerably fewer. All were based in Pittsburgh, unless otherwise noted here.

In the first issue of *Timepieces,* mention was made of a unique clock fashioned from leather by an inmate of the Western Penitentiary in Pittsburgh. Just as unbelievable is this tale found in *Timepiece Quarterly:*

> John P. Bakewell, glass manufacturer of Pittsburgh, October 1, 1830, was granted a patent for making clock wheels by the new glass pressing technique. The significance of this invention may not be appreciated at first, but prior to 1830 the only cheap or low-priced clocks possible were the wooden movement clocks, the wheels of which were far more easily worked than in brass. A glass clock wheel could be pressed with its gears (teeth) ready cut! It is averred that some clocks were made with pressed glass

wheels. Certainly the patent was granted and Bakewell was no fool of a glassmaker, as his history proves. Stamped brass clock parts sounded the death knell of wooden clock parts but what happened to the glass wheel idea?[1]

Samuel Davis was listed as a clockmaker in 1815, 1819, and 1826. Pittsburgh in 1815 was a thriving commercial center of 9,000 inhabitants. That year's directory listed Davis as one of the city's major clockmakers, with a shop on the east side of Market between Diamond and Fifth streets, and mentioned that he made both movements and cases. Where he came from or when he started work in Pittsburgh is not known.

The Historical Society of Western Pennsylvania possesses clock No. 31 by Davis, which was probably made in 1797.

The Cramer Directory of 1807 mentions that there were five clock- and watch-makers then in Pittsburgh (which at that time was the size of a village). Davis surely must have been one of them. His eight-day, brass movement clocks exhibit good craftsmanship; his cases are usually of solid walnut. An earlier writer said that Samuel mixed punch work and paint on his dials. While this is possible, it is not probable; punch mark artistry goes with brass dials. If the dial of No. 31 is typical, what appear to be punch marks around the dial perimeter and in the spandrels are actually painted gesso. That same writer also said that Samuel made very fancy clock hands; however, those on No. 31 are apparently replacements. It does appear true that he used Arabic numerals exclusively and he sometimes applied his signature in gold leaf. Naturally, some were made on special order, so their present locations are known.

Although no substantiating evidence has been found, two respected researchers report that Peter Freytit and Frederick Friend were listed in directories from 1813 to 1837 as clock- and watchmakers in Diamond Alley.

Although a maker of this name has not been listed in any compilations, the signature "Michael German, Heidelburg, Pa." appeared on the dial of a clock offered for sale near Boyertown, Pennsylvania, in the spring of 1972.

It has been repeatedly—though incorrectly—recorded that Frederick Heisley was a clockmaker in Pittsburgh from after 1820 to 1839. In fact, he never lived farther west than the banks of the Susquehanna River. His son, Frederick Augustus (1792–1875), is the Heisley who migrated westward to Pittsburgh. Presumably he learned his trade from his father and then moved to Pittsburgh in 1836. He was immediately listed in the 1837 directory. His advertisement illustrated a surveyor's

191

1. "Glass Clockwheels," *Timepiece Quarterly* 1, no. 2 (February 1949).

compass and stated that he made clocks and watches. Following a 1839 directory listing as a watch- and instrumentmaker, his name appeared intermittently from 1849 until 1873.

It is curious that a possible partnership not previously listed can be found at this late date. In the August 1972 issue of ANTIQUES, an article appeared entitled "Early Furniture of Western Pennsylvania," written by Robert W. McDermott. It contained photographs of a mahogany, Hepplewhite style, tall clock with fine inlay decoration, demonstrating that high quality cabinetmaking existed in Pittsburgh at the dawn of the nineteenth century. The dial is signed "Johnston & Davis, Pittsburgh." The clock is dated at approximately 1805. The only Davis clockmaker there was Samuel, who made clocks as early as 1797 and may have been listed in 1807. He definitely was named in the 1815 directory. According to pencilled notations inside the door and on the backboard, the Johnston and Davis clock was made for the Negley family. In his article on clockmakers of the area, George Swetnam also mentions a timepiece built specifically for Jacob Negley by S. Davis in about 1797, but no trace is found of any Johnston. Absolutely no conjecture can be offered as to Johnston's identity, unless he was perhaps a cabinetmaker who did not label his products.

Gideon Morgan created clocks, both as an individual and as a partner in Morgan & Hart. From the estimated manufacture date of a clock to be hence described, it is deduced that Morgan was at work well before his first directory listing. He may have been one of five unnamed clockmakers mentioned in the 1807 Cramer Directory. He was listed in the 1819 directory as a member of the Morgan & Hart firm whose shop was on Wood Street between Fourth and Diamond. Thus, he was not far from his contemporary, Samuel Davis. As with Davis, we do not know where Morgan came from or when he arrived in Pittsburgh; nor do we know his vital dates. Also, like Davis's apparent one-time partner, Johnston, the Hart of the partnership is not mentioned again. In the 1826 directory Gideon Morgan was listed alone.

The Morgan clock that helps us date its maker is in a Sheraton style case of cherry, inlaid with curly maple. It has a brass, eight-day movement, time and strike, with a sweep second hand and a moon phase. The weights are lead-filled brass shells. The owner and others feel it was made circa 1810.

Thomas Perkins began his clockmaking career in Philadelphia and was listed in the directories there from 1783 through 1799. He moved to Pittsburgh, probably in about 1810, and became one of the small group mentioned in Cramer's Directory. He was listed as a clock- and watchmaker on Market between Front and Second streets in the 1815 directory. Sometime in the 1830s he founded Thomas Perkins & Co., which was first listed in the 1837 directory. Described as clock- and watchmak-

192

Fig. 191. Handsome, well-proportioned clock in mahogany veneer case by Samuel Davis. The painted decorations are more typical of eastern Pennsylvania clocks, while the carved rosettes at the tips of the scrolls mark this as a western Pennsylvania piece. Courtesy of the Historical Society of Western Pennsylvania.

Fig. 192. The small circles surrounding the numeral ring and around the spandrels are gilt gesso. The hands appear to be replacements. Courtesy of the Historical Society of Western Pennsylvania.

ers with a shop on Market Street, the company had clocks reported to have had gold leaf signatures and arranged so that the escape wheel ran the reverse of the usual direction. The creation of the firm suggests a switch to repairing.

Around 1840 Perkins became interested in politics and was elected as one commissioner of Allegheny County, a position he held as late as 1850.

Z.B. Tannehill is listed by one earlier compiler as being at work around 1825, but his name has not been located in any directories nor has he been confirmed in any other way.

James Thomson (1790–1875), born near Chambersburg, may have obtained some early training from Alexander Scott, who was at work there by 1810 or even earlier. Thomson moved to Pittsburgh in 1812, where he opened a shop on Fifth between Wood & Market streets, which was in business until 1825. Though he advertised as a clock- and watchmaker, he more likely meant he was a watch repairer.

He entered into a partnership with Samuel Stackhouse for the construction of steam engines. These excellent engines were used in many of the steamboats that plied the three rivers. Later, the partners expanded into the building of iron steamships; their most famous was the *Michigan,* later renamed the *Wolverine* — it was America's first steel steamship.

The firm was dissolved in about 1840; Thomson, who had become interested in politics, was elected the city's mayor in 1841. After that he formed a partnership with Joseph Tomlinson to construct railroad engines and freight cars. In 1853 Thomson became the chief engineer of the Pittsburgh Gas Company, a post he held until 1875 and left shortly before his death.

Thomas Troth was included in the 1815 city directory as a watchmaker. Several authors confirm this; however, this is the extent of our knowledge of Troth, other than that his shop was on Second Street between Market and Ferry.

The 1837 directory listed John Wallace as a clock- and watchmaker at work at Market and Second. One of his pieces is described as sitting in a mahogany tall case and having an eight-day brass movement with well-made weights and pendulum, a brass-covered bob, conch shell spandrels, a moon phase and a calendar. While the conch shell and mollusk spandrels are frequently found on clocks made along the seaboard, Wallace is the westernmost maker coming to our attention who used them.

Although not made in America, there is an interesting tower clock at the Harmony Society Restoration at Old Economy.

While commercial clockmaking by individuals passed into limbo by the mid-nineteenth century, the rare individual clockmaker did not. In about 1866 a large outdoor clock was mounted on the Reineman, Meyran, and Siedle Jewelry Store

Fig. 193. The one-handed tower clock atop the Harmony Society Church has been in continual use since 1831.

at 42 Fifth Street in Pittsburgh. On July 4, 1887, it fell down, sustaining considerable damage. Subsequently, Otto Siedle acquired the clock and, with some alteration of his own, installed it in the attic of his home in Ben Avon. Three faces for it were built into the gables of his house, and the timepiece operated successfully well into the present century.

The University of Pittsburgh owns a mercury pendulum regulator tall clock bearing the name of Reinhold Siedle, Otto's father. Reinhold entered the retail business around 1846; whether he made this clock is not known.

Tailor George Awl (b. 1868) constructed a Chimes-of-Normandy timepiece in a case of a thousand pieces in the form of an oil well, which pumped and operated by the clock mechanism. It had an alarm attachment that would ring a gong, sound a horn, and flash a light—a devilish device, not for the light sleeper.

Andrew Milo, a deaf steam-fitter, built a special alarm clock that went off automatically every day at seven A.M. It not only sounded an alarm and turned on a light, but it also started a coffee pot, a toaster, an egg poacher, a radio, and, in the winter, a heater.

Mention must be made of a man who never made a timepiece, but who was intimately associated with time and left his imprint on America, Dr. Samuel Pierpont Langley. In 1867, at age thirty-three, he was the first fulltime director of the Allegheny Observatory of the Western University of Pennsylvania, now the University of Pittsburgh. Later he became the director of the Smithsonian Institution and dabbled in (the earliest) experiments with heavier-than-air aircraft. His arrival in Pittsburgh was during an era when universal accurate time was nonexistent. Correctly diagnosing the deficiency and the need, he set up a mechanism at the observatory whereby once a day he could accurately record sidereal time. He sold standard time to the city, which put it in the town clock at the old city hall. He later sold standard time to many railroads.

Probably the last timepiece of any unique quality made within this era is all the more remarkable because it is the brainchild of an amateur, the late Dr. Walter J. Teskey of Pittsburgh. This podiatrist, whose many hobbies included modelmaking, designed and built, at the request of architects, an unusual clock. Fitted into the street wall of the then-new (1958) Bell Telephone General Headquarters Building in Pittsburgh, the piece was a thirty-six inch world globe, internally illuminated and rotating one turn every four minutes. Lucite buttons on its surface marked 120 cities and places around the world. As each point passed the meridian, its name was flashed for two seconds onto a screen above the globe; the exact time at that location was displayed directly below it by a mechanical digital read-out.

Armstrong County

Armstrong County was named in honor of Colonel John Armstrong, who in 1756 destroyed Kittanning, the largest Indian town west of the Alleghenies, in retaliation for tribal depredations. Military action in the area did little to encourage settlement or industry, thus delaying official organization until 1800.

A charming vignette serves to introduce the county's sole clockmaker.

In the *Columbian* of June 21, 1828, is an advertisement of John Clugsten, in which he stated, among other things, that he had "commenced the manufacture of eight-day and thirty-hour brass clocks, in the frame building next door to Thomas Blair's office," which was on lot No. 122, on the north side of Market, a little above Jefferson Street, and opposite the old Register's office. He, however, made none of the thirty-hour and but five of the eight-day kind. Those which he did make were the long-case corner clocks, one of which was purchased by John Mechling, which is now owned by J.E. Brown; one by James McCullough, Sr., who still keeps it in good running order, the cost of both clock and case being $40; one by the late David Reynolds, which is still in the dining-room of the Reynolds House, but it has not been kept in running gear for several years; one by the late James Montieth, which became the property of his daughter, the late Mrs. Dr. John Gilpin, and was removed by Dr. Gilpin, several years before his death, to his homestead in Cecil County, Maryland; and the remaining one by the late James Matthews, which was sold with his other effects after his death. Mr. Clugsten's part of the work consisted in making, polishing, and fitting

194

the different parts of the machinery, and adjusting them to the dial-plate, which he did in such a way as to be creditable to Kittanning artisanship. There are attachments to those clocks showing the day of the month and the phases of the moon.[1]

Although the ownership and location of these fine clocks were known in 1883, it was a great stroke of luck to locate one a century later.

195

Fig. 194. Note extreme height of this John Clugsten clock. Courtesy of Dr. Douglas H. Shaffer.

Fig. 195. The lack of fancy adornment on the dial and hood bespeaks of the no-nonsense artisanship of country clockmakers. Courtesy of Dr. Douglas H. Shaffer.

1. Robert W. Smith, *A History of Armstrong County, Pennsylvania* (Waterman, Watkins & Co., 1883).

Beaver County

Beaver County, settled around 1725, was organized in 1800 from parts of Allegheny and Washington counties. Early on, beaver furs became a major article of trade—hence, the county's name. The region was also a center for launching military campaigns against the Indians during the last quarter of the eighteenth century.

There were no officially listed clockmakers for this county, although they did exist. From lineal descendants comes the brief account of two native artisans named Martin.

> Grandfather's uncle, Hugh Martin, was born in 1805 in Darlington Township. He attended grade school and Greersburg Academy in Darlington, married and in 1844 purchased the Thomas Sprott homestead in Darlington. Behind the main house there stood a three story straight-up log house, on the third story of which Hugh Martin had his clock shop. He made both grandfather and mantle clocks. We do not know whether he signed them or used some other form of brand name.
>
> At Uncle Hugh's death in 1880, the property came to my husband's grandfather, James Martin. He continued in the business but expanded to also make caskets, cabinets, and other furniture which he sold in Pittsburgh. In the fall of 1886, he took a wagon load of his wares, including all the clocks he had made up, and sold them. At that time the shop and all tools and equipment burned to the ground and grandfather never made another clock. Regretfully, we know of no surviving clock by either Martin.[1]

1. Letter received from Mrs. Fred Wallace, February 19, 1974.

196

197

Fig. 196. Clock by Michael Strieby, Greersburg. Courtesy of Raymond O. Hill.

Fig. 197. Dial and hood of the Strieby clock in fig. 196. Courtesy of Raymond O. Hill.

The *Book of American Clocks* includes Michael Strieby, of Greensburg, Pennsylvania, circa 1790–1830. Michael Strieby is, instead, assignable to Beaver County. Raymond O. Hill, the noted clock collector and historian, states:

The Strieby family made only tall clocks as far as is known. Which one of the family made the movements or the cases is not known. Jacob Strieby is the only one mentioned in Bausman's *History of Beaver County* as a clockmaker in Greersburg, now Darlington, Pa. Because of the mail mix-up between Greensburg and Greersburg, the latter was changed to Darlington. The movement of my Strieby clock is brass eight-day with strike on a bell on the hour. It has a moon phase, seconds bit, and days of the month. The dial is painted steel with red, white, and blue shields on all four corners. The name "Michael Strieby, Greersburg" appears on the dial. The mystery surrounding the name "Michael," and the fact that Jacob had a listing in the directory of the town and so far as is known never had his name on any of the known clocks, may never be solved. At one time there were four or five known Michael Strieby clocks in the vicinity.[2]

Figures 196 and 197 show a Strieby clock. The brass eight-day movement has fairly thick plates, rack and snail striking control, and steel milled pinions. Attention must be drawn to an odd feature—the winding arbors are not on the same level. There is a date dial; the hour hand is missing, as are the feet. The present owner believes the case was originally grained painted.

Because of a recent attempt to place the Strieby family in Indiana, the facts were rechecked. Again, Hill wrote:

Aaron Strieby came to America from Poland around 1750. His son, Michael, was born September 21, 1757. His travels brought him from eastern Pennsylvania to Pittsburgh about 1798. He moved up into Beaver County in 1802 to a settlement later called Greersburg, where he lived until his demise August 20, 1830. One of his sons was Jacob, born in 1796, died in 1885. He was apprenticed to his father to learn clockmaking, in which affiliated business he remained all his life. It is reiterated that four or five clocks exist with dials signed "Michael Strieby, Greersburg." One is described as somewhat country Chippendale in appearance, while the rest are termed plain. The hands and dials are mentioned as being consistent with the first quarter of the nineteenth century.[3]

2. Letter received from Raymond O. Hill, January 29, 1974.
3. Letter received from Raymond O. Hill, November 5, 1975.

Somerset County

Named for Somersetshire, England, Somerset County was set up from a section of Bedford and was established as early as 1795. Early military thoroughfares were cut by Generals Braddock and Forbes; the Great Cumberland Road, or National Pike, now U.S. Route 40, also cut through the county. Thus, the rather early settlement of an area west of the Alleghenies is explained.

The first clockmaker here, Michael Hugus (1775–1825), was actually born in Bucks County. His father, John, came to America from a French Huguenot colony in Germany in 1761. It is asserted that originally the family name was Hugo; and the story persists that the American Hugus family was somehow related to the famous Victor Hugo (1802–85). Michael was brought to Pleasant Unity in 1789. Where or from whom he learned his trade is not apparent. He most likely moved into the town of Somerset when or just before he married a local woman in 1801. He remained there as an active clockmaker until his death.

A clock by Michael Hugus, housed in a private home in Missouri, can be here described. It has an excellent brass movement and a cast steel bell, engraved "Ainsworth, Warr'n," which came from Warrington, England. Its heavy sheet iron dial is well preserved; the clock also has a day-of-month dial. On the rear of the imported brass calendar ring is engraved "Osborne Manufactory, Birmingham"; however, the balance of the movement seems to consist of parts made in Somerset.[1]

1. "Michael Hugus, Famous Clockmaker," *Laurel Messenger* (August 1964), p. 3.

199

Apparently, Hugus taught his trade to Samuel Hoffard (1801–48) who became an excellent clockmaker. Hoffard worked in Berlin. Many of his clocks are known; they reportedly resemble those made by Hugus. His cases are well proportioned; his dials are sharply and beautifully executed.

Hoffard clocks are fairly well-travelled. One found in Illinois is signed "Sam. Hofford, Berlin" and has both a calendar and a moon phase dial. Another, located in Virginia, reads "Sam'l Hoffard, Berlin, Somerset Cy." Its case is mahogany Chippendale; besides a moon phase, it has a handmade calendar hand, hour and minute hands, and a sweep second hand.[2]

There is good reason to believe that Hoffard taught his trade to the Heffley brothers, Daniel (1813–87) and Annanias (1817–76), who also worked in Berlin. The Heffley brothers must have been prodigious workers because they are believed to have shipped over one hundred orders to Ohio, in addition to supplying local and nearby markets.[3] It is not known how long Annanias continued in the trade, but Daniel labored at his clockmaking until at least 1867—quite a late date for tall case clocks, which are the principal type attributed to him.

There is one (unsubstantiated) reference to a maker named Adam Hoops, working somewhere in Somerset County probably around the 1790s to the 1810s. Perhaps this trace of information will stimulate further research on him.

Fig. 198. Tall, graceful clock by Samuel Hoffard, Berlin. Courtesy of Wesley G. Harding.

Fig. 199. Beautiful dial of the clock in fig. 198 indicates that the maker spelled his name "Hoffard," not "Hofford" as some authorities claim. "S.C." was long interpreted to mean South Carolina, whereas this was the abbreviation for Somerset County. Courtesy of Wesley G. Harding.

2. *Laurel Messenger,* (February 1965), p. 8.
3. Ibid.

Warren County

Because of Indian activities, little progress was made in the settling of Warren County until about 1794. The region, organized in 1800, was composed of what were formerly parts of Allegheny and Lycoming counties. This county was named for General Joseph Warren of Bunker Hill fame. Lumbering was long the principal industry; one would not, therefore, logically expect many artisans and craftsmen to have settled there.

The One Hand Clock Corporation, owned and operated by Colonel Fred E. Windsor, provides Warren County's only connection to clockmaking. As recently as this firm operated, there should be a wealth of information about it; however, there is not.

Brooks Palmer's *Treasury of American Clocks* contains only this reference: "One Hand Clock Corp. Warren, Pa. after W. W. I to ca. 1935. Dial (3 sizes: 9″, 10″, 12″ diameter) with single hand. 30-hour Spg. movement made by Ansonia. Not much data available. All records destroyed after death of president, 1935." The Warren County Historical Society offered almost identical information.

There are several things wrong with this information. First, the label "clock" is a misnomer; the product was rightfully a timepiece, as its sole function was time-telling—there was no striking. Second, Colonel Windsor did not pass away until February 19, 1936. Third, units with seven-inch dials were also made; one is owned by the Warren County Historical Society and others have been reported.

It would appear that this firm made its own dials, cases, and pedestal stands, and inserted Ansonia movements made to their specifications. If production continued until 1936, the company must have prearranged a six-year inventory of movements or changed suppliers because Ansonia was sold to Russia through Amtorg (a purchasing agency in New York City) in 1930.

Warren County also provides some clues to the identification of a mysterious clockmaker. In 1943 or 1944 there was published a list of names appearing on a large number of antique tall case clocks which had passed through the repair shop of Philadelphian John Conrad. Among the names was that of John Irvine Watt. Two early chroniclers simply listed him as "Pennsylvania, no date, tall clocks." The mystery began to unravel in 1971 when a Connecticut clock dealer offered for sale a clock signed "John Watt-Irvine." This piece is shown in figure 200.

Some research located the village of Irvine in Brokenstraw Township, Warren County. It was discovered that a John Watt settled in this county in 1797 and was listed in the censuses of both 1800 and 1810, as well as on tax lists for intervening years. To be sure, nothing was found in the records to prove that Watt was a clockmaker except that the family apparently came from Lancaster County, a stronghold of clockmakers. Therefore, it is safe to suppose that John Irvine Watt, of whom there is no other mention, was actually John Watt of Irvine.

Fig. 200. Relatively short (just under seven feet), top-heavy clock by John Watt, Irvine. Courtesy of Chester S. Osaski.

Westmoreland County

Formed from a section of Bedford County and named for the English county of the same name, Westmoreland County was organized in 1773. This date, early for a western county, is probably explained by the county's military background. Fort Ligonier was a base for an expedition against the French in 1758; it served as the jumping-off post in the expedition to capture Fort Duquesne; and it was used during Pontiac's Uprising and, finally, during the Revolution. The county sent a regiment to the siege of Boston. Such an origin, however, did little to attract such artisans as clockmakers, so their number is few.

William Gorgas was the fourth generation of that highly reputed family of Germantown and Ephrata clockmakers. He labored in Greensburg. Earlier historians set his working dates as approximately 1830 to 1850. However, a clock was recently placed on the market, the face of which is signed "William Gorgas No. 17." Oddly, on the bridge of this clock is written, in the maker's own hand, "William Gorgas Manuf-June the First 1814 No. 17." Obviously he did not make the clock in one day—most likely this was the day it was completed. The clock has an eight-day brass movement, with a moon phase and a sweep second hand, and is housed in a walnut Hepplewhite style case measuring eight feet and two inches tall. He is said, however, to have also made shelf clocks.

A clock set in a case typical of the pillar and scroll model but with a flat bottom (no feet) is illustrated in *Timepieces Quarterly* of November 1948. The tapered, freestanding pillars, the scroll top, and the three finials are all there; even the dimensions—34½ inches tall, 17¾ inches wide, and 6 inches deep—are appropriate. It has an eight-day brass movement, marked "T.C. Huggins, August 1, 1809, Mount Pleasant." Because that community is within Westmoreland County, one could infer that Huggins was a maker, or at least an assembler, yet no previous compilation of clockmakers' names mentions him.

Jacob Hugus (1768–1835), of Greensburg, bought property within the county in 1784. His brother Michael was a clockmaker in Berlin, Somerset County. Jacob operated a flour mill after 1816, but a descendant insists that he also made several tall clocks and, indeed, one was owned by a respected early collector.

Just as it is our desire to correctly record our early clock- and watchmakers, it is an equal duty to point out previous errors. Michael Strieby has, for a quarter-of-a-century, been listed as a tall case clockmaker in Greensburg circa 1790 through 1830. Actually, his abode was Greersburg, Beaver County.

Other Pennsylvania Counties

Collateral Horological Activity
in Other Counties

The following counties, while boasting no clock- or watchmaking activity, did have some collateral horological activity. Briefly recorded here, this state may pose some challenge to future researchers in this discipline.

Bradford County

Bradford County was home to two men listed in the horological field, neither of whom have been confirmed nor denied. J.K. Seem is mentioned by Palmer as being at work in Canton in 1868.[1] His patent, #73,127, facilitated an improvement on calendar clocks; it added a calendar consisting of three small discs attached to the back of a dial and the dial fitted to an old clock. The calendar information appeared through slots cut in the dials at the 12, 3, and 6 o'clock points. Andrew Hayes and Dalia Maria Miller's *Calendar Clocks* illustrates a steeple shelf clock by Ingraham and a cottage shelf clock by Ansonia which are both fitted with the Seem calendar. Mr. A.E. Huson, the renowned collector of O.G. clocks, confirms that he has seen the

---

1. Brooks Palmer, *A Treasury of American Clocks*, p. 362.

Seem calendar in one of these pieces. Mr. Seem later moved to Macomb, Illinois, where he applied for and received two more calendar mechanism patents.

William Chamberlin is mentioned by Drepperd as laboring in Towanda from 1838 into the 1850s.[2] Inquiries about these men were directed to the county clerk, the chamber of commerce, and the libraries in each community, but no answers were found.

Butler County

No authenticated clockmakers can be ascribed to Butler County, but what is claimed to be the oldest tower clock in the Western hemisphere is still on display in the Harmony Museum, in Harmony, Pennsylvania. Estimated to have been made in about 1650, it was brought from a German monastery by Father Rapp, who in 1803 left Germany with a large group of followers to seek religious freedom in America. In 1804 they acquired a tract of 5,000 acres near what is now Zelienople. The next year the Harmonie Society was formally set up.

The story of this clock was written by A.J. Whitehill, who not only examined the clock minutely but also made the parts necessary for its renovation to an operable condition. For those who are familiar with antique clocks, certain features readily assist a close identification of country of origin and probable age. It is almost certain that this ancient clock is German, and it most likely dates in the mid-seventeenth century. Every piece of the clock is handmade: the frame is of puddled iron; each nut and bolt were made for each other—there is no interchangeability; the original weights were stone blocks carefully hewn to size and fitted with a ring that was leaded into place so it could be attached to the winding drum by a twisted hemp line.

Whitehill made the brass bearings and sprocket wheels for each of the winding drums by hand. Likewise, he designed and installed an automatic winding mechanism.

2. Carl W. Drepperd, *American Clocks and Clockmakers*.

Fig. 201. Harmonite one-handed clock.

Cambria County

Cambria County cannot boast a bona fide, confirmed clock- or watchmaker, but this region did host some men of interest in the general field of horology.

According to a speech given by Richard Davis at a meeting of the Cambria County Historical Society on September 15, 1971, David R. Davis, watchmaker, came to Ebensburg from Montgomeryshire in the 1830s and made wooden watches and clocks in an abandoned log school at the southwest corner of Sample and Sugar streets. That he made wooden clocks is possible, even believable, but that he constructed wooden watches stretches credulity.

George Davis, a watchmaker and possibly the son of David, is also mentioned as working in Ebensburg around 1850.

The Sky carried advertisements in April 1832 and March 1834 for James Robinson, watch- and clockmaker.

The 1850 census listed two watchmakers in Johnstown: John Lutchan, sixty-six years old, from Maryland, and John Shoully, twenty-eight, born in Germany.

The Wiggins & M'Killop's 1876 directory of Johnstown and County lists Francis X. Sedelmeyer as a clockmaker in Conemaugh. It is strongly suspected, however, because of the date, that he was really a clock repairman.

Carbon County

Carbon County has four men listed in the horological field, none of whom have been confirmed or denied.

William R. Otis (1817–62) of Mauch Chunk (now Jim Thorpe), is the only name suggested as a clock- and watchmaker. He issued watch papers which plainly indicated that he also handled rings, chains, jewelry, keys, seals, gold pins, and similar items.[3] Such a specialized form of advertising fairly conclusively indicates that Otis operated a jewelry store and performed clock and watch repairing.

Inquiries to the usual authoritative sources proved almost fruitless, unearthing traces of only three men, whose names appeared on 1828 tax lists: Michael Gangware of Lausanne Township, and Jacob Klotz and Michael German of East Penn Township.

Centre County

One compiler listed Jacob Haller, of Aaronsburg, as working in the 1790s and through the 1810s. Linn's *History of Centre and Clinton Counties* places him as a clockmaker in 1810; he is also classified as a clockmaker in the assessment lists of 1812, 1820, and 1821. The secretary of the Northumberland County Historical Society has seen one of Haller's tall case clocks, and he described it as beautiful.

Elijah Reeves, of Bellefonte, advertised in the *Bellefonte Patriot* from June 18 to November 23, 1823, as a "clock and watch-maker . . . next door to the office of the

3. Dorothea E. Spear, *American Watch Papers* (American Antiquarian Society, 1952), p. 53.

Patriot. . . . He will work on the most reasonable terms for cash or country produce." Linn's *History* includes watchmaker Reeves among merchants and others in Bellefonte who advertised between 1821 and 1829. The Centre County Library and Historical Museum has a grandfather clock made by Elijah Reeves.

A tall, double-door shelf clock, signed "Thomas Weaver, Centre County," was exhibited at the annual Convention of the National Association of Watch and Clock Collectors, Inc. in Pittsburgh in June 1973. The name Thomas Weaver, possibly applying to more than one person, is associated with Aaronsburg several times between 1836 and 1842 and in several contexts, but clockmaking is not mentioned. This, however, does not rule out Weaver as a clockmaker.

Linn's list of advertisers also included one William Alloway as a watchmaker; however, no further identification has been found.

If credence may be placed in a narrative, two other clockmakers heretofore unknown may be discovered. George Shultz, a native of Philipsburg, tells this story about his two brothers, John, born in 1804, and Henry, born in 1808. Described as "born mechanics," the boys were taken to see a windmill when they were quite young. Upon their return home, John set to work with his pocket knife and carved a complete windmill (on a small scale). He later made a miniature working model of a sawmill.

In 1818 their mother was given a wooden Yankee clock. "John and Henry, after much careful and critical examination of it, commenced making wooden clocks, too. They had already constructed a very good turning lathe and now they sent to Philadelphia for some mahogany of which to make the wheels and pinions of their clocks. I think they made about ten or twelve of them, all together, by working at them at such times as they had no business of greater importance at hand. A few of them they sold, and the rest of them they gave away as presents to some of their friends."[4]

Henry later became a first-rate smith and machinist, while John developed into an excellent carpenter.

Clinton County

The author encountered local pride tempered with honest interpretation in Clinton County. The county quite naturally had names of men who had been referred to as

4. Letter received from Robert J. Allison, curator, Clearfield County Historical Society.

watchmakers or clockmakers in their lifetimes, but, in all reality, they were probably repairmen. One such man was Charles O. Moyer, who lived in the county from 1919 to 1929. In 1893 he wired the giant Ferris Wheel that turned at the Chicago Exposition.

A clipping from a January 1974 issue of the *Express* revealed a practice often found in the making of antique clocks.

> Handsome grandfathers' clocks had an interesting history seventy years ago— 1904. Clinton County Auditor, William D. Kintzing, had sold to School Director, John F. McCormick, a grandfather's clock that had an interesting history. The clock was made in Dunnstown in 1799 or 1800 by a cabinet maker named Fergundus, and was a beautiful specimen of cabinet making. The works were brought from Philadelphia and put in the handsome cherry wood case. It was a correct timekeeper and also showed all the phases of the moon. The clock was given by Washington Dunn in 1844 to his daughter, Mary, as a present on the occasion of her marriage to T.C. Kintzing.

Delaware County

Even the half dozen or so early compilations came up almost empty-handed for Delaware County. Only the names of the following men have been suggested.

Charles A. Ladomus (1782–1858), a scion of French nobility and the chosen interpreter for Napoleon, came to America in 1822 and two years later established his home and business in Chester. A silversmith, he was good at mathematics, music, and astronomy, and was generally described as a walking encyclopedia.

Jacob Ladamus, the eldest son of Charles, learned to make and repair both clocks and watches from his father. He later moved his work to Philadelphia, where his wife's father, Henry Ducommun, also appeared in directories as a clock- and watchmaker. Jacob operated at 33 S. Fourth Street from 1843 to 1847 and at 246 High Street from 1848 to 1850.

Lewis Ladomus, Charles' second son, also adopted the profession from his father and, though he lived in Chester, he worked in Philadelphia, where the directories placed him at 413½ High Street from 1845 to 1850.

Charles' third son, Joseph Ladomus (1828–1912), was a jeweler and watchmaker who assumed control of the family business at the age of twenty. He also traveled the country to repair old English clocks.

Joseph H. Ladomus (1854–1934), the grandson of Charles, conducted a watch-making and jewelry business at Third Street and Edgemond Avenue and was known throughout the county as an expert in his trade.

While these five men may not have been makers in our sense, their family saga is, nonetheless, worthy of mention. Two more men, one named Latham (no first name has been found) and the other named Joseph Smith, have been suggested as clock-makers, yet no evidence exists.

The name of Dr. John Worrall appears in the tax lists of 1800 as a watch cleaner in Marple. His son, Dr. Thomas Worrall, is mentioned in the 1807 tax lists of Upper Providence Township as a clockmaker. Although a practicing physician, he is reputed as having been quite skilled in making and repairing fine complicated machinery, especially clocks.[5]

Erie County

Although there was no supporting data, one source mentions the Lovell Manufacturing Company as making clocks in Erie County from the 1850s to the 1880s; another source simply dates it around 1893. Richard Wright, president of the Erie County Historical Society, set the record straight by checking with Edward Doll, former president and general manager of the company. Lovell was organized in 1882 and did not manufacture timepieces; however, they bought clocks and sold them under the Lovell name. This practice was discontinued in about 1890. Mr. Lovell was a sales agent as early as 1872 for the American Clock Company.

Fayette County

Fayette County, organized in 1783, was named for General Lafayette. President

---

5. George Smith, *History of Delaware County* (Philadelphia: Ashmead, 1862), p. 516.

Washington made a dramatic test of the U.S. Constitution when he quelled the Whiskey Rebellion here in 1794.

If the long-lived Benjamin Campbell (1749–1843) left a record of his clockmaking activities, it has not been found. Although he was born at London Crossroads, Chester County, Pennsylvania, it is unlikely that he practiced his trade there. That he was at work in Hagerstown, Maryland, from 1775 to 1792 is confirmed by the Washington County Historical Society of Hagerstown. Perhaps there was too much competition in the region, for he finally moved to Uniontown, Pennsylvania, in Fayette County, where he continued his trade until 1830, finally passing away at the age of ninety-four.

The *Western Telegraph and Washington Advertiser* of April 26, 1796 contained the following advertisement:

> Merimee, William, Watch Maker, Informs the public, and his friends in particular, that he has now returned from Kentucky and intends, as usual, to carry on the Clock and Watch-making Business, at Brownsville, formerly known by the name of Redstone Old Fort.

Greene County

It has already been noted that verified clockmaker Jacob Wolf, long ascribed to Waynesburg in Greene County, actually belonged to Waynesburg, now Waynesboro, in Franklin County. Luckily, the names of two unverified clockmakers turn up in Wolf's stead. L.K. Evans wrote: "A. Leonard, pioneer clock and watch maker, carried on his trade at the Inn of Barnet Rinehart. Here he manufactured and repaired clocks, watches and jewelry on the shortest notice and at a modest price."[6] The time that Rinehart's Inn operated was about 1810 to 1820.

The 1850 census of Marion Township, Greene County listed Dominick Haas, thirty-six years old and born in Germany, as a clockmaker who owned real estate worth $800. The date suggests that Haas was more likely a repairman.

6. L.K. Evans, *Early Merchants of Waynesburg,* p. 173.

Huntingdon County

Huntingdon County claims only one substantiated artisan in the clockmaking field. Humphrey Griffith was born in Wales and made clocks in London; the date of his emigration to America is not known, but he was in Huntingdon in 1818 before moving on to Ohio.[7] Griffith built fine tall case clocks and decorated them in a unique way: in addition to signing his dials, he signed his cases in Welsh script.

The Huntingdon County Historical Society and other sources could locate no other makers.

Indiana County

Indiana County has only one listed clockmaker, and even he has been neither confirmed nor denied. H. Boyd is mentioned by Drepperd as being at work in Blairsville during the 1830s.[8] He is described as a clock- and watchmaker and a silversmith. Some of his eight-day tall clocks with painted dials are reported.

The usual sources for other names yielded no additional information.

McKean County

We cannot officially document any clock- or watchmakers in McKean County, but we did learn of one fellow, a jack-of-all-trades, who lived in the area. An inquiry was made to the McKean County Historical Society. The society's records contained no mention of a clockmaker, but the curator wrote to say: "my father-in-law had mentioned that Smethport did have a very special clockmaker."[9] A subsequent letter continued the story: "I do know that August Smith was considered an outstanding clockmaker. I have seen an old wooden clock that [he] had made."[10]

7. James W. Gibbs, *Buckeye Horology* (Columbia, Pa.: Art Crafters, 1971), pp. 45, 46.
8. Carl W. Drepperd, *American Clocks and Clockmakers* (Boston: Charles T. Branford Co., 1958), supplement, p.7.
9. Letter received from Marian M. McKean, January 1, 1974.
10. Ibid., April 16, 1974.

Contact was made with Mr. Smith's daughter, who reported:

> My father, August A. Smith, was born near Clermont in McKean County, May 17, 1864, and later moved to a farm near Smethport. He was a perfectionist in everything he did. He valued praise for his work more than money. Perhaps he made a clock and sold it. He could repair anything if it could be repaired. In his later life, most of his time was spent repairing clocks and watches. He showed me wheels he had made from bone and wood for antique clocks which, of course, had to be perfect to work correctly. At one time he was called to work on the clock on top of the county courthouse. He repaired clocks and watches that had not been properly repaired by professionals, so he had a reputation for his fine work. He died November 25, 1943.[11]

Monroe County

Monroe County is a sparsely settled, mountainous area with little industrial development. To find there no full-fledged clock- or watchmaker is therefore not at all surprising. Yet the county was not totally devoid of men skilled in this art.

John H. Mellick (1818–55), originally from New Jersey, was listed in the 1850 census as a clock- and watchmaker. His dating suggests that he actually was a repairer, an idea supported by the absence of any product bearing his name. However, he must have been very good at his trade because the census listed one Joseph Heckman, sixteen, most likely an apprentice, as living in his household.

Samuel Mellick (b. 1828), born in Hawley, Wayne County, was listed in the 1860 census as a watchmaker. This, again, quite likely meant he was a repairer. He, too, must have been a talented tradesman, for the census listed Daniel Smith, twenty-two, Peter Williams, eighteen, and Edward P. Mellick, seventeen, all watchmakers, as living in his home. Edward Mellick was the son of John; however, the relationship between John and Samuel is not known.

All of the above lived in Stroudsburg and none are listed in the usual reference books, perhaps because of their rather late date.

Tax records list Xavier Eckhardt as a clockmaker in Stroud Township in 1828, but no confirmation of this has been discovered.

11. Letter received from Roxy Johnston, April 25, 1974.

Northumberland County

John Beitzel, single freeman, was assessed as a clockmaker in 1808 in Sunbury. Reportedly from Chambersburg, this watchmaker lived or worked on Front Street, and later "carried on from the county jail, while serving for bigamy."[12] Jacob Bright, also listed as a watchmaker, lived on the south side of Chestnut Street, between Front and Second, in about 1830.[13] Both men were probably only repairers.

Jacob Cope was a clockmaker in Watsontown around 1800. In 1943 or 1944 a list was published of the antique tall clocks that had passed through the repair shop of John Conrad in the Philadelphia area. Included was one clock signed "Jacob Cope – Watsontown." Several other Cope clocks are extant and are usually engraved with his name on the pendulum bob rather than signed on the dials.

Perry County

A trading post was opened in 1750 to tap the great Indian pathways which crossed the area. Organization did not come until 1820 when it was formed from part of Cumberland County and named for Commodore Oliver H. Perry, hero of the Battle of Lake Erie.

Although Perry County is bereft of any clockmaker, there is an amusing tale about traveling clock and watch repairmen, entitled *Early Perry County Watch and Clockmakers*, written by Henry W. Shoemaker.

> The recent sojourn of an octogenarian, watch and clockmaker at the historic stone mansion of Miss Sue A. Kline, of near Liverpool, Perry County, has put noted historian J.W. Shiebley in a reminiscent mood.
> "In the old days," he remarked, "these traveling watch and clockmakers would often spend a winter in a mansion like the old Fetter brick chateau in Landisburg, where there would be a score of tall clocks, mantel clocks, block sundials, and pocket clocks, as old-timers called the pocket sundials, to regulate and put in order. In the Fetter

---

12. Everts and Stewart, *The History of Northumberland County* (Philadelphia, 1876), p. 43.
13. Herbert C. Bell, *History of Northumberland County* (Chicago: Brown, Funk, and Co., 1891), p. 465.

home there were tall grandfather clocks on the stairs, in the drawing rooms, the library, and the kitchen, all of which must synchronize in their striking and chiming, as also the smaller clocks on the shelves in the upstairs apartments, and some of the huge eighteenth-century watches also had sweet musical chimes in minor key, while all types of sundials had to be adjusted."

At the Kline mansion the aged traveling artisan repaired a dozen tall clocks, including the master clock, nine feet tall, built during the Revolution by that most celebrated clockmaker, Henry Doll, of Harrisburg, who ranked with Kline, of Reading, Seneca Lukens, of Horsham, the Sollidays, of Hilltown, and old "Daddy" Stretch of Philadelphia, as among the greatest of Pennsylvania clockmakers.

The aged clock-mender who recently stayed at the Kline home was trained in Austria, and his descriptions of the treatment of apprentices, girls as well as boys, clearly showed that training had commenced for Nazi barbarities three-quarters of a century ago. The 'prentices sat at a long bench, the boys working on the wheels, the girls winding the springs; if a mistake was made or any slackening of products, a functionary known as the *mannszuchter,* or the "disciplinarian," placed a red hot file at the lobe of the delinquent's ear, but despite the torture the victim must go on working without interruption in fear of graver punishments.

"America is a fine country," said the aged sage to the junoesque chatelaine of the Kline homestead, "and more work is accomplished here by rewards and increased pay than the cruel task-masters I worked under in old Vienna."

From the Kline dwelling, the tottering but skillful old Austrian "footed it" to Selinsgrove to put the clocks in order for the Schoch family who possess several beautiful timepieces brought from Switzerland by their ancestor, Major Anthony Selin, an original member of the Society of the Cincinnati, and also to do some work for the noted historian and Alpine club founder, W.M. Schnure.

Union County

Albert Benedict has been named as a clockmaker in Lewisburg in the 1860s. Additional proof, however, is lacking, and the late date is suggestive of repairing rather than of making.

J. Berkly has also been noted as a clockmaker in Lewisburg, from about 1800 to 1820. In addition to signing his clocks with the usual name and place, he appended the title "clockmaker." He built movements of the hang-up type, often popularly called wag-on-the-wall; this was perhaps his only production variety. The majority of the purchasers of these movements made their own arrangements for casing them. Hence, Berkly clocks would be found in a variety of cases, differing in both style and quality.

Upon mention of a clockmaker named Ely, one usually thinks of Hugh Ely of New Hope, Pennsylvania, and Trenton, New Jersey; however, John Ely is twice referred to as a clockmaker in early nineteenth-century Mifflinburg.

Clockmaker Philip Franck worked in New Berlin. One source dates him in the early nineteenth century, which is too vague; another suggests that he toiled from the 1800s to the 1850s, which seems too long. Oddly, a historical society in another county had knowledge of Franck and pinpointed his time in New Berlin as about 1835.

Certainly, more should be verified about the artisans of Union County. For example, Solomon Kleckner is noted but not documented as a clockmaker in Mifflinburg. One authority says he worked in about 1830, while another believes the longer period of 1818 to 1860 is correct.

Sometimes a slight difference in spelling causes difficulty in identification. Two reputable early writers assert that John Sharf made tall clocks in Mifflinburg, one dating him from 1820 to 1826, the other from the 1820s to 1860. However, the same historical society that offered data on Franck states that J. (John) Scharf worked in Selinsgrove, Snyder County, and his brother (not named) made clocks in Mifflinburg.

Peter Withington is said to have been a Mifflinburg clockmaker, perhaps in 1820.

J.K. Housen, of Lewisburg, issues watchpapers proclaiming himself a watch- and clockmaker and a jeweler. A safe translation might set him as a jewelry store proprietor who could do repairing.

Washington County

Early records attribute a mahogany-cased tall clock, with an unusual steel movement and a dial marked "Cannonsburg, 1841," to Alexander Cooke. This has since been disproved as the evidence shows that Cooke made all of his clocks during the 1790s. Each is numbered on the signature plate; to this date, the lowest number reported is seven and the highest is forty-five. That Cannonsburg was laid out as a town in 1786 and was set up as a borough in 1802 serves as additional proof. Alexander Cooke, a clockmaker, was among the taxables at that time.

George Lewis was active in Cannonsburg in the 1830s as a cabinetmaker and, perhaps, as a casemaker. Combination metal and wood hang-up movements—now called wag-on-the-walls—bearing his name on the dials are reported. Some even appeared in cherry tall cases, possibly of his own make. One such clock appeared at the convention of the National Association of Watch and Clock Collectors, Inc. in Pittsburgh in June 1973.

In 1795 Jedidiah Hd. Post, self-styled "Watch Maker in the Town of Washington," advertised a reward for the return of a stolen watch. No conclusive data about him has been found.

Crumrine's *History of Washington County* lists John DeLille, Thomas Hutchinson (manufacturer of the "tall Dutch Clocks"), and Thomas Wells as clock- and watchmakers. None of these men are confirmed in other sources (although a Thomas Hutchinson was listed in Philadelphia from 1816 to 1820).

W.H. Jenney, of West Alexandria, advertised in the 1826 directory as a general job carpenter and gunsmith who also repaired clocks and watches, and G.W. Aiken was a sometime clock peddler working out of Prosperity.

Counties With No Horological Activity

So far as can be determined by fair investigation, no clock- or watchmaking as we know it occurred in the following counties of Pennsylvania: Blair, Cameron, Clarion, Clearfield, Crawford, Elk, Forest, Fulton, Jefferson, Lackawanna, Lawrence, Lycoming, Mercer, Mifflin, Potter, Sullivan, Susquehanna, Tioga, Venango, Wayne, and Wyoming.

Patents, Bibliography, and Index

Horological Patents Issued to Pennsylvanians

Pennsylvania, developed early in the history of America and widely industrialized, could be expected to host a multitude of ingenious men. That this proved to be true is attested by the uncommonly long list of persons to whom patents in the field of horology—considered in its widest scope—were issued. To my knowledge, the only state surpassing Pennsylvania in this field of endeavor is New York.

For use of this list I am indebted to George H. Eckhardt and his *United States Clock and Watch Patents 1790–1890* (1960).

BAILEY, J.   Buckingham   December 7, 1887   #353,840
     Clock for transmitting electric signals
BAKEWELL, J.P.   Pittsburgh   October 1, 1830
     Glass wheels for clocks
BALDWIN, M.W.   Philadelphia   June 1, 1858   #20,403
     Attachment for watches to ascertain the time without looking at the watch
BEIDLER, G.A.   Philadelphia   March 16, 1875   #160,867
     Ratchet watch key
BERGER, L.   Danville   March 10, 1874   #148,405
     Calendar clock and watch
BEYERLE, J.F.   Reading   September 20, 1887   #370,038
     Striking clock for timing watches
BITNER, A.   Lancaster   October 10, 1882   #265,568
     Watch regulator

BITNER, A.	Lancaster	November 28, 1882	#268,354
Dust proof watch plate			
BITNER, A.	Lancaster	March 13, 1883	#273,938
Dust proof watch			
BOCK, M.	Hughesville	October 1, 1878	#208,563
Clock case			
BOCK, M.	Hazelton	June 11, 1889	#405,004
		October 7, 1890	#437,965
Timepiece keys			
BOSS, J.	Philadelphia	May 3, 1859	#24,820
Manufacture of watch cases			
BRIDGE, E.W.	Philadelphia	November 19, 1872	#133,196
Toy Watch			
BRIDGE, E.W.	Philadelphia	August 27, 1877	#194,645
Toy clock			
BROWN, G.H., and WELTEROTH, H.J.	Blossburg	January 22, 1884	#292,282
Apparatus for adjusting beat of pendulum			
CARROLL, N.	Philadelphia	October 10, 1865	#2,182
Sundial			
CASSIDY, P.B.	Pittsburgh	April 8, 1884	#296,675
Clock winding device			
CHABOT, C.	Philadelphia	December 25, 1883	#290,858
Machine for making watch pendants			
CHAPPATTEE, E.C.	Philadelphia	November 8, 1887	#373,011
		July 9, 1889	#406,816
Watch cases			
CHASE, E.T.	Philadelphia	June 18, 1889	#405,394
Clock attachment			
CONSTERDINE, J.A.	Philadelphia	February 22, 1881	#238,089
Watch protector			
CRAWFORD, J.M.	Philadelphia	July 17, 1883	#281,465
		May 5, 1885	#317,096
Illuminated clock			
CROSBY, A.C.	Union	December 11, 1866	#60,343
Watch jeweling tool			
CUPIT, A.	Philadelphia	March 6, 1883	#273,471
Clock winding device			
CUSTER, J.D.	Norristown	November 24, 1830	
Clocks			
CUSTER, J.D.	Norristown	February 4, 1843	#2,939
Watches			
DATES, J.H.	Philadelphia	May 27, 1890	#428,717
Stop clock			

DEVER, P.	Glen Riddle	February 22, 1876	#173,848
Watch chain and key combined			
DEVLIN, J.	Philadelphia	August 14, 1860	#29,575
Lever escapement for watches			
DRAWBAUGH, Daniel	Eberly's Mills	January 14, 1879	#211,332
Earth-Battery for electric clock			
DRAWBAUGH, Daniel	Eberly's Mills	August 9, 1887	#367,898
Magnetic clock			
ENGLE, S.D.	Hazelton	April 24, 1866	#54,135
Watches			
ENGLE, S.D.	Hazelton	January 11, 1870	#98,677
Dust ring for watch frames			
ESLER, R.B.	Philadelphia	February 15, 1876	#9,005
Watch charm			
EVANS, L.	Pittsburgh	February 24, 1874	#147,918
Stem winding watch			
FELIMAN, B.J., and	Franklin	April 12, 1887	#360,955
REESE, W.H., Jr.			
Advertising clock			
FENIMORE, W.	Philadelphia	February 11, 1868	#74,325
Watch dust-cap			
FENIMORE, W.	Philadelphia	May 30, 1871	#115, 455
Watch case spring			
FOGG, C.M.	Philadelphia	April 8, 1890	#425,375
Watch bow fastener			
FREYMOUTH, B.F.	Philadelphia	December 22, 1814	
Alarm bell to be fixed to a clock or watch			
GANSTER, G.P.	Reading	December 4, 1877	#197,771
Clocks and gas regulating mechanism			
GANSTER, G.P.	Reading	November 16, 1880	#234,557
Combined clock winding and gas clock mechanism			
GANSTER, G.P.	Reading	December 19, 1882	#269,278
Clock-work escapement			
GANSTER, G.P.	Reading	October 9, 1883	#286,418
Apparatus for winding clocks by currents of air			
GEARY, M.W.	Lock Haven	April 13, 1886	#339,875
Watch key			
GOLDSBOROUGH, J.	Philadelphia	April 9, 1872	#5,757
Watch key or chain			
GRAESSLE, W.T.	Philadelphia	September 10, 1889	#410,831
Watch pendant winding and setting device			
HAAS, E.	Philadelphia	June 30, 1885	#321,021
Watch case			

HAINES, W.	Philadelphia	April 16, 1878	#202,344
		October 29, 1878	#209,340
Adjustable watch key			
HAMM, W.B.	Philadelphia	July 8, 1873	#6,759
Watch chain charm			
HAWKINS, M.C.	Edinborough	August 1, 1876	#180,579
Watch regulator			
HEITEL, J. and J.W., and	Philadelphia	November 17, 1868	#84,060
GEISSLER, J.L.			
Watch escapement			
HERWIG, H.	Media, Pa.	January 22, 1889	#396,655
HEXMER, C.J.	Philadelphia	August 14, 1888	#387,974
Assignor to Philadelphia Time Telegraph Company. Electric clock synchronizing system			
HIRST, C.C.	Philadelphia	December 14, 1880	#235,529
		October 11, 1881	#248,260
Safety watch pendant			
HOFFIGER, P.T.	Philadelphia	September 30, 1873	#143,285
Clock or watch key			
HOPKINS, C.	Philadelphia	June 9, 1868	#78,803
Watch rejeweling tool			
HOPKINS, C.	Philadelphia	August 31, 1869	#94,208
Apparatus for rejeweling watches			
HOYLE, D.P.	Pittsburgh	October 12, 1880	#233,249
Railway timepiece			
HUFFNAGLE, A.	Philadelphia	February 10, 1874	#7,164
Watch chain and memento			
HUMBERT, A.	Philadelphia	November 29, 1870	#109,620
Combining keys with watches			
HUMBERT, A.	Philadelphia	December 6, 1887	#374,535
Watch case spring			
JENNET, J.	Meadville	September 7, 1858	#21,425
Time keeper escapement			
JUNGERMAN, E.	Gettysburg	March 25, 1884	#295,873
Electric alarm for spring clocks			
JUNGERMAN, E.	Gettysburg	April 22, 1884	#297,520
Automatic winding signal for spring clocks			
JUNGERMAN, E.	Gettysburg	April 29, 1884	#297,694
Automatic winding reminder for clock			
KENNEDY, S.A.,	Attleborough	December 3, 1867	#71,624
HOLT, S.W., and	Philadelphia		
GERLACH, Jr.			
Electric clock			
KENNEDY, S.A.	Attleborough	February 1, 1870	#99,321
Electric clock			

KENNEDY, W.K.	Pleasant Mount	November 1, 1887	#372,540
Watch case			
KILBORN, L.J.	Pennsylvania	October 13, 1809	
Casting clock wheels			
KRONERSBERG, E.	Philadelphia	November 20, 1888	#393,159
Clock synchronizing mechanism			
LEEDS, G.H., and THORPE, C.W.	Philadelphia	May 20, 1873	#139,166
Striking works of clock			
LILLE, S.M.	Philadelphia	August 13, 1878	#206,887
Time clock			
LOVELL, G.S.	Philadelphia	August 11, 1865	#2,044
		October 10, 1865	#2,190
Clock fronts			
McGLYNN, J.H., and HOWELLS, W.P.	Wilkes-Barre	December 27, 1887	#375,497
Alarm clock			
McNUTT, E.	Philadelphia	November 2, 1875	#169,458
Watch regulator			
MASCHER, J.F.	Philadelphia	February 18, 1859	#22,883
Alarm clock			
MATTHEWS, W.	Philadelphia	November 4, 1890	#439,965
Clock chimes			
MERSHON, R.S.	Philadelphia	April 26, 1859	#23,810
Time keeper regulator			
MERSHON, R.S.	Philadelphia	November 24, 1863	#40,726
Watch key			
MIFFLEIN, L.	Germantown	May 21, 1867	#64,892
Solar chronometer			
MILLER, H.	East Hanover	May 5, 1825	
Astronomical clock			
MINK, F.	Philadelphia	April 5, 1890	#423,532
		April 8, 1890	#425,382
		October 28, 1890	#439,414
Assignor to Keystone Watch Case Company. Watch bow fastener			
MOSELEY, C.S., and BITNER, A.	Lancaster	August 12, 1879	#218,556
Watch safety pinion			
MUCHLE, E.A.	Philadelphia	November 26, 1867	#71,505
Magic watch-case			
MUELLER, T.	Philadelphia	September 16, 1879	#219,593
Manufacture of watch case bezels			
MUELLER, T.	Philadelphia	September 16, 1879	#219,594
Assignor to Hagstoz & Thorpe. Manufacturing watch case centers			

MUELLER, T.	Philadelphia	September 16, 1879	#219,595
Assignor to Hagstoz & Thorpe. Manufacturing watch pendants			
MUELLER, T.	Philadelphia	April 27, 1880	#226,870
Device for making bezels and backs for watch cases			
MUELLER, T.	Philadelphia	June 28, 1881	#243,392
		December 5, 1882	#268,713
Watch crowns			
MUELLER, T.	Philadelphia	December 5, 1882	#268,714
Watch pendant			
MUELLER, T.	Philadelphia	March 13, 1883	#273,759
		July 3, 1883	#280,394
Watch cases			
MUHR, P.	Philadelphia	March 11, 1890	#423,174
Watch case spring			
MUMA, J.	Hanover	July 13, 1858	#20,888
Watch escapement			
MYERS, L.	Philadelphia	September 10, 1872	#131,175
Striking clock			
NICHOLAS, W.A.	Philadelphia	September 18, 1883	#285,154
Watch protector			
PAULUS, E.	Philadelphia	August 10, 1858	#21,146
Time keeper escapement			
PAULUS, E.	Philadelphia	November 5, 1867	#70,465
Watch key			
PAULUS, E.	Philadelphia	April 25, 1868	#3,167 & 8
Watch top plate			
PAULUS, E.	Philadelphia	November 3, 1868	#83,788
Winding clock for watches			
PENNINGTON, H.	Philadelphia	July 19, 1887	#366,683
Window clock			
POWELL, J.B.	Philadelphia	August 2, 1859	#24,997
Machine for winding clock			
POWELL, J.G.	Philadelphia	January 4, 1876	#171,850,1,2
		July 19, 1881	#244,663
Toy watches			
POWELL, J.G.	Philadelphia	June 4, 1878	#204,606
Escapement for toy watches			
POWELL, J.G.	Philadelphia	June 4, 1878	#204,607
Toy watch and clock			
PURDY, W.B.	Huntingdon	February 21, 1865	#46,496
Universal timepiece			
REMPE, H.	Hutzdale	July 16, 1889	#407,243
Stem winding and setting watch			

RICE, J.W.	Pittston	January 18, 1876	#172,499
		April 11, 1876	#176,060
Clock winding device			
RICHMOND, A.B.	Meadville	October 30, 1877	#196,702
Pendulum clock			
SCOTT, W.W.	Pittsburgh	April 25, 1876	#9,247
Watch chain charm			
SEEM, J.K.	Canton	January 7, 1868	#73,127
Calendar clock			
SHAW, T.	Philadelphia	May 27, 1879	#215,777
Time Clock			
SMITH, W.D.	Pittsburgh	December 19, 1882	#269,475
Alarm apparatus for eight-day clocks			
SMITH, W.D.	Pittsburgh	February 26, 1884	#294,338
SMITH, W.D.	Pittsburgh	February 3, 1885	#311,540
Alarm clock			
SOMMER, H.B.	Philadelphia	October 3, 1886	#16,927
Watch display case			
SPELLIER, L.H.	Doylestown	May 30, 1882	#258,818
Electric motor for clocks			
SPELLIER, L.H.	Philadelphia	November 17, 1885	#330,632
Contact maker for electric clocks			
SPRINGER, C.	New Castle	May 12, 1868	#77,848
Watches			
STATZELL, P.M.	Philadelphia	September 27, 1859	#25,589
Method of operating independent second hand of stop watch			
STATZELL, P.M.	Philadelphia	May 21, 1872	#126,908
Watch dust protector			
STECHER, M.	Philadelphia	June 28, 1887	#365,493
Electric alarm clock			
STOVER, S.F.	Perkasie	January 10, 1882	#252,062
Watch staff and jewel holder			
STRODE, T.T.	Mortonville	September 25, 1860	#30,166
		August 1, 1865	#49,169
Calendar clock			
STUFFT, R.L.	Scottdale	July 6, 1886	#345,192
Watch case spring			
STUFFT, R.L.	Scottdale	December 21, 1886	#354,666
Combined dust ring and case spring for watches			
THORNHILL, J.H.	Wilkes-Barre	October 30, 1888	#392,140
Stem winding and setting watch			
VOTTI, C.	Philadelphia	April 11, 1882	#256,255
Calendar clock			

VOTTI, C.	Philadelphia	December 4, 1883	#289,789
Signal device for winding clock			
VOTTI, C., and	Philadelphia	December 30, 1884	#15,673
NEWMAN, G.C.			
Clock case			
WILBY, F.H.	Philadelphia	Jannuary 26, 1875	#159,238
Device for making watch case bezels			
WILBY, F.H.	Philadelphia	February 16, 1875	#159,993
Forms for watch case backs			
WILSON, G.J.	Reading	March 10, 1868	#75,505
Watch case			
WILSON, R.	Williamsport	July 3, 1832	
Timepiece alarm			
WILSON, W.W.	Pittsburgh	July 5, 1859	#1,115
Sundial			
YEAKEL, A.M.	Perkasie	October 5, 1886	#350,407
		May 21, 1889	#403,820
Stem winding and setting watch			
ZAHM, H.L. and E.J.	Lancaster	October 1, 1867	#69,381
Watch regulator			

Bibliography

Abbott, Henry G. *The Watch Factories of America—Past and Present.* Chicago: George K. Hazlett, 1888.

Allison, Robert J. Clearfield County Historical Society. Letter to author.

The American Heritage History of Colonial Antiques 1785–1865. Ed. Marshall B. Davidson. Marion, Ohio: American Heritage Publishing Co., 1967.

Andrews, Willard I. Assistance in obtaining Ellicott and related data, including the *Buffalo Courier Express,* February 25, 1935.

ANTIQUES *Magazine.* "Jacob Wolf, Clockmaker" (June 1954); "James and Marshall Wilkins" (May 1973); and photograph of a Charles Young clock (February 1974).

Atkinson, W. Ross. Information on watchmaking at Lancaster, Pennsylvania, and the Hamilton Watch Company.

Auge, Moses. "Clocks and Watchmakers of Montgomery County." *Sketches,* vol. 1 (1895). The Historical Society of Montgomery County.

Baer, James A., Jr. "The Furniture and Furnishings of Monticello." ANTIQUES *Magazine* (July 1972).

Bailey, John S. "The Early Clock-Makers (Of Bucks County)." Paper read before the Bucks County Historical Society, October 27, 1885.

Barnhart, Freda G. Annie Halenbake Ross Library, Lock Haven, Pa. Letter to author.

Barnsly, Mrs. E.R. "Property of Job Hollinshead, Clock and WatchMaker." Excerpt from *Newton Enterprise,* March 15, 1951.

Barr, Lockwood. "William Faris, 1728–1804." *Maryland Historical Society Magazine* (December 1941).

Barrington, S.H. "Custer and His Clocks." *N.A.W.C.C. Bulletin* 3, no. 10, whole no. 30 (October 1949).

——. "David Rittenhouse." *N.A.W.C.C. Bulletin* 7, no. 3, whole no. 63 (April 1956).

——. "Early Pillar and Scroll–1788." *N.A.W.C.C. Bulletin* 4, no. 1, whole no. 31 (December 1949).

Bast, A. Robert. "A Masterpiece by Daniel Rose of Reading, Penna." *Timepieces Quarterly* 1, no. 4 (February 1950).

Beacham, N.F. Abby Aldrich Rockefeller Folk Art Collection, Williamsburg, Virginia. Letter to author.

Beaver, J. Kenneth. Series of articles on Daniel Drawbaugh, published in the *Patriot* and the *Evening News,* Harrisburg, Pa.

Biographical Directory of American Congress, 1774–1827. Washington, D.C.: Government Printing Office, 1928.

Blackson, Walter. Letter to author.

Blaine, Harry S. "John Fitch, Clockmaker." *N.A.W.C.C. Bulletin* 4, no. 4, whole no. 34 (June 1950).

Bonnage, Robert. Beaver Falls Historical Commission. Letter to author.

Bowman, John F. "Lancaster's Part in the World's Watchmaking Industry." Paper read before the Lancaster County Historical Society, May 1945.

Bowser, Edna H. Cameron County Historical Society. Letter to author.

Boyer, Robert J. Letter to the author.

Briner, Donald M. Historical Society of Perry County. Letter to author.

Brown, James V., Public Library. Williamsport, Pa. Photostatic copies of material from books on various clockmakers.

Brumbaugh, G. Edwin, F.A.I.A. Letter to author.

Bucks County Historical Society. Correspondence and photographs.

Bugbee, Monica H. Lehigh County Historical Society. Letter to author.

Burris, Mrs. Leroy. Historical Society of Montgomery County. Letter to author and various bulletins.

Castle, William A. Correspondence and photograph.

Cauffman, Louise C. "A George Hoff Clock." *Timepieces Quarterly* 1, no. 4 (February 1950).

Chandlee, Edward E. *Six Quaker Clockmakers*. Philadelphia: David McKay, 1943.

Christian Forrer—The Clockmaker and His Descendants. Rutland, Vt.: Tuttle, 1939.

Clinton, Ruth. Information extracted from an article on the Ellicotts in the *Buffalo Courier Express,* February 25, 1935.

————. Correspondence, information, and photographs.

Cockley, Eber. Letter to author.

Colonial Records.

Conner, Amy. Historical Society of Carroll County, Maryland. Letter to author.

Conrad, John. List of clocks in Philadelphia area.

Crossman, Charles S. "A Complete History of Watch and Clock Making in America." Published in the *Jewelers' Circular* in 1889, 1890, and 1891.

Cummins, Mrs. R.I. Radnor Historical Society. Letter to author.

Davis, Lee. Research information on York County, along with photographs of York County clocks.

Davis, Richard. "Cambria County Clockmaking." Paper read before the Cambria County Historical Society, September 15, 1971.

Davis, Russell J. Letter to author.

Delaware County Historical Society. Letter to author.

Drepperd, Carl W. *American Clocks and Clockmakers*. Enlarged edition. Boston: Charles T. Branford, 1958.

Dworetsky, Lester, and Dickstein, Robert. *Horology Americana*. Roslyn Heights, N.Y.: Horology Americana, 1972.

————. *John N. Solliday, Shelf Clock*. Roslyn Heights, N.Y.: Horology Americana, 1972.

Dyke, Samuel E. "Clock and Watch Makers of Lancaster County, 1750–1850." *Journal of the Lancaster County Historical Society* 77, no. 4 (Michaelmas 1973).

————. "Clockmakers of Lehigh and Northampton Counties." Compiled from tax records. Courtesy of Ruth S. Kramer and the Lehigh County Historical Society.

Eberlin, Merle B. Clarion County Historical Society. Letter to author.

Eckhardt, George H. "The American Cuckoo Clock Company." *N.A.W.C.C. Bulletin* 6, no. 8, whole no. 58 (April 1955).

————. "The Clocks of the Historical Society of Pennsylvania." *N.A.W.C.C. Bulletin* 7, no. 4, whole no. 64 (June 1956).

————. "J. Wilbank—Bell Founder and Clockmaker." *N.A.W.C.C. Bulletin* 5, no. 3, whole no. 43 (April 1951).

————. "Pennsylvania Clockmakers." *Historical Society of Montgomery County Bulletin* 3 (October 1942).

————. *Pennsylvania Clocks and Clock Makers*. New York: Devon-Adair, 1955.

————. *United States Clock and Watch Patents 1790–1890*. New York: privately printed, 1960.

"Edgehill-Randolph Papers." Supplied by the University of Virginia Library.

Egle, William Henry. *The History of the Counties of Dauphin and Lebanon in the Commonwealth of PA: Biographical and Genealogical*. Philadelphia: Everts and Peck, 1883.

"The Joseph Ellicott Clock." Information was extracted from this article published in the *Grosvenor Library Bulletin* 17, no. 2 Buffalo (December 1934).

Ellicott, V.L. Letter to author.

Elliott, William C. Letter to author.

Engle, Stephen D. "Stephen D. Engle and His Famous Clock." *N.A.W.C.C. Bulletin* 5, no. 2, whole no. 42 (February 1952).

Evans, Charles W. *Biographical and Historical Accounts of the Fox, Ellicott and Evans Families*. Buffalo: Baker, Jones, 1882.

Eyester, George A. Letter to author.

Ford, Edward. *David Rittenhouse, Astronomer–Patriot 1732–1796*. Philadelphia: University of Pennsylvania Press, 1946.

Frazier, Arthur H. "The Stretch Clock and Its Bell at the State House." *Pennsylvania Magazine of History and Biography* 98, no. 3 (1974).

Fretz, Annie M. "Louis H. Spellier and His Electric Clock." Paper read before the Bucks County Historical Society, May 2, 1936.

Gabler, Mrs. R.F. Kittochtinney Historical Society. Letter to author.

Gibbs, James W. *Buckeye Horology—A Review of Ohio Clock and Watchmakers*. Columbia, Pa.: Art Crafters, 1971.

————. "Daniel Drawbaugh, Tragic Genius." *N.A.W.C.C. Bulletin* 7, no. 3, whole no. 63 (April 1956).

————. *Horological Tour of Philadelphia*. Columbia, Pa.: Mifflin Press, 1968. Guidebook published for N.A.W.C.C. Silver Jubilee Convention.

———. "Horology Escalated." *N.A.W.C.C. Bulletin* 13, no. 2, whole no. 132 (February 1968).

———. "Religious Sect Clockmakers." Part 1. *N.A.W.C.C. Bulletin* 16, no. 1, whole no. 167 (December 1973).

Part 2. *N.A.W.C.C. Bulletin* 16, no. 2, whole no. 168 (February 1974).

Part 3. *N.A.W.C.C. Bulletin* 16, no. 3, whole no. 169 (April 1974).

Part 4. *N.A.W.C.C. Bulletin* 16, no. 5, whole no. 171 (August 1974).

Part 5. *N.A.W.C.C. Bulletin* 16, no. 6, whole no. 172 (October 1974).

Glatfelter, Charles H. Adams County Historical Society. Letter to author.

Gobrecht, Edward J. Letter to author.

"Grandfather Clockmakers of Reading." *Historical Review of Berks County* (July 1948).

Greening, Helen. Pike County Historical Society. Letter to author.

Hagey, Mr. and Mrs. Walter. Letter to author.

Hannon, Jean O. Letter to author.

"Hanover, Pa. Clockmakers." *Evening Sun,* 3d ed., March 4, 1944.

Harmonie Historical Society. Letter to author.

Heebner, Donald S. *History.*

Heilman, H.H., Jr. Letter to author.

Helfter, Mrs. Clyde E. Buffalo and Erie County Historical Society. Correspondence and photographs.

Helms, James K. "The Lost Planetarium of David Rittenhouse." *Historical Society of Montgomery County Bulletin* 11 (October 1939).

Herald Press Book Publishing Division of Mennonite Publishing House, Scottsdale, Pa. Correspondence and research information.

Herr, Doris W. Letter to author.

Hill, Raymond O. Correspondence and photographs.

Hocker, Edward W. "The Hageys Made An Unusual Record As A Clockmaking Family." *Norristown Timers Herald,* August 31, 1973.

Hollingshead, Paul. Letter to author.

Hommel, Rudolf P. "Jacob Godschalk of Towamencin and Philadelphia, Clockmaker." Paper read before the Historical Society of Montgomery County, February 22, 1945.

Hoover, Gladys L. Beaver County Historical Research Department. Letter to author.

"Horsham Man Old Clockmaker." *Ambler Gazette,* September 6, 1928.

Hugus, N.F. Letter to author.

Jacobs, Eugenia Y. Washington County Historical Society. Letter to author.

Jacobs, Penelope. "Famous Local Residents (of York)." *N.A.W.C.C. Bulletin* 8, no. 6, whole no. 77 (December 1958).

James, Arthur E. *Chester County Clocks and Their Makers.* West Chester, Pa.: Horace F. Temple, 1947.

———. Letter to author.

Jauch, Fred W. Extracts from Pittsburgh City Directory.

Jones, Richard W.S. Letter to author.

Kauffman, Brian W. Letter to author.

Keck, Mrs. O.J. Butler County Historical Society. Letter to author.

LaFond, Edward. "Clocks of Western Pennsylvania." Paper read at the N.A.W.C.C. National Convention, June 21, 1973.

———. "Frederick Heisely Strikes Again." *N.A.W.C.C. Bulletin* 13, no. 3, whole no. 133 (April 1968).

Lancaster County Historical Society. Letter to author.

Lockwood, Luke V. *Colonial Furniture in America.* New York: Castle Books, 1957.

Lowe, Harold A. Letter to author.

Lukens, Grace. Lukens family history.

McCaulley, Samuel A. "Jacob Hagey—Colonial." *N.A.W.C.C. Bulletin* 3, no. 3, whole no. 73 (April 1958).

McCollough, Robert Irving. "Hamilton Watch Company—Lancaster, Penna., U.S.A." Part 1. "The Ezra F. Bowman Era." *N.A.W.C.C. Bulletin* 11, no. 9, whole no. 115 (April 1964).

Part 2. "A Railroad Watch is Born." *N.A.W.C.C. Bulletin* 12, no. 1, whole no. 119 (December 1965).

Part 3. *N.A.W.C.C. Bulletin* 12, no. 6, whole no. 124 (October 1966).

Part 4. *N.A.W.C.C. Bulletin* 12, no. 8, whole no. 126 (February 1967).

McDermott, Robert W. "Early Furniture of Western Pennsylvania." ANTIQUES *Magazine* (August 1972).

McKean, Marion M., and Johnston, Roxy. McKean County Historical Society. Letter to author.

Marsh, John L. Edinboro State College. Information on the One Hand Clock Corporation.

Martin, Levi E. *Biographical Memorial of John Eberly and Genealogical Family Register of the Eberly Family.* Harrisburg, Pa.: Press of the United Evangelical Publishing House, 1896.

Martin, Sheila W. "Bucks County Clockmakers." *Panorama—The Magazine of Bucks County* (January 1970).

Mead, Helen H., and Putnam, H.C., Jr. Warren County Historical Society. Letter to author.

"Mennonite Clockmakers." A compilation from the Lancaster Mennonite Conference Historical Society and Ira D. Landis.

Miller, Andrew H., and Miller, Dalia W. *A Survey of American Clocks —Calendar Clocks.* Elgin, Ill.: Antiquital, 1972.

Milne, David. Letter to author.

Mitman, K.H. Letter to author.

Moore, N. Hudson. *The Old Clock Book.* New York: Tudor, 1911.

Moyer, Mrs. James S. Boston Area Public Library. Letter to author.

Moyer, Jane S. Easton Area Public Library. Letter to author.

Mulhollen, Betty J. Cambria County Historical Society. Letter to author.

Neth, Elliott. Correspondence.

Newton, Craig A. Columbia County Historical Society. Letter to author.

Niebling, Warren H. *History of the American Watch Case.* Philadelphia, Pa.: Whitmore, 1971.

———. "The Keystone Watchcase Company." *N.A.W.C.C. Bulletin* 13, no. 8, whole no. 138 (February 1969).

Nutting, Wallace. *Complete Clock Book.* Revised and enlarged edition by William B. Jacobs, Jr. Lordship, Conn.: Edmund-Bradley, 1973.

———. *Furniture Treasury.* Vol. 2. New York: Macmillan, 1948.

Orr, Sylvester H. "Clockmakers in Pennsylvania of the 18th and 19th Centuries." Paper read before the Historical Society of Montgomery County, April 24, 1926.

Palmer, Brooks. *The Book of American Clocks.* New York: Macmillan, 1950.

———. "Solliday Clock Family, A Puzzler." *New York Sun.*

———. *A Treasury of American Clocks.* New York: Macmillan, 1967.

Parker, William. Letter to author.

Partridge, Albert L. "Peter Stretch, Clockmaker." Paper read before the Boston Clock Club.

Pennypacker Auction House. Kenhorst, Pa.

Pickens, Ruth G. "Jacob Wolf, Clockmaker of Waynesburg, Pa." *Spinning Wheel* (June 1954).

Pleasants, J. Hall, and Sill, Howard. *Maryland Silversmiths, 1715–1830.* Harrison, N.Y.: R.A. Green Publisher, 1972.

Prime, Alfred Coxe. *The Arts and Crafts in Philadelphia.* Series 1, 1771–1785. Series 2, 1786–1800. The Walpole Society, 1929.

Reed, Herbert P. "Berkshire Furnace." *Historical Review of Berks County* (Spring 1978).

Rinker, Harry L., and Heisey, John W. York County Historical Society. Letter to author.

Ritter, Oscar A. "Early Philadelphia Watchmakers." *N.A.W.C.C. Bulletin* 1, whole no. 13 (September 1946).

Robacker, Earl F. "Tick-Tock Time in Old Pennsylvania." *Pennsylvania Folklife* 9, no. 4 (Fall 1958).

Roberts, Charles R. "Grandfather's Clocks." Paper read before the Lehigh County Historical Society, 1922.

Roberts, Stoudt, Krick, and Dietrich. *History of Lehigh County, Pennsylvania.* Allentown, Pa.: Lehigh Valley Publishing Co., 1914.

Roberts, Mary Carter. Maryland Department of Economic Development. Letter to author.

Ross, Jane. "Quest of John Fitch." *Early American Life* (February 1979).

Rothrock, David. Letter to author.

Rothrock, Henry S. Letter to author.

Rubicam, Milton. "David Rittenhouse, LL.D., F.R.S."

Ruth, John Lowry. Translation of a paper written in German by John Fischer, entitled "John Fischer, Clockmaker and Engraver of York."

———. "Pages From The First Clockmaker's Catalog of Record." *Timepieces Quarterly* 1, no. 2 (February 1949).

Salisbury, Ruth. Historical Society of Western Pennsylvania. Allegheny County clock information and photographs.

Sallada, Elizabeth. Information from the private Solliday Family genealogical records and information on various Bucks County clockmakers.

Sampsell, Jeanne Z. Union County Historical Society. Letter to author.

"Samuel and Charles Solliday." Excerpts from the *Bucks County Intelligencer.*

"Samuel S. Grosch Clock Article." *Timepieces Quarterly* 1, no. 1 (November 1948).

Sandwich, Charles M., Sr. Letter to author.

Schiffer, Margaret B. *Furniture and Its Makers of Chester County, Pennsylvania.* Philadelphia: University of Pennsylvania Press, 1966.

Schwenkfelder Family Genealogical Record.

Shaffer, Douglas H. "A Survey of the American Spring-Driven Clock, 1840–1860." *N.A.W.C.C. Bulletin,* supplement no. 9 (Winter 1973).

Shanaberger, Mark E. "Angelus Clock." *Timepieces Quarterly* 1, no. 2 (February 1949).

———. "Pillar and Scroll Clock Cases Tell Their Own Story." *Timepieces Quarterly* 1, no. 1 (November 1948).

Sheffer, John M. Letter to author.

Shellenberger, David A. Information and photographs.

Shellenberger, Frederick J. "Grandfather's Clocks." Paper read before the Bucks County Historical Society, May 23, 1911.

Shoemaker, Alfred L. "Reading's First Artist." *Historical Review of Berks County* 13, no. 3 (April 1948).

"Sketch of Isaiah Lukens." *Historical Society of Montgomery County Scrapbook* (A7/2A), p. 26.

Smart, Charles E. "Heisley Family." *N.A.W.C.C. Bulletin* 13, no. 2, whole no. 132 (February 1968).

———. "The Hershey Family." *N.A.W.C.C. Bulletin* 13, no. 2, whole no. 132 (February 1968).

Smiley, Flora W. "The Drawbaugh Electro-Magnetic Clock." *American Horologist and Jeweler* (June 1953).

Smith, George. *History of Delaware County.* Philadelphia, Pa.: Ashmead, 1862.

Smith, Marlin R. Correspondence.

Smith, Robert W. *History of Armstrong County, Pennsylvania.* Waterman, Watkins & Co., 1883.

Smith, Wayne K. "The First Clockmaker of Harrisburg."

Snyder, Charles F. Letter to author.

Snyder, John R., Jr. "The Bachman Attributions: A Reconsideration." ANTIQUES *Magazine* (May 1974).

Somerset County Courthouse records.

Spangler, L.S. "Critical and Biographical Notes on Rudolph Spangler, Clockmaker." *Timepieces Quarterly* 1, no. 1 (November 1948).

Spany, Robert E. Letter to author.

Spear, Dorothea. *American Watch Papers*. American Antiquarian Society, 1952.

Steinmetz, Mary O. "Early Clockmakers of Berks County." *Historical Review of Berks County* (October 1935).

Stewart, Charles. "Evolution of the Clock as a Measure of Time." Courtesy of W.B. Drinkhouse, treasurer of the Northampton County Historical and Genealogical Society.

Stokeley, James. "The Rittenhouse Exhibition." *Pennsylvania Magazine of History and Biography* 56 (1932).

Stoltz, Victor, and Parkhurst, E.H., Jr. "William Wallace Dudley and His Masonic Watch." *N.A.W.C.C. Bulletin* 13, no. 6, whole no. 136 (October 1968).

Stoudt, John. *Early Pennsylvania Arts and Crafts*. New York: A.S. Barnes, 1964.

Stow, Charles Messer. "Philadelphia Had 300 Clockmakers." *New York Sun*, from a series of three articles.

Stretch, Carolyn Wood. "Early Colonial Clockmakers in Philadelphia." *Pennsylvania Magazine of History and Biography* 56 (1932).

Swetnam, George. "Clockmakers and Watchmakers of Western Pennsylvania." *N.A.W.C.C. Bulletin* 9, no. 8, whole no. 90 (February 1961).

Swinehart, Fred C. "Early Pennsylvania Clocks and Their Makers." Paper read before the Historical Society of Montgomery County, April 26, 1941.

Tesky, Walter J. Miscellaneous information on Allegheny County.

Thomen, Harold O. Centre County Library and Historical Museum. Letter to author.

Tillman, Cornelia. Historical Society of Dauphin County. Letter to author.

Tinkom, Margaret B. "Dr. Christopher Witt, Citizen Extraordinary 1675–1765." *The Germantown Crier*, magazine of the Germantown Historical Society.

United States census reports.

Wallace, Mary V. Letter to author.

Walters, Elizabeth D. Monroe County Historical Society. Letter to author.

Watson, Vette. "Four Pittsburgh Clockmakers." *Timepieces Quarterly* 1, no. 3 (May 1949).

Western Telegraph and Washington Advertiser, December 29, 1975.

Wewer, William. Information from the Pennsylvania Archives.

Whisker, V.E. Excerpts from article in the *Bedford Gazette*.

Wilson, Conrad. Chester County Historical Society. Letter to author.

Workman, Arthur. "Clock Dial Painting." *Timepieces Quarterly* 1, no. 4 (February 1950).

Wright, Richard. Erie County Historical Society. Correspondence and information.

York County Historical Society. Correspondence and census data.

Zerbe, Karen A. Historic Bethlehem, Inc. Letter to author.

Index